BOLLINGEN SERIES LXXXV

Selected Works of Miguel de Unamuno

Volume 5

Selected Works of Miguel de Unamuno

Edited and Annotated by

Anthony Kerrigan and Martin Nozick

Miguel de Unamuno

The Agony of Christianity

and Essays on Faith

Translated by Anthony Kerrigan

*Annotated by Martin Nozick
and Anthony Kerrigan*

Bollingen Series LXXXV · 5
Princeton University Press

THIS IS VOLUME FIVE OF THE
SELECTED WORKS OF MIGUEL DE UNAMUNO
CONSTITUTING NUMBER LXXXV IN BOLLINGEN SERIES
SPONSORED BY BOLLINGEN FOUNDATION.
IT IS THE THIRD VOLUME OF THE
SELECTED WORKS TO APPEAR

Printed in the United States of America by
Princeton University Press
Princeton, N.J.

Table of Contents

Contents

Translator's Note

BY AGONY, UNAMUNO means death throes, indeed, but the death throes of any dubious, any doubtful, any doubting man all his life. By Christianity, he means the West, properly so-called, the area where the *corrida* of Christianity, the running of the black bulls of Christianity, is—or has been—celebrated, played out (in both senses). The Decline of the West? Unamuno speaks of this phenomenon in Chapter VII, where he suggests that what the Romantics (Napoleon chief among them) did not foresee was that the Cossacks would turn "Democratic" and the democratic Left would turn Cossack, that the Church would turn Revolutionary and the Revolution would turn Ultramontane (over the mountains to Moscow or Mao everything seems better). The Romantics did not dream of Bolshevism/Fascism/Maoism. Nor did they foresee "the chaotic disorder which the agonic Oswald Spengler attempts to render by the architectonic music of his *Der Untergang des Abendlandes*, which is simply the agony of Christianity." And there we have a Baroque—but concise—definition of our book's title.

And, what of the "desert Muslimism" of which Unamuno speaks in this book? In its peace—and in its warfare—"it becomes Christianized . . . which is to say it becomes agonic, it agonizes in the throes of proselytism." The dogmatic Libyan Chief of State offered, in 1972, the Catholic Irish Republican Army the arms it needed—if it would turn Muslim! And in

1973, in Uganda, Amin Dada, another military dictator, was forcibly turning a country only 10% Moslem into an all-Islamic state, and doing so by naked terror, beginning with the "enforced mass conversions to Islam among the troops." ("Behind Uganda's Ordeal," C. Munnion, London.)

What is to be done? We agonize. We agonize in any case. We might as well do it on purpose (like the rich young farmer who could afford to farm "on purpose" in Kingsley Amis's softly Gnostic *Green Man*, a ghostly book which includes a parody of the fruity "with-it" cleric of the ephemeral English moment).

A procreative man, Unamuno fought death, fought it alongside Christianity, whose message may be love—procreative love rather than some other watered variety—but whose "buena nueva," "glad tidings," good news is, or was, war on death.

Unamuno glosses the battle, the permanent revolution against death. He glosses, he adverbializes, Western man's "agony," which is Greek for struggle: that of agonist, protagonist, antagonist—with, in, and against his individual life-role, whatever it may be, and whether or not it be all three.

When Unamuno put together this gloss on his reading against death, in exile, in Paris, he did not see his Parisian exile in a romantic light. He viewed it, felt it, much as an Athenian viewed proscription, when Athens was integral. He took it as a terrible sentence against himself—even if it was self-imposed. He lived to view it (in retrospect) as having been a wrong-headed move by himself, and even contra-indicated as any kind of medicine for his country's ill.

The Paris of the senses, of the bittersweet *joie de vivre* and its consequent hangover *cafard*, did not exist for him, though he was as sensually farfetched, as deeply sexual, even as perverse, as James Joyce in the same city, whatever the obvious and different appearances of their public characters: that of the rebellious Irish-pagan Catholic Celt and that of the heterodoxical Castilian-Catholic Basque who said he believed in a Christ from Tangiers.

For Unamuno, the Christian God was a "working hypothesis" (as Martin Nozick writes in his book on Unamuno), but he doubted the conclusions. Such was his Agony as well as his Tragic Sense of Life, which were not only books by Unamuno but novels of his life.

Agony, struggle, *la moral de batalla*, mean life, while peace means, as it did for Don Quixote, the end, death. And Christ had come—whatever His other, contradictory messages—to bring "not peace but a sword." And Agony itself, in short, is a death agony against final death, against total death. (As, coition, the struggle and little death, is the only means to keep humanity eternal.) And now when Christianity and the West are under sentence of the final penalty (even as "the race of the monks of the West," as foretold in this book), and the death-rattle is electronically amplified the better to be heard, the agony is all the more painfully agonizing. Now that Europe, the West, seems doomed, all that is left to us is resistance.

The Resistance itself is based on contradiction: "Whoever affirms his faith upon a basis of uncertainty does not and cannot lie," Unamuno wrote in his *Tragic Sense of Life*. He did not seek a synthesis of thesis and antithesis any more than did Pascal or Proudhon, as he announces here, but abided by contradiction, even by strife. "Men seek peace, they say, but do they . . . ?" he asks in Chapter III of *The Agony*.

What is to be done? "Struggle for its own sake," says Unamuno in his Prologue to the Spanish edition of *La Agonía del cristianismo* (a prologue addressed solely to the Spanish reader, and placed at the end of this present edition in English), "even without hope— and even against hope. . . ." Concepts are of scant help: "What is grace? Another tragic evasion." And, elsewhere: "What is philosophy? Metaphysics, perhaps." And "What is justice? In morality it is something. In religion it is nothing." On the very first page of Chapter VI he tells us that both hope and memory are illusions. And hope is the shadow of the past, just as memory is the shadow of things to come.

As for Christianity, it is nevertheless "essentially grace and sacrifice," not Law, not Duty (which are legal concepts). And Politics? "Christian Democracy is in the same category as 'blue chemistry.'" As for constructive Christian action: "Social work done by . . . Catholics . . . has as little to do with Christianity as has Pasteur." And as for revolutionary seminarians: "Then there are those poor devils [devil, *diabolos*: slanderer] who claim that Jesus was a great democrat, a radical revolutionary, a real Republican! Christ's passion still goes on." Thus in Chapter IV.

There have been two previous renderings into English of *The Agony of Christianity*: Pierre Loving's (New York, 1936), translated from the French version, which had been the first-published edition of Unamuno's book; and an edition by Karl Reinhardt (New York, 1960), from Unamuno's Spanish original, published after the French of Unamuno's manuscript. We have collated our version with them both. The numbering here of the chapters of *The Agony of Christianity* is in accordance with the Loving translation, which is the order of the French version, the first version of the book to be published, and of the *OC²* (the standard text for our series), and also of the Candamo edition (which is perhaps the most carefully edited Unamuno printed text in Spanish). Reinhardt, who often omits lines and some other matter in his English version, follows the order found in *OC¹*. Our version of the essay "What is Truth?" was collated with the excellent translation made by John Upton and published in *The Centennial Review* (Fall 1958), and from it a better word was often borrowed.

ANTHONY KERRIGAN

Palma de Mallorca
1973

I

The Agony of Christianity

I die because I do not die.

St. Teresa of Jesus

I. Introduction

CHRISTIANITY IS ONE of the values of the universal spirit with roots in the deepest recesses of human individuality. The Jesuits say that with Christianity we resolve the *business* of our own personal and individual salvation: and even though it is mainly Jesuits who say so, treating the matter as one of divine economics, we can do worse than accept their concept as a preliminary postulate.

Since it is of purely individual concern, and therefore of universal interest, I am forced to explain briefly the personal and private reasons why I undertook the piece here proffered.

The military tyranny reigning in my poor Spanish fatherland exiled me to the island of Fuerteventura, where I was able to enrich my inner religious, and even mystic, experience. I was taken off the island by a French sailing vessel, which brought me to French soil, so I could establish myself here in Paris, where I am writing this, in a kind of cell near the Étoile, here, in this Paris layered with history, saturated with social and civil life, where it is almost impossible to find a single corner from before History, a corner which will survive History. Here, I cannot contemplate the sierra, crowned nearly all year long with snow, upon which I nurture the roots of my soul in Salamanca; nor contemplate the plain, the steppe, at Palencia, where my eldest son has his home, and which assuages my spirit; nor the sea over which I daily watched the sun rise on Fuerteventura. The river here, this Seine, is not the Nervión of my native Bilbao, where the sea's pulse, the ebb and flow of its tides, can be felt. Here, in this cell, when I first arrived in Paris, I fed myself on reading, chance reading, for chance is the root of liberty.

In these particular circumstances—religious and Christian circumstances, I venture to say—I was approached by P. L. Couchoud with a request to contribute a *cahier*, to his series *Christianisme*. And it was he who suggested, among others, the present title: *The Agony of Christianity*. The fact is that he knew my work *The Tragic Sense of Life*.

When P. L. Couchoud came to me with his request, I was reading the *Enquête sur la monarchie*, by Charles Maurras—how far from the Gospels!—in which we are served up some tinned goods containing meat already rotten, a product of the slaughterhouse of the dead Count Joseph de Maistre.

In this deeply anti-Christian book I read about the 1903 program of *L'Action Française*, and of how "a true nationalist puts his country before all else, and as a result conceives, conducts and resolves all political questions in relation to the national interests." When I read this passage I recalled the phrase "My kingdom is not of this world" and I thought that for a true Christian—if indeed a true Christian could be found in public life—every political or other question should be conceived, conducted, and resolved in relation with the individual's interest in eternal salvation, in relation with his interest in eternity. And if the fatherland founders? The fatherland of a Christian is not of this world. A Christian should sacrifice his country to truth.

4

Truth! . . . "You can no longer deceive anybody," wrote Ernest Renan; "the mass of humanity, gazing into the eyes of the thinker, puts the question to him squarely: *Is not the truth fundamentally sad?*"

On Sunday, November 30, of this year of grace—or disgrace—1924, I attended divine services in the Greek Orthodox Church of St-Étienne nearby, in the rue Georges Bizet, and, reading the inscription above on the great painted bust of Christ which fills the tympanum, the Greek words "I am the way, the truth, and the life," I once again felt myself on an island and wondered—or dreamed rather—whether the way and life are the same thing as the truth, whether there isn't some contradiction between truth and life, whether it is not truth that kills illusion and life that maintains it. And then I thought of the agony of Christianity, the agony of Christianity in itself and in each of us. Though, in actual fact, is there any Christianity outside each one of us?

And hence the tragedy. For truth is something collective, social, even civil; truth is what we agree to be true and by which we understand each other. And Christianity is something individual and incommunicable. And thus the reason why it agonizes in each one of us.

Agony, ἀγωνία, means struggle. He who lives in the throes of struggle, struggling against life itself, lives in agony, agonizes. And he struggles against death as well. Its spirit is summed up in the ejaculation of Teresa of Jesus: "I die because I do not die."

What I am about to narrate here, my reader, is my own agony, my struggle for Christianity, the agony of Christianity in me, its death and resurrection at each moment of my inner life.

The Abbé Loyson, Jules-Théodose Loyson, wrote his brother Père Hyacinthe, on June 24, 1871: "It seems here even to those who have most supported you and who hold no prejudice, that you write too many letters, especially at the moment in which all attention is absorbed by matters of general interest. It is feared that it is all part of a tactic by your enemies to draw you on to this terrain and crush you there."

Well now: in the religious sphere, and especially the Christian sphere of things, there is no question of dealing with grand general religious interests, eternal and universal, without assigning them a personal character, and I would say even an individual character. Any Christian, to demonstrate his Christianity, his agony for Christianity, should say of himself *Ecce Christianus*, in the way Pilate said *Ecce Homo*. He should display his Christian soul, his soul of a Christian, the soul he has fashioned in his struggle, in his agony of Christianity. And the end of life is to fashion a soul, an immortal soul; a soul of one's own making. Because at the hour of death one bequeaths a skeleton to the earth, but a soul, a piece of work, to history. Or such is the case when one has lived, that is, when one has wrestled with the life that passes, wrestled it for the prize of the life that remains. And life, what is life? Even more tragic, what is truth? For if truth is not to be defined since it is truth that does the defining, since it is the definer, neither is life to be defined.

* * *

A French materialist—I no longer remember who it was—said that life is the aggregate of functions resisting death. And thus did he define it agonically, or if you prefer, polemically. Life was, then, for him, struggle—agony—against death, and also against truth, against the truth of death.

We speak of the "struggle for life," but this struggle for life is "life" itself, and is at the same time the "struggle."

And it is worth meditating on the biblical legend of Genesis according to which death was introduced into the world by the sin of our first ancestors wishing to be like gods; that is, they wished to be immortal, in possession of the knowledge of good and evil, of the knowledge which bestows immortality. And later, according to the same legend, the first death was a violent one, a murder, Abel's death at the hands of his brother Cain; a fratricide to boot.

One wonders how wild beasts usually die—lions, tigers, panthers, hippopotami—in their jungles or deserts; whether they are most commonly slain or die a so-called natural death, lying down in some corner to die alone and in solitude, like the greatest of saints, in the manner that the greatest saint of all doubtless died, the Unknown Saint—unknown primarily to himself and one who was perhaps born dead.

Life is a struggle, and solidarity with life is struggle and is forged in the struggle. I shall not forbear repeating that what most unites us as human beings are our discords. And what most unites each one with himself, what constitutes the intimate unity of our life, is our inner discords, the interior contradictions of our discords. One only makes peace with oneself in order, like Don Quixote, to die.

And if such is our physical or corporeal life, then our psychic or spiritual life is, in turn, a struggle against eternal oblivion—and against history. For history, which is the thought of God upon man's earth, lacks an ultimate human finality and is bent on oblivion, on unconsciousness. And all of man's effort is to lend a human finality to history, a super-human finality, as Nietzsche might say, Nietzsche who was the great conjurer of that absurdity: social Christianity.

II. Agony

Agony, then, is a struggle. And Christ came to
bring us agony: struggle and not peace. He himself
told us so: "Think not that I am come to send peace
on earth: I came not to send peace, but a sword. For
I am come to set a man at variance against his father,
and the daughter against her mother, and the daughter-in-law against her mother-in-law. And a man's
foes shall be they of his own household" (Matt. 10:
34-36). He remembered that His people, those of His
house, His mother and His brothers, took Him for a
madman. And also that "when his friends heard of it,
they went out to lay hold on him: for they said, He
is beside himself" (Mark 3:21). And then, again:
"I am come to send fire on the earth; and what will I,
if it be already kindled? But I have a baptism to be
baptized with; and how am I straitened till it be accomplished! Suppose ye that I am come to give peace
on earth? I tell you, Nay; but rather division: for
from henceforth there shall be five in one house
divided, three against two and two against three. The
father shall be divided against the son, and the son
against the father; the mother against the daughter,
and the daughter against the mother; the mother-in-
law against her daughter-in-law, and the daughter-
in-law against her mother-in-law" (Luke 12:49-53).

"And what of peace?" we shall be asked. For another similar set of passages from the Gospel might
be reproduced, passages even more numerous and

9

more explicit, which speak to us of peace. But the point is that this peace is the fruit of war and that war is the fruit of peace. And herein lies the agony.

Someone may say that peace is life, or death, and that war is death, or that it is peace: for they are almost indifferently assimilated one to the other; and further, that peace in war—or war in peace—is life in death, the life of death and the death of life, which is agony.

Pure conceptism? Conceptism is St. Paul, and St. Augustine and Pascal. The logic of passion is a conceptist logic, polemical and agonic. And the Gospels are swollen with paradoxes, with bones that burn.

And just as Christianity is always in agony, so is Christ.

Our Spanish crosses, our Spanish Christs are terribly tragic: they represent the worship of Christ in agony, not yet dead. The dead Christ, turned to earth, becomes peace, the dead Christ buried by the other dead is the Christ of the Holy Burial, Christ lying in His sepulchre. But the Christ worshiped on the cross is the agonizing Christ, the One who cries out: *Consummatum est!* And it is this Christ, the Christ of "My God, my God, why hast thou forsaken me?" (Matt. 27:46), that agonic believers worship. And among these believers are many who believe they do not doubt, who believe that they believe.

The way to live, to struggle, to struggle for life and to live on the struggle, on faith, is to doubt. We have already said as much in another work, recalling the Gospel passage: "Lord, I believe; help thou mine unbelief" (Mark 9:24). A faith that does not doubt is a dead faith.

And what is it to doubt? *Dubitare* has the same root—that of the numeral *duo*, two—as *duellum*, struggle. Doubt, Pascalian, agonic or polemical doubt, not Cartesian or methodic doubt, doubt of life (life is struggle) and not doubt of the way (method is way) supposes the duality of combat.

As we learned from the catechism, faith is to believe in what we did not see. To believe in what we see—and what we do not see also—is reason, science; and to believe in what we shall see—or shall not see—is hope. And all of it is belief. I affirm, and believe, as a poet, as a creator, my eyes on the past, on recollection; I deny, I disbelieve as a rational being, a free citizen, my eyes on the present, and I doubt, I struggle and agonize as a man, a Christian, looking into the unrealizable future, into eternity.

Among my Spanish countrymen, my Spanish people, an agonic and polemical race, there is the cult of Christ in His agony. But there is also the cult of Our Lady of Sorrows, *La Dolorosa*, with her heart pierced by seven swords. This Virgin is not precisely the Italian *Pietà*. With us the devotion is not so much to the Son lying dead in the lap of His mother as to the Mother herself, the Virgin Mother, who agonizes in sorrow with her Son in her arms. It is the cult of the Mother in agony.

We also boast, I shall of course be told, the cult of the Infant Jesus, *el Niño de la Bola*, the child holding the globe of the world, the cult of the Nativity, and of the Virgin who gives life by suckling the Child.

I shall never in my life forget the sight I saw on the feast of St. Bernard, in 1922, at the Trappist monastery of Dueñas, near Palencia. The Trappists were singing a solemn *Salve Regina* to Our Lady in her chapel, the scene illuminated with beeswax candles. Above the high altar stood a statue, of no great artistic value, of the Virgin Mother clothed in blue and white. She seemed to be depicted after her visit to her cousin St. Elizabeth, before the birth of the Messiah. Her arms outstretched toward Heaven, she seemed to long to fly there with her tender, tragic burden, the Unconscious Word. The Trappists, young and old, some scarcely of an age to be fathers, some beyond that age, filled the chapel with the chant of their litany.

Janua coeli! they implored, *ora pro nobis!* Gate of Heaven, pray for us. The chant was a cradle song, a lullaby to death. Or rather, a cradle song to not being born. The singers seemed to be dreaming of unliving life, of reliving it back toward infancy, sweet infancy, so they might taste on their lips again the heavenly taste of maternal milk and return to the sheltered, tranquil sanctuary of the womb, there to sleep the sleep of the unborn for centuries, *per omnia saecula saeculorum.* This aspiration, so closely resembling the Buddhist Nirvana—itself a monastic conception—is also a form of agony, however it may seem the opposite.

In the *Journal* of Père Hyacinthe—*Father* Hyacinth, let us not forget—whom we shall discuss at greater length later on, we read under the date of July 9, 1873, when he was awaiting a child of his mystico-carnal marriage, a passage on the immortality of the soul and the resurrection of the flesh: "May he rest in peace beneath his mother's heart for at least the nine months' sweet sleep granted him!" This sweet dreamless sleep was the prenatal earthly paradise of which the Trappist Fathers of Dueñas were dreaming.

On the other hand the Portuguese mystic Frei Tomé de Jesus, in his book *Os trabalhos de Jesus,* tells us of the travails suffered by Our Lord Jesus

Christ in the nine months he spent confined in His Mother's womb.

The suffering of monks and nuns, of the solitaries of both sexes, are not those of sexuality, but rather of maternity and paternity, that is, of finality. They suffer to think that their flesh, bearer of the spirit, will not be perpetuated, will not propagate itself. On the threshold of death, at the end of the world, of their world, they tremble with a desperate hope in the resurrection of the flesh.

The Trappists of Dueñas were chanting *Mater Creatoris, ora pro nobis!* Mother of the Creator! The human spirit longs to create its creator, the one who will endow it with eternal life. *Mater Creatoris!* Mother of the Creator! Hear the cry of anguish, the cry of agony!

The Virgin was called Mother of God, Θεοτόκος, *deipara.* "And blessed is the fruit of thy womb" (Luke 1:42) is said of the Word for whom everything that has been made was made (John 1:3). Not alone the soul, but also the human body, the body which is to be resurrected, yearns to create the Word, that the Word may in turn create the soul and render it eternal: and create the body, cradle and sepulchre of the soul, the body where the soul is born and dis-born, dies and dis-dies. To be dis-born is to die, and to dis-die is to be born. Such is the dialectic of agony.

Perhaps one of those poor Trappists was even then praying for my conversion. For he was praying, without knowing it, for his own conversion.

Thus Christianity agonizes.

But what is Christianity? For we must proceed, they say, by definitions.

III. What is Christianity?

CHRISTIANITY MUST BE DEFINED agonically
and polemically in terms of struggle. Perhaps it
would be better to determine first what Christianity
is not.

In Spanish, the oracular suffix *ismo* of *cristianismo*,
"Christianism," carries with it the suggestion that
Christianity is a doctrine like Platonism, Aristotelian-
ism, Cartesianism, Kantianism, or Hegelianism. But
this is not the fact of the matter. On the other hand
we also have the splendid word *cristiandad*, which,
signifying as it does the quality of being a Christian—as the word humanity signifies being a human
being—has come to mean the community of Christians: Christendom. But this is manifestly an absurdity, for community kills Christianity, which involves
only isolated souls. No one, of course, speaks of
Platonianity, Aristotelianity, Cartesianity, Kantian-
ity, or Hegelianity. And Hegelianity, the quality of
being Hegelian, could not be the same as Hegelity,
the quality of being Hegel. Nevertheless, we do not
distinguish between Christianity and *Christity*. For
the quality of being Christian is the quality of being
Christ. The Christian makes himself a Christ. St.
Paul sensed this fact, for he felt Christ being born,
agonize, and die in him.

St. Paul was the first great mystic, the first Christian properly so called. Though St. Peter was the first

to whom the Master appeared, St. Paul beheld Christ within himself; Christ appeared to him, even though he believed that Christ had died and been buried (1 Cor. 15:3-8). And when he was caught up to the third heaven, without knowing whether in his body or out of it, for concerning such matters only God knows (many centuries later Teresa of Jesus will repeat the same thought) he heard "unspeakable words" ("dichos indecibles," in Spanish, "unspeakable speakings," ἄρρητα ῥήματα), an antithesis very much in the style of agonic mysticism (which is the mystical agony), which proceeds by antithesis, paradoxes, and even by tragic play upon words. For mystic agony plays upon words, plays upon the Word. It plays at creating the Word, as perhaps God played at creating the World, not so as to play with it later but to play in creation, inasmuch as the creation was a game. Once created, He delivered it over to the disputes of men and the agonies of the religions in search of God. And as for St. Paul, when he was caught up to the third heaven, to paradise, he heard *unspeakable words* not given to man to speak (2 Cor. 12:4).

Whoever feels incapable of understanding and sensing this experience, of knowing it in a biblical sense, of engendering and creating it in himself, let him renounce the comprehension not only of Christianity, but of anti-Christianity as well, of history itself, of life itself, of reality, of personality. Let him take up what is commonly called politics—aye, party politics at that—or let him turn to scholarship, devote himself to sociology, or to archeology.

Whoever or whatever one knows with mystic knowledge, through the interpenetration of essences, whether it be Christ, or any living, eternal man, or any and all human or divine power, it always comes to the same: that the knower becomes, in knowing, the known; the lover, in loving, the beloved.

When Lev Shestov, for example, discusses the thoughts of Pascal, he appears disinclined to grasp the fact that to be a Pascalian is not merely to accept his thoughts: it is also to be Pascal, to become Pascal. For my part, it has chanced that on several occasions, whenever I have encountered in some book a man rather than a philosopher or a savant or a thinker, when I encountered a soul rather than a doctrine, I have exclaimed: "But I have been this man myself!" And thus I have lived again with Pascal in his own century and place, and I have lived again with Kierkegaard in Copenhagen, and so with others. And are these phenomena perhaps not the supreme proof of the immortality of the soul? May not these people live in me as I live in them? I shall know, after death, if I thus live on in others. Though even today may not some number of people outside me feel they live in me, even if I do not feel myself in them? What consolation! Leon Shestov opines that "Pascal carries with him no solace, no consolation," and further, that "he annihilates every kind of consolation." Many would agree, but how erroneously! There is no greater consolation than that which springs from dis-consolation, just as there is no more creative hope than that found in the hopelessly despairing, the desperate.

Men seek peace, they say. But do they—really? They are also said to seek liberty. Not so. They look for peace in time of war—and for war in time of peace. They seek liberty under tyranny—and tyranny when they are free.

And as far as liberty and tyranny are concerned, we should not say *homo homini lupus*, man acts like

16

a wolf among men, but rather *homo homini agnus*, man acts like a lamb among men. The tyrant did not make the slave; the slave created the tyrant. A man offered to shoulder his brother, carry him on his back, and it was not the brother who forced him to do so. Man is essentially idle, and in his idleness he is horrified by responsibility.

Returning once again to the subject of mystic knowledge, let us recall the words of Spinoza: *Non ridere, non lugere, neque detestari, sed intelligere*: we should neither laugh, nor lament, nor detest—only understand. But—*intelligere*: understand? NO; rather know in the biblical sense: love—*sed amare*. Spinoza spoke of "intellectual love"; but Spinoza was, like Kant, a bachelor and may have died a virgin. Spinoza and Kant and Pascal were bachelors; they were never, apparently, fathers; and neither were they monks in the Christian sense of the word.

Christianity, or better, Christendom, from the time of its birth in St. Paul, has not been a doctrine, though it has expressed itself dialectically. It has been a way of life, of struggle, an agony. The doctrine has been the Gospel, the Glad Tidings. Christianity has been a preparation for death and resurrection, for eternal life. If Christ be not risen from the dead, then we are of all men most miserable, cried St. Paul.

We could speak of "Father" Paul or "Father" St. Paul, for he was a Holy Father as well as an apostle; but it would occur to no one to speak of Father Spinoza or Father Kant. And one can speak—should speak—of Father Luther, of the monk who married; and one cannot speak of Father Nietzsche, with his progressive paralysis, though there be those who think that Nietzsche's *beyond good and evil* is the same as the *sola fide* of Father Luther's *enslaved will*.

17

Christendom has been the cult of a God-man, who was born, suffered, agonized, died, and arose from the dead to transmit His agony to those who believed in Him. Christ's passion has been the center of the Christian cult. And the Eucharist, the symbol of His passion, is the body of the Christ who dies and is interred in each of those who commune with him.

There is a necessary distinction, as has been repeatedly asserted, between Christianity, or rather Christendom, and evangelism. For the Evangel, the Gospel, is in truth a doctrine.

Perhaps the misnamed "primitive Christianity," the supposed Christianity before the death of Christ, evangelism, contains another, non-Christian, Judaic religion, strictly monotheistic, and the basis of theism.

So-called primitive Christianity, the Christianity of Christ—something as absurd as the Hegelianism of Hegel: Hegel was Hegel and not a Hegelian—was apocalyptic, as has been endlessly demonstrated. Jesus of Nazareth believed in the impending end of the world, and that is why He said: "My kingdom is not of this world." Perhaps He believed in the resurrection of the flesh, in the Judaic manner, rather than in the immortality of the soul in the Platonic manner, and believed also in a Second Coming. Proofs for these beliefs can be found in any honest exegetical work, assuming that exegesis and honesty are compatible.

And in that world to come, in the kingdom of God, whose impending advent was awaited, the flesh would not have to be propagated, would not need to be engendered, for death was destined to die.

The Gospel according to St. Matthew records, in a cardinal passage which is of the very essence of Chris-

18

tianity, that after the Pharisees tempted Jesus by asking Him whether or not it was lawful to pay the tribute to Caesar, that is, to the Roman Empire, He
answered: "Render unto Caesar the things which are
Caesar's; and unto God the things which are God's,"
then the Sadducees came to Him on the same day,
and they, who unlike the Pharisees did not believe in
the resurrection of the flesh and a life to come, asked
Him, in that cardinal passage (22:23-33): "Master,
Moses said, If a man die, having no children, his
brother shall marry his wife, and raise up seed unto
his brother." And they continued: "Now we once had
among our people seven brothers, and the first died
after marriage, and, having no issue, left his wife to
his brother; and the same thing happened with the second brother, and the third, and so on until the seventh,
and the wife died last. Therefore in the resurrection
whose wife shall she be of the seven? for they all had
her." And Jesus replied: "Ye do err, not knowing the
scriptures, nor the power of God. For in the resurrection they neither marry, nor are given in marriage,
but are as the angels of God in heaven. But as touching the resurrection of the dead, have ye not read that
which was spoken unto you by God, saying, I am the
God of Abraham, and the God of Isaac, and the God
of Jacob? God is not the God of the dead, but of the
living. And when the multitude heard this, they were
astonished at his doctrine."

And thus the agony of Christianity followed its
course, between the Pharisees on one side and the
Sadducees on the other.

And later when Jesus died and the spirit of Christ
was reborn in the souls of the faithful, to agonize in
them, then the belief in the resurrection of the flesh

originated and along with a belief in the immortality of the soul. And that great dogma of the resurrection of the flesh in the Judaic manner and of the immortality of the soul in the Hellenic manner came to its agonized fruition in St. Paul, a Hellenized Jew, a Pharisee, who stammered it out in his potent polemical Greek.

Once the anguish attending on the expected end of the world had faded away, once it became clear that the kingdom of God was not about to appear in the world of the living and the dead, of the faithful and the infidel—"Thy kingdom come!"—then those primitive listeners to the words of Jesus, who had received Him with palms on the entry into Jerusalem, felt each one a foreboding of his own individual world's end, of the end of his own world, of the world which was himself, of the world he bore within himself, felt an intimation of his own carnal death, and of his own religion, his own Christianity. Under pain of death, of perishing altogether, each one had to create an individual religion, a *religio quae non religat*: a paradox, in short. For as human beings we live together, but each one dies alone, and death is the supreme solitude.

With the disillusion concerning the end of the world and the beginning of the kingdom of God on earth, history died for the Christians, in so far as those primitive Christians, the evangelists, those who heard and followed Jesus, may be said to have possessed a sense of history. They perhaps knew of Isaiah and Jeremiah, but these prophets had about them nothing of the spirit of a Thucydides.

P. L. Couchoud is in the right when he says (in *Le Mystère de Jésus*) that the Gospel "does not pretend to be history, chronicle, factual narrative, or biography." It is called "glad tidings" (Rom. 10:15). And St. Paul calls it a "mystery" (Rom. 16:25). The Gospel is a revelation of God.

But this divine revelation, this mystery, perforce became Christian history. History, however, implies progress, change; whereas revelation cannot progress, even though Comte Joseph de Maistre, using an agonic dialectic, spoke of "the revelation of the revelation."

The resurrection of the flesh, the Judaic hope— Pharisaic, psychic, almost carnal—entered into conflict with the immortality of the soul, the Hellenic, Platonic, pneumatic, or spiritual hope. And therein lies the tragedy, the agony, of St. Paul—and of Christianity. For the resurrection of the flesh is something physiological, something completely individual. But only a recluse, a monk, a hermit can carnally rise in his flesh and live alone—if such a feat is to live— alone with God.

The immortality of the soul, on the other hand, is a spiritual matter, a social matter. Whosoever creates for himself a soul, whosoever creates a work, lives in it and through it lives in other men, in Humanity, for as long as Humanity lives. And thus he lives in History.

And nevertheless, the Pharisees, the people from among whom sprang the belief in the resurrection of the flesh, awaited a social life, a historical life, a life as a race. For the true deity of the Jews is not Yahweh but the Jewish people. In the eyes of the rationalist Jewish Sadducees, the Messiah is the Jewish race itself, the Chosen People. And they believe in their own immortality. Hence the Judaic concern with physical propagation, with having numerous children, with peopling the world with them, and hence their preoccupation with a patriarchate.

And hence, again, the preoccupation with *proles*: progeny, race. And we have the case of the Jewish Karl Marx attempting a philosophy of the prole-tariat and theorizing on the population law of the Protestant pastor Malthus. The Jewish Sadduceans, being materialists, sought the resurrection of the flesh in their progeny, and also, of course, in money. And St. Paul, the Jewish Pharisee, being spiritualist, sought the resurrection of the flesh in Christ, in a historical Christ rather than in a physiological one. (I will explain later what I mean by historical: an ideal rather than a real concept.) St. Paul sought the resurrection in the immortality of the Christian soul, the immortality of History.

And hence we have doubt, *dubium*, and struggle, *duellum*, and agony. The Epistles of St. Paul offer us the highest example of agonic style: not dialectic, but agonic, for there is no dialogue in it, but only strife and contention.

IV. The Word and the Letter

"And the Word was made flesh and dwelt among us (and we beheld his glory, the glory as of the only begotten of the Father)" reads the beginning of the Gospel According to John (1:14). And this Word, which was made flesh, died after the passion, after the agony, and the Word became the Letter.

That is, the flesh became skeleton, the Word became dogma, and the rains of heaven washed down the bones of the skeleton and carried its salt off to sea. Such was the work of Protestant exegesis, the work of the men of the Letter, the men of the Book. For the spirit, which is speech, the word, oral tradition, breathes life; but the Letter, which is the Book, kills. Though the Apocalypse contains a mandate to eat a book, whoever eats a book is bound to die. The soul, on the contrary, breathes through words.

"The Word was made flesh, and dwelt among us. . . ." Here we stand before the controversial question, the agonic question *par excellence*, the question of the historical Christ.

And who or what is the historical Christ? The answer depends on the manner in which History is felt and understood. Whenever I repeat that I am surer of the historical reality of Don Quixote than of Cervantes, and that Hamlet, Macbeth, King Lear, or Othello created Shakespeare rather than he them, people think I am indulging in paradoxes, in rhetorical figures of speech, expressing myself "in a manner of speaking," when in fact I am expressing an agonic doctrine.

First, we must distinguish between the reality and the personality of the historical person. The word *reality* is derived from Latin *res*, thing, and *personality* is derived from *persona*, person. Karl Marx, the Jewish Sadducee, thought that things mold men and direct them, too; hence his materialist conception of history, his historical materialism, which we might also call realism. But we who wish to believe that men, persons, mold and exercise direction over things, nourish within ourselves, in doubt and agony, a faith in a historical, personalist or spiritualist, conception.

Persona, in Latin, was the actor in a tragedy or comedy, who thus played a part or enacted a role. Personality is the accomplishment of a person in History.

Who or which was the historical Socrates: the Socrates of Xenophon, of Plato, or of Aristophanes? The historical, immortal Socrates was not the man of flesh and blood and bone who lived in such-and-such an epoch in Athens, but the one who lived in each of those who heard him, and from each and all of them was formed the Socrates who left his soul to humanity. And he, Socrates, lives therein.

A melancholy doctrine! No doubt. But the truth is essentially sad. "My soul is exceeding sorrowful unto death!" (Mark 14:34.) It is difficult to console oneself with History. Sorrowful is one's soul unto death, but the flesh is what makes it sorrowful. "O wretched man that I am! who shall deliver me from the body of this death?" (Rom. 7:24) cried St. Paul.

And this body of death is carnal man, physiological man, the human "thing." The other, who lives on in others, in History, is historical man. However, he who lives in History strives also to live in the flesh, strives to root the immortality of his soul in the resurrection of the flesh. Such was the agony of St. Paul. History, moreover, is reality—as much or more than nature. The person is a thing, Spanish *cosa*, and *cosa* is derived from *causa*, cause. So even the narration of History is History. The personal doctrines of Karl Marx, the Jewish Sadducee, who believed that things make men, have produced things—among them the Russian Revolution. Lenin was, indeed, much closer to the truth of historical reality when, on being told that some doctrine was at odds with reality, he exclaimed: "So much the worse for reality!" All of which shows how faithful he was to Hegel!

The Word made flesh strives to live in the flesh, and when death supervenes, it dreams of the resurrection of the flesh.

> It was at first the idea of the Messiah and of the blessed age he was to inaugurate which gave rise to the thought of the unjust fate of the faithful who will have died before his coming. In order to remedy this injustice it was granted that they should be reborn, and, to complete the equality, that they be reborn as they had been when alive. Thus arose the astonishing dogma of the resurrection of the body, in contrast to the Greek notion of the immortality of the soul.

Thus, T. Zielinski, in *La Sibylle*.

The general belief was that the Word had been brought to life. But the Word, which is Christ, spoke but did not write. In only one passage in the Bible— and hence thought to be apocryphal—at the beginning of chapter VIII of the Fourth Gospel, we are told that when the Pharisees brought before Jesus the woman taken in adultery, He bent down to the ground and wrote with His finger, without reed or ink, in the dust of the earth, in letters which the wind would carry away.

But if the Word, the *Palabra* of Low Latin, did not write, St. Paul, the Hellenized Jew, the Platonizing Pharisee, did write or, more correctly, did dictate his Epistles. With St. Paul the Word becomes a Letter, the Gospel becomes a Book, becomes the Bible. And Protestantism, the tyranny of the Letter, makes its appearance. St. Paul begot St. Augustine, and St. Augustine begot Calvin and Jansenius. And perhaps Keyserling was not so far from the truth when he asserted that during Christ's life neither the likes of Paul, or of Augustine, or of Calvin would have followed Him.

Behold here the inner law of religious contradictions. The Prologue of the Fourth Gospel is the work of a bookman, a man of letters, of a biblical and not an evangelical man. And so it commences with the declaration that in the beginning was the Word: ἐν ἀρχῇ ην ὁ λὸγος. It does not say ἐν αρχῇ ἦν ἡ γράφη: in the beginning was the Scripture, the Letter, the Book. Certainly not! Even in man's embryonic process the skeleton follows the flesh.

And thus the Letter appeared, the Epistle, the Book, and the evangelical became the biblical. And then—fount of contradictions!—it was precisely the evangelical element which harbored hope in the death of History. And out of that hope, dashed by the death of the Messiah, out of Hellenized Judaism, out of a Platonizing Pharisaism, was born a faith in the resurrection of the flesh.

The Letter is dead; no life can be found there. The Gospel according to Luke (24) relates that when the disciples of the Master gathered about His tomb on the Saturday after His death, they found the stone rolled away and the body of the Lord not there: "And it came to pass, as they were much perplexed thereabout, behold, two men stood by them in shining garments: And as they were afraid, and bowed down their faces to the earth, they said unto them, Why seek you the living among the dead?" That is: Why seek the Word among bones? Bones have nothing to say.

The immortality of the soul, of the soul which manifests itself in writing, the soul which is the spirit of the Letter, is a pagan philosophic dogma. It is a sceptical dogma, and it is accompanied by a tragic query. A reading of Plato's *Phaedo* should suffice to convince us of this truth. Perhaps those pious pagans dreamed of dying like the Trappists of Dueñas, to fall asleep forever in the bosom of the Lord, or in the bosom of Demeter, the Virgin Mother, to sleep there dreamlessly, coming to an end like the men of the primordial age, the golden age, of whom Hesiod says "that they died as though they were overcome with sleep": θνῆσκον δ' ὥσθ' ὕπνω δεδμημένοι.

St. Paul made the Gospel biblical, changing the Word into the Letter. Quite naturally he has been called the Apostle of the Gentiles, rather than the Apostle to the Pagans. For pagan, from Latin *Paganus*, literally means man of the land, *pagus*, a villager, a peasant, *pagensianus*. And the peasant, the man of the fields, is—another contradiction!—a man of the Word and not of the Letter.

The true pagan was unlettered. Is it not true that the countryside is the domain of the spoken word while the city is the fief of the written word? The *Volksgeist* of the German Romantics is worth little credence.

The illiterate, the unlettered, are the very ones to be enslaved by *alpha* and *beta*, by the alphabet and the Letter. A peasant's head is brimful of literature. His traditions have a literary origin; some man of letters invented his legends. The popular songs of the countryside are made from liturgical music.

The Pauline religion—the religion of the Letter, perhaps even the written Word—was the religion of the cities, of the urban masses, of the workingmen of the great population centers. It was like Bolshevism, which will never penetrate the Russian peasantry, the villagers, the Orthodox pagan peasants, attached as they are to their traditional spoken word.

We are in the presence of a whole world of contradictions!

And thus we have the agony of Christianity in St. Paul and in the Pauline religion which had its source in him; or better, in the religion which begot him. Here was the tragedy of *Paulinity*: the struggle between the resurrection of the flesh and the immortality of the soul, between the Word and the Letter, between the Gospel and the Bible. And the agony continues. "The thesis of the *Phaedo* is no more than a subtlety. I much prefer the Judeo-Christian system of the resurrection," wrote Renan. And if you read the *Choses passées* of the ex-Abbé Alfred Loisy, you will find yourself witness to another agony.

And with the Letter was born dogma, that is, decree. Struggle, agony, became absorbed in dogma and by dogma, because of its very nature, the contradictory nature which is congenital with dogma—for the Letter kills. And then followed the agony of dogmatism, the battle against heresies, the struggle of ideas against thought. But dogma continued, then, to live on in the heresies, just as faith lives on in doubt and from doubts. Dogma sustained itself on negation and reaffirmed itself by negations.

At last arose the greatest of all the heresies since Arianism, which lived on in the new heresy: the Reformation initiated by Huss, Wyclif, and Luther. Since the Reformation cut our Europe in two, Christianity has ceased to exist, we read, and so then the question is asked: Where is mankind to be found for each and every human being? And the answer is: In his fatherland. Or so I read in a piece called "La déesse France" in Charles Maurras's *Enquête sur la monarchie*.

The Reformation, which was a detonation of the Letter, sought to bring the Word to life in the Letter; it sought to extract the Word from the Book, the Gospel from History, and it brought to life the old latent contradiction. And then and there agony did indeed become the very life and fiber of Christianity!

The Protestants, who established the sacrament of the Word—a sacrament which killed the Eucharist—chained the Word to the Letter. And they set about teaching people to read rather than to listen.

And it is a curious fact—though it may only serve to amuse us as an anecdotic aside—that the mother tongue of Ignatius Loyola, founder of the Society of Jesus, is the same language as that of the Abbé de Saint-Cyran of Port-Royal, and the same language as that of my parents and of all my ancestors, that is, *Euskera*, or Basque, and that it became a written language thanks to the Protestant movement. For the translation of the New Testament into Basque by Jean de Liçarrague, a French-Basque Huguenot from Briscous (the Basque Berascoya), was one of the first books, perhaps precisely the second, to appear in Basque.

The attempt was made to establish the Word by means of the Letter, but the agony increased. Bossuet quite aptly said: "You change, therefore you are not truth!" But back came the answer: "You do not change, therefore you must be dead!" And the Church and the Reformation joined battle one against the other, and even within themselves: the Roman Church became Protestantized, and the Reformation became Romanized.

The final outcome was the end of the paganized Christianity petrified in the Holy Roman Empire, the Christianity characterized by the struggle between the Papacy and the Empire, between *Sacerdotium* and *Imperium*. This marked the end of the United States of the West; and the era of national states began, the era of the goddess France and the goddess Germany, the goddess England and the goddess Rome—and the poor demi-goddess Italy. And henceforth so-called Christian citizens could unite in the service of some patriotic, national, or socio-economic cause, but never again for an exclusively religious purpose. Spanish traditionalism will raise its banner of "God, Fatherland, and King!" Mazzini will cry out for "God and the People!" But this God is no longer the God of that Christ who fled to the wilderness when the mob wanted to proclaim him King.

During one of our Spanish Civil Wars, the Civil War of 1873 to 1876, in my native Basque country, the Carlist General Lizárraga—his name the same as that of the Huguenot who translated the Bible into Basque, and the same name my own children bear on their mother's side—advancing on the Liberals, hurled toward Heaven the unconscious blasphemy "Long Live God!" One may well call out "As God lives . . . !" But to say "Long live God!" in the subjunctive case, or in the optative . . . ? Or perhaps indeed even in the imperative . . . !

The Reformation attempted a return to life by way of the Letter, and went on to nullify the Letter. For free inquiry constitutes death for the Letter.

V. Abishag the Shunammite

THE FIRST BOOK OF KINGS, commonly called the Third Book of Kings, begins:

> Now King David was old and stricken in years; and they covered him with clothes, but he gat no heat. Wherefore his servants said unto him, Let there be sought for my lord the king a young virgin: and let her stand before the king, and let her cherish him, and let her lie in thy bosom, that my lord the king may get heat. So they sought for a fair damsel throughout all the coasts of Israel, and found Abishag a Shunammite, and brought her to the king. And the damsel was very fair, and cherished the king, and ministered to him: but the king knew her not.

And then we are told that Adonijah, son of Haggith, rose up saying he would reign once David was dead, and he assembled his followers. But the prophet Nathan said to Bath-sheba, the mother of Solomon, that it was he, Solomon, and not Adonijah who was to succeed David. And he caused her to go in to the great king, her companion in sin, to draw from him a promise that his successor on the throne should be Solomon, the son of their sin, and not Adonijah, who was already busy offering up sacrifices and comporting himself like a king. The prophet Nathan abetted Bath-sheba in her endeavor. In the meantime, poor Abishag, the unique—and still—virgin wife of the great king, continued in her attempts to bring him heat in his last days, all unaware of any conspiracy.

David swore to Bath-sheba that Solomon would be his successor on the throne.

> Then Bath-sheba bowed with her face to the earth, and did reverence to the king, and said, Let my lord king David live for ever.
> And King David said, Call me Zadok the priest, and Nathan the prophet, and Benaiah the son of Jehoiada. . . . And bring him down to Gihon . . . and anoint him there king over Israel: and blow ye with the trumpet, and say, God save king Solomon.

And they did so, amidst a great multitude. And meanwhile poor Abishag of Shunam, innocent of all these political doings, continued to give warmth with her kisses and caresses to David on his deathbed.

The followers of Adonijah, Jonathan, the son of the high priest Abiathar, and others dispersed. But Adonijah, fearful of Solomon, "arose, and went, and caught hold on the horns of the altar." And then he "came and bowed himself to king Solomon."

The second chapter relates the counsels David gave Solomon, the son of his sin, as David lay dying. And then: "So David slept with his fathers, and was buried in the city of David."

Though the biblical text does not say so, David must have died in the arms of Abishag, the Shunammite, his last wife, who gave him warmth with her kisses and caresses on his deathbed, who rocked him perhaps in his last sleep with a mother's lullaby. For Abishag, the virgin, whom David never knew just as she never knew him except in desire, was the last mother to the great King.

And so Solomon sat on the throne of David, his father, and Adonijah, the rejected pretender, sought out Bath-sheba and persuaded her to ask Solomon to give him, "to wife," Abishag the Shunammite, the

widow of David. Solomon was outraged at the wili-
ness of his elder brother, who thus attempted to take
the throne from him, and he vowed to have him killed.

Solomon was a wise king—and a sensual one.
Versed in political life, he was a civilized king. And
we hear nothing more of poor Abishag, the Shunammite, who had languished with love by the side of
her now dead king, lying by the side of the husband
of her virginity, mourning him with hot tears, and
wanting him back alive. Meanwhile Solomon reigned
and kept a harem. Is not the symbolic significance of
the story plain?

David has always been for Christians a symbolic
figure, one of the prefigurations of the God-Man, of
Christ. The soul in love strives to give him warmth
in his death-agony, his final agony, with the kisses
and embraces of incandescent love. And since the soul
cannot know, as Abishag could not know, its Beloved,
and since the Beloved—and this is more terrible
still—can no longer know the loving soul, the soul
despairs in its love.

To know, in the biblical sense, is synonymous with
the act of carnal union—and spiritual union—by
means of which children are engendered, children of
flesh and spirit. And this sense of the word deserves
some meditation.

In Genesis, Adam and Eve were commanded to
increase and multiply (1:28), before they were for-
bidden under pain of death to taste of the fruit of the
tree of knowledge of good and evil (2:17), which,
according to the serpent, would make them like gods.
And yet, a widespread popular Christian tradition has
stubbornly persisted in taking original sin—commonly understood as the fall of our first parents in Paradise—to mean carnal temptation. And with that sin

and that fall, History began, and so did what we call progress.

To know, biblically to know, then, is in effect to engender, and all vital knowledge presupposes a penetration, a fusion in the depths of the spirit, a fusion of the knowing spirit with the thing known; all the more so if the thing known is another spirit, as is often the case; and still more so if the thing known is God, God in Christ, or Christ in God. Hence the mystics speak of spiritual marriage and say that mysticism is a species of meta-erotic love, a beyond-love.

This type of knowledge, mystical or creative, then, is quite unlike what we call rational knowledge— though who the devil knows what rationalists mean by reason! *Ratio* is one thing, and *Vernunft* another. I read, for example, in Lev Shestov, who was a rationalist, this statement on Pascal: "The basic condition of the possibility for human knowledge consists, I repeat, in the fact that truth can be perceived by any normal man." But what does he mean by a "normal man"? The everyday common man, the "average man" of the English language, the German *Durchschnittsmensch*? That is to say, some creature of phantasy: *Phantasia, non homo,* to use the expression of Petronius. It was these poor normal men who perceive nothing but rational truth whom Comte Joseph de Maistre, another agonic man, had in mind when he wrote, not without a touch of hauteur: "They have nothing but their reason!" Poor human reason—and not divine, creative truth!

Le pur enthousiasme est craint des faibles âmes
Qui ne sauraient porter son ardeur et son poids.

So wrote Alfred de Vigny, another Pascalian man, in his *La Maison du berger*. And it should be noted that enthusiasm, Spanish "endiosamiento," ἐνθουσιασμός, signifies "to be possessed by a god." The enthusiast is a man possessed by a god, transformed into a god, pervaded by God. And this is something which can happen to a poet, to a creative man, but never to a normal or average man.

> Et n'être que poète est pour eux un affront

"And to be merely a poet is for them an affront." And in their turn the rationalists clamor: "They have nothing to offer but verse!" The poets thus offer their poetry. And who offers truth?

Poor Abishag, the Shunammite, a soul hungering and thirsting for spiritual maternity, wildly enamored of the Great King who lay dying, did her best to sustain him, to breed with him, to give him life, to revive him with her mad kisses and embraces. And she buried him within her. David, for his part, deeply loved the poor girl who warmed him on his deathbed, but he could no longer know her. An awful fate for David, and awful for Abishag! Who suffered more?

Which is the more terrible for a soul: not to be able to love, or not to be loved? Not to be able to know or not to be known? Not to be able to beget or not to be able to be begotten upon? Not to be able to create life or to be unable to receive life? St. Teresa of Jesus pitied the Devil because he cannot love. And Goethe said of Mephistopheles that he was the power who, wishing to do evil, effects good; wishing to destroy, he builds. The truth is that hatred, and even more so envy, are forms of love. True atheists are madly enamored of God.

A great Spanish political figure, Don Nicolás Salmerón, used to say that one lost the virginity of faith only to acquire the maternity of reason. But there is also a maternal virginity, or a virginal maternity. But sometimes virginity, literally speaking, is lost without subsequent maternity—or paternity—and this happens most especially when the blood is en- venomed by a certain vice. And then there are eunuchs, such as the Ethiopian eunuch in the service of Candace, of whom the Acts of the Apostles make mention and who achieved procreation of the spirit.

The poor soul hungry and thirsty for immortality and the resurrection of the flesh, hungry and thirsty for God, for the God-Man in the Christian fashion, or the Man-God in the pagan fashion, consummates its maternal virginity by embracing the eternal agonist.

Other books tell of how Israel went from mono- cultism to mono-theism, and yet other books again tell of what it means when a God becomes man or a man becomes God. In this book I wish only to speak of the profound meta-erotic (mystical, if you will) experience and of what constitutes the agony of a soul steeped in the agony of its God, of the agony of love and knowledge: of knowledge, which is love, and of love, which is knowledge.

The soul delivered over to the agony of love and of knowledge scarcely takes any heed of the doings of Solomon—of his political feats, of history, of civili- zation, not even of his temple, which is to say, the Church. And if such a soul does take any heed at all, it will be merely to rekindle its agony and, in the end, because a soul, every soul, is the daughter of contra- diction. But Abishag need not, aye, need not forever reject Adonijah. Imagine her married to him, the mother of his children, and Adonijah continuing his contest with his brother Solomon—and Abishag still enamored of David. For there is only the one great love, the first and the last. Imagine Abishag the Shunammite, her soul rent, her love for David at war with her duty to Adonijah, son of David. Imagine that tragedy!

Would the embraces and kisses of Abishag ever work the miracle of bringing David back to life?

A miracle! Here we come face to face with one of the most confusing of concepts, especially now that faith in the miracles of faith has been displaced by faith in the miracles of science.

"Savages are not astonished by the applications of scientific discovery," we hear said. When a savage sees an airplane in flight or hears a recording, he is not, apparently, overly impressed. Why should he be? He is accustomed to seeing the miracle of an eagle in flight, the miracle of a man or a parrot talking, and one miracle the more does not overwhelm him. The savage lives amid mysteries and miracles. And the savage who is born and reared among a people called civilized never loses his faith in miracles, if not in miracles of faith, in miracles of science.

One day, a lecture on astronomy was given in the hall of a social club. The audience, made up of employees from commercial and industrial establishments, some manual workers among them, men of no scientific background, were astonished when they heard from the lecturer—that is, from Science itself—of the millions of miles that lay between Sirius and the sun. "But how could such a distance have been measured?" the audience wanted to know. And they answered themselves: "The miracles of science!" The following day an ingenuous man tried to explain how the measurement was made, and when they realized that, though somewhat more complicated, the method was much the same as the one used by a surveyor to measure land or to calculate the height of a mountain, their reaction was one of contempt for science. Among their number were certain social mystics, of the kind who salivate when the talk turns to socialism . . . "scientific socialism." Scientific socialism, indeed—the kind that produced the Bolshevik miracle!

Maurras wrote (in his *Enquête sur la Monarchie*, p. 481):

> I do not know what General André, who passes for a Positivist, thinks on this head, but his master and mine, Auguste Comte, always considered Catholicism the necessary ally of science against anarchy and barbarism. He often used to say: let those who believe in God become Catholics, and those who do not believe in God become Positivists. . . . He sent one of his followers to Rome, to the Gesú, to consult the Jesuits. A misunderstanding marred the meeting; but on quitting the company of the Jesuits, the representative of Comte uttered the following grave words: *When the political storms of the future make manifest the intensity of the modern crisis, you will find the young Positivists just as ready to die for you, as you are ready to be massacred for your God.*
>
> Divided as to the things of heaven, Positivism and Catholicism are often in accord on earth. One kind of Positivist is M. Accard, a follower of Bonald and of Taine, who figures in one of Paul Bourget's novels. . . .

....

> The Church and Positivism tend to fortify the family. The Church and Positivism tend to support political authority as having its source in God or the highest laws of nature. The Church and Positivism are friends of tradition, of order, of the fatherland, of civilization. In short: the Church and Positivism have the same enemies. In addition, no French Posi-

tivist would ever forget that if the Capetian dynasty made France, the bishops and the clergy were their first collaborators.

All the above may have to do with the kingdom of Solomon and the dissensions between Solomon and Adonijah: it is of the essence of Catholicism, but it has nothing to do with the kingdom of David, and even less with his agony, with that agony which constitutes life for Christianity.

And what of Abishag's love: what was that? Faith? Hope?

I have just finished reading in the *Variété* of the poet Paul Valéry his "La Crise de l'esprit," where he writes: "But hope is only man's mistrust of the clear foresight of his mind. Hope suggests that any conclusion unfavorable to us *must be* an error of the mind."

Auguste Comte asked that "those who believe in God become Catholics." Louis Veuillot, another precursor of *L'Action Française*, addressing the cunning Henri Rochefort, told him: "Monsieur le comte, you are so divertingly original, but we lesser folk are in need of God, or at least in need of people who believe in God." But inasmuch as Veuillot drew a fine distinction between *croire en Dieu* and *croire à Dieu*, between believing in God and believing that there is a God, people not native to France, such as myself, scarce can understand this business of needing people who believe in God. And we must renounce any possibility of understanding it, inasmuch as the self-same Veuillot tells us that "French is not to be learned merely by wanting to learn it: one must be born to it." And he adds: "And why learn French?" Then:

Because French is a beautiful and noble language. One does not know French, speak French, write French, without knowing many other things which go into the making of what used to be called an *honnête homme*, an honorable man. French poorly tolerates the lie. In order to speak French it is imperative to possess a fundamental nobility and sincerity. Here you may dissent, citing Voltaire. But Voltaire, though he was no fool, spoke a desiccated language, already notoriously debased.

I will not cite Voltaire, who was certainly no Jesuit—though perhaps something worse—and will merely admit to being forever limited by an inability to distinguish between believing in God and believing that there is a God, or by not knowing the manner in which people who believe in God are simply to "become Catholics." And as for being ready to be massacred for the God of the Jesuits—that must be political talk. Men allow themselves to be massacred for an idol. The truth is that very few have enough soul to warm their God in His agony and make Him live, to imbue agony with life.

And will that David whom Abishag wished to revive with her kisses and embraces, will that Christ in agony, cause God the Father to save us? And here we speak of *justification*, which pertains to morality.

I have been reading Lev Shestov on the terrible dilemma with which Erasmus confronted Luther: if we are not saved by good works but only by the grace of God, a grace which God is free to bestow upon some and deny to others, "where, then, is justice?" And Shestov continues:

> Erasmus was not interested in discussing the Bible or Saint Paul. Like everyone else he condemned Pelagius and accepted the doctrine of Saint Augustine concerning grace, but he could not accept the monstrous thought that God was *beyond good and evil*, or that our *free will*, our consent to submit to the Law, be left, meaninglessly, to the supreme

tribunal; that before God, in short, man possesses no defense, not even justice. Thus wrote Erasmus, and thus have thought and still think nearly all men; one might even say, more simply, all men.

All men, perhaps; but not all Christians! Christians can not believe in such a manner. And as for God's being "beyond good and evil": nothing of the sort! The "beyond" here, the German *Jenseits*, is a Germanic formula belonging to the progressive thinker Nietzsche. God is *within* good and evil, encompassing them both, just as eternity is *within* the past and the future, encompassing them both, in this sense *beyond* time. And justice—what about justice? It is something in morality; in religion it is nothing.

VI. The Virility of Faith

PÈRE HYACINTHE, of whom we shall speak at good length later, and whose childhood memories centered around "the Catholic sadness of his family's hearth, the suffering soul of his revered father, and the melancholia of his good mother," this poor Père Hyacinthe, who dreamed of finding the Church in the garden and the cell of his monastery, at one time corresponded with Ernest Renan, and once wrote to him (May 11, 1891) thus:

> Is it an illusion? Is it only a memory? Is it still a hope? Allow me, allow my candid and robust faith as a spiritualist and a Christian, this last hypothesis. In any case, I believe so firmly in the survival of souls and their final salvation, that I do not despair of finding myself in entire accord with you in some other world, if not in this one.

Père Hyacinthe's candid and robust faith did not comprehend the fact that illusion, memory, and hope are not three hypotheses but only one: that hope is a memory, and that both hope and memory are illusions, and that faith, according to St. Paul, "is the substance of things hoped for" (Heb. 11:1). Paul speaks of what is hoped for as being an act of will. But does not memory also depend on the will? And the same Paul says, with a Pindaric note in his voice, that eating, drinking, feasting, and the Sabbath "are a shadow of things to come," σκὶα τῶν μελλόντων (Col. 2:17). And memory is as much if not more a shadow of things to come as, or than, hope is the shadow of the past.

In the *Journal* of Père Hyacinthe we read under the date of October 18, 1892: "The thinker affirms or denies; Renan's intellectual power did not carry him beyond doubt. He lacked *virility*."

A lack of virility! For this friar, this Father, it was all a question of virility! For this man who wished to leave the seed of his flesh in this world where the dead resurrect, it was a question of virility: the feat of transcending doubt, of affirming or denying, of believing or not believing—and not to believe is to believe since "I do not believe in the resurrection of the dead" can be phrased as "I believe that the dead do not rise again, that the dead die." Faith the daughter of virility! Affirmation or negation, dogma, the sons of virility!

Virility derives from *vir*, man, the male of the human species. The same root serves to form *virtus*. And, according to Christian theologians (albeit the words Christian and theologian imply a contradiction), faith is, at least in Spanish, "una virtud teologal": "teologal" and not "teológica," which would be "theological," a theological virtue. But there are no theological virtues, unless it be *furor theologicus*, which fathered the Inquisition. But let us examine briefly this notion of virility, since our father-friar appears to think that to affirm or deny, to get "beyond doubt," is more a matter of the will than it is even of intellectual potency. Let us examine the will and the will to believe.

The pragmatist William James, another Christian in despair, another of those in whom Christianity agonized, wrote an entire essay on the will to believe

Has this will anything to do with virility? Is virility a source of will?

Schopenhauer, who thought that it was, and who considered the virile organs to be the center of will, praised and admired the Spanish for being of the same mind as himself and cited certain popular expressions current in Spain in defense of his views— rather coarse expressions, for the names of these organs are bandied about by Spaniards in the belief that such a practice makes them men of action, decision, will. Awesome blasphemies abound about the holy name, which ought to be sacrosanct, and one is reminded of the phrase in Petronius' *Satyricon*, concerning a man who *putabat se colleum Jovis tenere*. But is this will?

The Spanish word for will, *voluntad*, is a word without living roots in current colloquial language. In French, *volonté* is closely related to *vouloir*, low Latin *volere*, classic Latin *velle*. But in Spanish we have no derivative of this Latin root: for *vouloir* we say *querer*, from Latin *quaerere*, to seek, quest, and from our *querer* we get *querencia*, a substantive applied only to animals and which designates the attachment they build up or feel instantly for a certain place or person. The real Spanish word to express what issues from the organs of virility, an expression of desire and not will, is *gana*.

Gana! An admirable word! *Gana*, which is probably of Germanic origin—though Spanish is the most Latin of the Latin languages, even more Latin than Italian, and the language containing the fewest Germanic elements—*gana* partakes of the words desire, humor, appetite, longing. We Spanish feel or have *ganas*, in the plural, to eat and drink, and to rid ourselves of the unassimilated surplus. There are *ganas* to work and, even more, *ganas* to do nothing at all. As the man said: "It's not that I don't have *ganas* to work, it's simply that I have *ganas* not to work." And the *gana* of not-doing is *desgana*: dis-desire, want of appetite. "Virility" all by itself moves on to its own suicide, down the road to solitude, to eunuchism—which is the end stop for wilful abulics, those who wilfully lose all desire, wilfully lose their will.

How accurate and how profound is the phrase "spiritual lust"! The lust of the solitary onanist in the style of poor Huysmans, another soul in agony, in spiritual contention, when he was *en route* to monastic Christian faith, the faith of these lonely souls who renounce carnal paternity. A Spaniard will say: "No me da la real gana!" "I don't royally feel like it!" "No me da la santísima gana!" "I don't Most Holy feel like it!" He doesn't give a royal, Most Holy damn! And he will also say: "It doesn't come from my . . . organs of virility" (to use a euphemism). But what does all that mean now? What is the source of his royal, Most Holy *gana* then?

La gana, as we have said, is not an intellectual faculty. And it can express itself in *des-gana*, lack of appetite or desire. Instead of will, *voluntad*, it engenders *noluntad*, a word we can put together from *nolle*, not to want. And this *noluntad*, daughter of *desgana*, leads to *nada*, nothingness.

Nada! Another fine Spanish word, brimming with life, with abysmal resonances! It was the word which poor Amiel, still another agonizing solitary—and how he wrestled with virility!—engraved in Spanish in his *Journal intime*. That word *Nada!* The nothingness in which faith based on virility, and the virility of faith, finally end.

Nada! Here is the word at the bottom of our special brand of Spanish nihilism—or better, our *nada-ism*, to distinguish it from the Russian variety—which already appears in St. John of the Cross, and which is palely reflected in Fénelon and Mme Guyon, and which is called Quietism in that Aragonese Spaniard Miguel de Molinos. *Nada*-ism has never been better defined than it was by the painter Ignacio Zuloaga, when he showed a friend his portrait of *The Wineskin-Seller of Segovia*, a monster rendered in the manner of Velázquez, a deformed and maudlin dwarf, and exclaimed: "If you could only see what a philosopher he is! . . . He says nothing!" *Nada*! It was not that the monster-philosopher said there was nothing or that everything was as nothing or comes to nothing, but simply that he said nothing. Perhaps he was a mystic submerged in St. John of the Cross's dark night of the soul. Perhaps all the monsters of Velázquez are mystics of this strain. Perhaps Spanish painting is the purest expression of the virile philosophy of Spain. The wineskin-seller of Segovia, by saying nothing about nothing, is freed from the obligation of thinking. He is a real free-thinker.

The faith of virility? Rather than faith, rather than the will to believe, what exists is a longing to believe, *ganas* to believe. And this longing and desire issues from the flesh, which according to the Apostle, "lusteth against the Spirit" (Gal. 5:17). And yet he speaks also of the "lusts of our flesh, fulfilling the desires of the flesh and the mind," *the will of the flesh*, θελήματα τῆς σαρκός (Eph. 2:3). Of the flesh that grows sad after it has sown its seed, the while "the whole creation groaneth and travaileth in pain" (Rom. 8:22). Despite everything, we must propagate the flesh. And at the same time we must husband our virility for the engendering of spiritual children. Which shall save us? The children of the flesh through the resurrection of the flesh, or those of the spirit through the immortality of the soul? Perhaps these two forms of survival are mutually contradictory in themselves.

Yet the flesh, according to St. Bernard—precursor of nature-loving Franciscan piety, so understanding of "Brother Pig," the body—is a truly good and faithful companion and comrade to the good spirit: "Bonus plane fidusque comes caro spiritui bono." And is there any need to cite Juvenal's "mens sana in corpore sano"? But then, perhaps the perfectly healthy body is possessed of a soul sunk in the abyss of Nothingness—like the soul of the wineskin-seller of Segovia.

Ganas to believe, a craving to believe! St. John of the Cross speaks of the "appetite for God" in his *Ascent of Mount Carmel* (Bk. 1, Ch. X). And this same appetite for God, whenever God Himself does not inspire it, that is, when it does not follow upon grace, "is of the same substance and nature as if it were near-matter and a natural object," and "it is nothing but nature and will remain so unless God were to inform it."

Appetite is blind, says the mystic. But if it is blind, how can it believe, since "seeing is believing"? And if it does not see, how can it affirm or deny?

"All that is in the world, the lust of the flesh, and the lust of the eyes, and the pride of life . . . is of the world," says the first of the epistles attributed to the Apostle John (1 John 2:16). And to seek God so that our flesh may be resurrected is as much lust of the flesh as it is to seek God in the world. And if it is agonic to try to propagate Christianity by the sword, by brandishing Christ, by crusades, it is agonic madness to try to propagate it by carnally engendering Christians through carnal proselytism, by vegetative propaganda.

A Crusade represents a form of virility—and it is a product of free will and not of grace. A crusade constitutes one of the most agonic acts of Christianity. Whoever sets out to impose a certain faith on someone else by the sword is seeking first to convince himself. He asks for signs, he asks for the chance to work a miracle, to buttress his own faith. And every crusade by the sword ends in the conquest of the conqueror, the conquistador by the conquered. And the conqueror, the conquistador, becomes a *nada*-ist.

An active monkhood, a way of husbanding virility in celibacy, is a necessity. The author of *La Peau de chagrin*, Honoré de Balzac, who left behind him so many children of the spirit—an entire race of them—and not a single child of the flesh, so far as we know, once wrote a profound study of provincial life, of prurient itches in the provinces, titled the *Curé de Tours* (where we read those admirable lines about the "*città dolente* of old maids" apropos of Mlle Salomon who became a mother while remaining a virgin), terminating this psychological gem with an immortal page on celibacy. He begins by presenting the terrible Pope Hildebrand: only a celibate may be infallible, only one who husbands his carnal virility may imprudently affirm or deny, and say "I excommunicate you in the name of God!" thinking the while "God in my name excommunicates you! *Anathema sit!*"

And Balzac goes on to speak of "the seeming selfishness of men who carry within themselves a science, a nation, a body of laws . . . in order to give birth to new nations or new ideas": what Balzac calls "the maternity of the masses"; maternity, mind you, and not paternity, just as he says "give birth to"—rather than "beget," *enfanter* and not *engendrer*—new nations. And he adds that these men must combine in their powerful being "the teats of a woman with the force of God." The force of God is virility. Is God male or female? In Greek, the Holy Ghost is neuter, but it is identified with Santa Sophia, Hagia Sophia, Holy Wisdom, which is feminine.

The husbanding of virility is a necessity, but does it resolve the agony? *L'agonie* is the title of the last part of that "frightful philosophical study," as its author himself calls *La Peau de chagrin*. At the end, Rafael de Valentin, the prot-agonist, that is, the one who agonizes, who struggles, the protagonist being the principal agonist, this Valentin dies with his teeth sunk in his wife's breast, and she, Pauline, cries out to the old retainer Jonathas: "What do you want? . . . He's mine. I killed him. Didn't I foresee it all?"

And let the reader not be surprised that in this study of the agony of Christianity we make reference to these two works of Honoré de Balzac, who was an evangelist and a Christian, in his fashion. Let us, however, return to St. Paul.

The Apostle Paul knew not woman and he recommended those who were capable of denying themselves to abstain from touching one (1 Cor. 7:1). Thanks to this continence, Paul was enabled through the gospel to beget in Christ Jesus (1 Cor. 4:15) not children of the flesh, but children of God (Rom. 9:8), children of the freewoman and not the bondmaid (Gal. 4:22-23). To those who had wives he recommended that they live as though they had none (1 Cor. 7:29). But for the man who felt himself weak, for whoever felt that he did not do the good which he would but the evil which he would not (Rom. 7:19), whoever was not animated by the will of the spirit of God but by the lust of the flesh, daughter of the earth, it were better that he marry than burn (1 Cor. 7:9). Woman thus is merely a remedy for concupiscence.

A remedy for concupiscence! Poor women! But woman "shall be saved in childbearing" (1 Tim. 2:15), if she can do nothing else. For man does not issue from woman, but woman from man (1 Cor. 11:9; Eph. 5:23), since Eve was fashioned from the rib of Adam. Nonetheless, the Virgin Mother, of whom the virile Apostle to the Gentiles never (of course) ever speaks, was not born of one of Christ's ribs, but instead Christ was born of woman (Gal. 4:4).

Christ was born of woman! Even the historic Christ, who came back from the dead. Paul tells us that Christ was first seen by Peter—he does not say that Peter saw Christ, but that Christ was seen by Peter, in the passive—and the last by whom Christ was seen was by Paul himself, "the least of the Apostles" (1 Cor. 15:9). But the fourth Gospel, which might be called the feminine Gospel, tells us that the first person to whom the risen Christ appeared was a woman, Mary Magdalen, and not a man (John 20: 15-17). Christ was seen by Peter, and heard by Mary Magdalen. When he appeared before her, in spiritual body, in a vision, she did not recognize him until she heard him lovingly call "Mary!" And then she replied "Rabboni": which is to say, Master. And Christ, who was not a mere apparition, a mere silent figure, but the Word, the Logos, spoke to her: Jesus said to her:

"Touch me not." The person who felt a need to touch in order to believe was Thomas, a man. Thomas had to see the imprint of the nails in Christ's palms and touch them with his finger, to see by touch. And to him Jesus said: "Because thou hast seen me, thou hast believed: blessed are they that have not seen, and yet have believed" (John 20:24-30). And thus it is said that faith consists in believing what has not been seen but heard. And after Christ said "Touch me not" to Mary Magdalen, He added: "For I am not yet ascended to my Father: but go to my brethren, and say unto them, I ascend unto my Father, and your Father; and to my God, and your God." And Mary went to tell what she had seen, and above all, what she had heard.

The Letter is seen, but the Word is heard. Faith enters by the ear. Paul himself, on being "caught up to the third heaven" heard "unspeakable words, unspeakable speakings." The Samaritan woman heard Christ; and Sara, though past the age, was delivered of a child of faith; and Rahab, the harlot, was saved by faith (Heb. 11:11-31). What more need be said? Unless to add that if not a woman, at least it was a eunuch, Queen Candace's favorite, an Ethiopian eunuch, who, after first reading Isaiah, then believed upon hearing the words of the Apostle Philip (Acts 8:26-40).

Faith is passive, feminine, the daughter of grace, and not active, masculine, or a product of free will. The beatific vision is a benefit in another life, but is it vision or hearing? According to Paul's polemic, faith here below comes from Christ, who rose from the dead, and not from the flesh, from that Christ who was virgin, of whose body all Christians are members (1 Cor. 6:15).

Pagan mythology offers us a man, a male god who, without recourse to woman, begets a daughter: for Jupiter begot Minerva from his own head.

What, then, of faith? A truly living faith, a faith living on doubt and never carrying the believer beyond doubt, the faith of Renan, is a will to know transformed into a will to love, a will to comprehend become a comprehension of will, and not a craving to believe, that ends, by way of virility, in nothingness. And such a faith is an agonic struggle, constant strife.

Virility, will, *ganas* are one thing; quite another is faith, femininity, woman, and the Virgin Mary. And the Virgin is the Mother of Faith: mother of faith by virginity.

"Lord, I believe; help thou mine unbelief" (Mark 9:24). "I believe" here means "I want to believe," or better, "I have a craving to believe," and represents the high point of virility, of free will, which Luther called "enslaved will," *servum arbitrium*. "Help thou mine unbelief" represents the high point of femininity, which is that of grace. And faith, albeit Père Hyacinthe wants it otherwise, emanates from grace and not from free will. Whoever craves to believe does not believe. Virility by itself is sterile. The Christian religion has, however, conceived the idea of a pure maternity, without recourse to man, of a faith by pure grace, by effective grace.

Faith by pure grace! The Angel of the Lord came into the house of Mary and, hailing her, said: "Fear not, Mary: for thou hast found favor with God." And he announced to her the mystery of Christ's birth; and she asked "How shall this be, seeing I know not man?" and the angel enlightened her. And Mary said: "Behold the handmaiden of the Lord; be it unto me according to Thy word." And the angel departed from her (Luke 1:26-38).

Full of grace, κεχαριτωμένη: only one woman is so called, and she is the symbol of pure femininity, of virginal motherhood, one who had no need to be carried beyond doubt because she had never doubted. Nor had she any need of virility. "Blessed are the poor in spirit: for theirs is the kingdom of heaven! Blessed are the pure in heart: for they shall see God!" (Matt. 5:3, 8).

"Virgin's thread" is a name given certain tiny threads which float in the wind and upon which spiders launch themselves into the open air and even into hurricanes, spiders which Hesiod (in *Works and Days*, 777) calls "airy-swinging." Seeds may be winged, as we know, equipped with tufts. But these spiders spin from their own entrails these frail filaments on which they hurl themselves into unknown space. A terrifying symbol of faith! Here faith hangs on Virgin's thread.

It is said that when the scorpion finds itself surrounded by fire and menaced by the flames, it sinks its poisoned barb into its own head. Is not our kind of Christianity and our kind of civilization a representation of this suicidal instinct?

The Apostle says of the polemic of agony that whoever struggles, whoever agonizes, is victorious over all: πᾶς δὲ ὁ ἀγωνιζόμενος πάντα ἐγκρατεύεται (1 Cor. 9:25). He himself, Paul, fought his own good fight, agonized through his own good agony, τὸν καλὸν ἀγῶνα ἠγώνισμαι (2 Tim. 4:7). Was he victorious? In that strife, to conquer is to be conquered. The triumph of agony is death; and this kind of death is perhaps life eternal. Thy will be done, on earth as it is in heaven, and let it be done in me according to Thy word: the act of engendering is also a kind of agony.

VII. So-Called Social Christianity

WHAT IS ALL this talk about social Christianity? What is this business of the social kingdom of Jesus Christ, with which the Jesuits make our ears ring? What has Christianity, true Christianity, to do with society here below, on earth? What is all the talk about Christian Democracy?

"My kingdom is not of this world" (John 18:36), said Christ when He saw that history was not coming to an end. And again: "Render therefore unto Caesar the things which be Caesar's, and unto God the things which be God's" (Luke 20:25). We must also recall the circumstances in which this last cardinal sentence was uttered.

Those who pursued and attempted to destroy Christ decided to ask Him if it was licit or not to pay tribute to Caesar, the invader, the enemy of the Jewish fatherland, the temporal authority. If He said yes, He might be presented before His people as a bad Jew, a traitor to His people; and if He said no, He might be accused of sedition before the imperial authorities. When the question was put to Him, Jesus asked for a piece of money and, pointing to the effigy on the coin, asked: "Whose image and superscription hath it?" They answered, "and said, Caesar's." And He: "Render therefore unto Caesar the things which be Caesar's, and unto God the things which be God's." The meaning seems clear: give to Caesar the world, society, the money which is Caesar's, the world's, society's; and give to God the soul which is to be raised with the body. Thus simply did Christ dispose of the entire socio-economic question; He had already said that it would be more difficult for a rich man to enter the kingdom of heaven than for a camel to pass through the eye of a needle; and He made it clear that His "glad tidings" had nothing to do with socio-economic questions or national questions, nothing to do with international democracy or demagogy, and nothing with nationalism.

The fourth Gospel reveals why the scribes and Pharisees caused Christ to be condemned, or rather, the pretext they used: He was no patriot: "Then gathered the chief priests and the Pharisees a council, and said, What do we? for this man doeth many miracles. If we let him thus alone, all men will believe on him: and the Romans shall come and take away both our place and nation. And one of them, named Caiaphas, being the high priest that same year, said unto them, Ye know nothing at all, nor consider that it is expedient for us, that one man should die for the people, and that the whole nation perish not" (John 11:47-50).

Clearly they sought to destroy Him because of His lack of patriotism: because His kingdom was not of this world, because He showed no interest in political economy, or in democracy, or in patriotism.

But after the reign of Constantine, when the Romanization of Christianity began and when the Letter—and not the Word—of the Gospel began to grow into something like the law of the Twelve Tables, then the Caesars set about trying to protect the Father from the Son, and God from Christ and from Christendom. And thus was born that horrendous entity known as Canon Law. And thus the judicial, worldly, social concept of supposed Christianity was consolidated. St. Augustine, man of the Letter, was a jurist from the start, a petty lawyer. And so was St. Paul—though he was also a mystic, so that the mystic and the jurist contended within him. On one side stood the law; on the other, grace.

Law and duty are not Christian religious sentiments but legal concepts. Christianity is essentially grace and sacrifice. And all that business about Christian Democracy is in the same category as "blue chemistry." Is it possible for the man who supports a tyranny to be as much a Christian as the one who supports democracy or civil liberties? The answer to the question is that the Christian, as Christian, has nothing to do with such a question.

But since the Christian is a man in society, a civic being, a citizen, how can he be disinterested in social and civic life? Ah! The fact is that Christianity demands perfect solitude. The ideal being in Christianity is the Carthusian who leaves father and mother and brothers for Christ, who gives up founding a family, renounces being a husband and a father. And this ideal is impossible—if the human race is to survive, if Christianity in the sense of a social and civic community of Christians is to survive, if the Church itself is to survive. And herein lies the most terrible aspect of the agony of Christianity.

There is no room in history for the anti-historic, for the negation of history. Or for the resurrection of the flesh or the immortality of the soul, or the Word or the Letter, or the Gospel or the Bible. History is a matter of burying the dead so that we may live from them. The dead rule in history, and the God of Christ is not a God of the dead but of the living.

Pure Christianity, evangelical Christianity, sets itself to finding eternal life beyond the confines of history and encounters only the silence of the universe which so terrified Pascal, whose life proved a Christian agony.

History, on the other hand, is also the thought of God in this world of men.

The Jesuits, those degenerated sons of Iñigo of Loyola, come chanting the ballad of the social kingdom of Jesus Christ, and, using this political criterion, set about dealing with political and socio-economic problems: for example, the defense of private property. Christ has nothing to do with either private property or with socialism. Neither has the divine anti-patriot's side which was pierced by a lance until blood and water flowed—causing a blind soldier to believe—anything to do with the "Sacred Heart" of the Jesuits. The soldier was blind—clearly—and he saw as soon as he was touched by the blood of Him who had said that His kingdom was not of this world.

And there are those other poor devils—devil, *diabolos*: slanderer—who claim that Jesus was a great democrat, a radical revolutionary, a real republican! Christ's passion still goes on. For He must still endure, suffer Himself to be made into a radical socialist by some and into a nationalist by others, here a Freemason and there a Jesuit! Christ, in the eyes of the high priests, scribes, and Pharisees of Judaism, was an anti-patriotic Jew.

"Certainly the temptation is great for a priest who abandons the Church to become a democrat. . . . Such was the fate of Lamennais. One of the very wise decisions of the Abbé Loyson was to resist on this head all seductions and to refuse all overtures which the progressive party never fails to make to those who break official ties." Thus writes Renan. But the Abbé Loyson, or more to the point, Père Hyacinthe, mar-

ried and founded a family, had children and became
a citizen. And, when he saw himself reproduced in the
flesh of others, with no need to wait for his own resurrection, he must have felt the birth of a longing to
live on in the immortality of history, and thus began
his concern with social questions.

Let us not forget, and let it be said with all due
reverence, that Christ was an unmarried man, and
this fact alone must have been enough to make Him
appear anti-patriotic to His biblical com-patriots.

No, no: democracy, civil liberties, dictatorship, or
tyranny have as little to do with Christianity as does
science. Social work done by Belgian Catholics, for
example, has as little to do with Christianity as has
Pasteur.

It is not the mission of Christianity to resolve socio-
economic problems, to solve the problem of poverty
amid wealth, to redistribute earthly goods, the world's
goods. And such is the case even if we accept that to
redeem the poor from their poverty also means to redeem the rich from their riches, just as to redeem the
slave is to redeem the tyrant; so that we must abolish
the death sentence not so much to save the condemned
as to save the executioner. And yet all this is not the
mission of Christianity. Christ summons the rich and
the poor, slaves and tyrants, the condemned and the
executioners. In the face of doom, of the end of the
world and of death, what do poverty and riches
amount to, what difference slavery or tyranny, to be
executed or to be the executioner?

"The poor always ye have with you," said Christ.
But not, as some of those who call themselves social
Christians affect to believe, in the interests of practic-
ing almsgiving, which they call charity, but because
there is always a civic society, fathers and sons, and

this civic society—civilization—carries poverty in its wake.

In Spain, the beggar begs for alms "for the love of God," and, whenever the alms are not given, the refuser says "Pardon me, brother, *por Dios*, for God's sake!" Since the beggar begs in the name of God, he is called a *pordiosero*. And inasmuch as the other person, the one assumed to be rich, asks for pardon in the name of God, *por Dios*, he, too, could be called a *pordiosero*. And so *pordioseros* they are, beggars, both of them, the beggar and the begged.

In Jerusalem, on May 13, 1901, Père Hyacinthe noted:

> Madame Yakovlew, wife of the Russian consul at Jerusalem, deplores, as do we all, the fact that Christian churches have made Jerusalem into a city of ignorance, filth, sloth, and beggary. And it will be the same wherever priests rule. Only read Zola's *Lourdes*. Mme Yakovlew points out that we have maligned the ancient Greeks and Romans: they possessed the idea of a single unique God and their statues were no more than symbols. Their customs were no more corrupt than those prevalent today, while their dignity of character and that of their life was greater. So what has Christianity come to offer?

Certainly not an end to ignorance or filth; nor has it come to introduce dignity of character or of life, what men of the world call dignity.

A Spanish priest, Jaime Balmes, wrote a book comparing Protestantism to Catholicism in relation to civilization. Good enough: Protestantism and Catholicism may be judged in their relationship to civilization. But Christianity, evangelical Christianity, has nothing whatever to do with civilization; and nothing to do with culture.

Christianity has nothing to do either with Latin culture, with a minuscule *c* all curved and nicely rounded, or with Germanic *Kultur* and its capital *K* of four spiked tips like a *cheval-de-frise*.

Since Christendom cannot live without or outside civilization and culture, Christianity agonizes. And so does Christian civilization, which is an innate contradiction. And both—Christianity and what we call Graeco-Roman or Western civilization—live through this agony, live off this agony. The death of one of the two would mean the death of the other. If the Christian faith, agonic and despairing, dies, our civilization will die; if our civilization dies, the Christian faith will die. And we must go on living in this agony.

Pagan religions, religions of the State, were political; Christianity is apolitical. But ever since it became Catholic—and Roman to boot—Christianity became paganized by its transformation into a State religion. We have even known a Papal, Pontifical State! The Church became political. And its agony grew.

Christianity is pacifist? The question seems devoid of sense. Christianity is above—or, if you will, below—such secular distinctions, such purely moral or perhaps merely political notions as pacifism or militarism, martial spirit or civil. Christianity is over and above the phrase *si vis pacem, para bellum*, if you want peace, prepare for war, which is easily converted into *si vis bellum, para pacem*, if you want war, prepare for peace, prepare yourself for it in peace.

We have already referred to Christ's saying that He came not to bring peace among families, but fire and division and the sword—πῦρ, διαμερισμόν, μάχαιραν (Matt. 10:34). But when He was caught by surprise on the Mount of Olives by those who came to take

Him, and His people asked Him if they should defend themselves with the sword, He answered that they should suffer thus far, *for the time being*, and He healed the ear of the servant of the high priest whom they had wounded (Luke 22:50-51). And He admonished Simon Peter who had drawn his sword and wounded the servant of the High Priest, Malchus, saying: "Put up thy sword into the sheath" and added "For all they that take the sword shall perish with the sword" (John 18:11 and Matt. 26:51-52).

The fourth Gospel, which is attributed to John, is the only one which tells us that the disciple who drew his sword in defense of the Master was Simon Peter, the rock upon which the Apostolic Roman Catholic Church is said to be built, the presumed founder of the dynasty which established the temporal power of the popes and preached the Crusades.

The fourth Gospel is often considered the least historical—in the materialist or realist sense. But in a more profound sense, in an idealist or personal sense, the fourth Gospel, the symbolic Gospel, is much more historic than the other three, the synoptic Gospels. It expresses more authentically—it made and continues to make—the agonic history of Christianity.

And it is in this fourth Gospel, which is the most historical precisely because it is the most symbolic of the four and also the most living, it is in this Gospel that the symbolic founder of the pontifical Roman Catholic dynasty is told that he who takes up the sword shall perish by the sword. In September of 1870, the troops of Victor Emmanuel of Savoy entered the Rome of the papacy by the sword. And the agony of Christianity was intensified again, the agony which had begun on the day on which the Vatican

Council had proclaimed the Jesuitical doctrine of the infallibility of the Pope.

The militia of the Cross was founded on this militarist dogma, a dogma engendered in the heat of battle, in a company mustered by an ex-soldier, by a military man who was wounded and no longer fit for the militia of the sword. And Loyola mustered his militia within the Roman Church and based it on discipline, *discipulina*, whereby the disciple, *discipulus*, does not learn, *non discit*, but passively receives his orders, the dogma: not the doctrine or learning of the master or teacher, but the orders of his chief, in accord with the third degree of obedience which Loyola extolled to the Fathers and Brothers of the Portuguese Province. And that, indeed, is agony!

Can anyone, then, expect the Roman Church to preach peace? Not long ago, the bishops of Spain in a collective document spoke of the war for the civil protectorate—civil! protectorate!—waged in Morocco by the Kingdom of Spain, not the Spanish nation, and called it a *Crusade*! And it can be called a crusade inasmuch as the soldiers carry the Cross as a symbol as well as a weapon with which to bash infidel heads—bash them with a Cross wielded in the manner of a mace. Terrifying struggle, terrible agony!

If the Catholic Church wishes to be Christian, it can preach neither war—nor peace. Louis Veuillot writes:

> The ruins of peace are more difficult to repair than the ruins of war. A bridge is more quickly replaced, a house more quickly rebuilt, an orchard more quickly replanted than a brothel is erased. As for men, they replace each other on their own, and war kills fewer souls than peace does. There is not a sin-

gle positive article against war in the *Syllabus*. It is
peace above all else which wages war against God.

It is impossible to set down more blasphemies.
Would Veuillot have written the same words after
Sedan? Would he write them today? Perhaps so, for
these men never admit to error. In any case, war
builds more brothels than peace. And it is not so certain that men ("cela" he calls them, *cela*!: "cela
repousse tout seul") replace each other on their own,
or that war kills fewer souls than peace. War saddens
and darkens the soul. And so does peace. The *Syllabus* may not contain a positive article against war,
but the Gospels do contain arguments against both
war and against peace, as well as arguments in favor
of war and in favor of peace. And the fact is that war
and peace are both things of this world, which is
not the kingdom of Christ. Abishag the Shunammite
had nothing to do either with the workings of Solomon's peace or with the war between Solomon and
Adonijah.

The struggle, the agony of Christianity, is not a
matter of either war or peace in this world. And it is
also useless to ask whether mysticism is action or
contemplation, for it is active contemplation and con-
templative action.

Nietzsche spoke of that which is beyond good and
evil. Christianity is beyond war and peace, or better:
this side of war and peace.

The Roman Church, or let us say the Jesuit
Church, preaches peace: the peace of conscience, implicit faith, passive submission. Lev Shestov says
truly enough: "Let us remember that the earthly keys
to the kingdom of heaven were bestowed upon St.
Peter and his successors, precisely because Peter

knew when to sleep, and slept while God, having descended among men, made ready to die on the Cross." St. Peter knew when to sleep, or slept without knowing it. And St. Peter it was who denied the Master until awakened by the cock which awakes the sleeping.

VIII. Absolute Individualism

By way of rejoinder to all our questions we are told that both Christianity and Western or Graeco-Roman civilization will disappear together and that, via Russia and Bolshevism, another civilization, or whatever you care to call it, will emerge: an Asiatic, Oriental civilization, with Buddhist roots— a communist civilization. For Christianity stands for radical individualism. And yet, the true father of Russian nihilist sentiment is Dostoevsky, a despairing Christian, a Christian in agony.

And here we meet head-on with the fact that there are no more intrinsically contradictory concepts, concepts which lend themselves more easily to contradictory applications, than those of individualism and communism, or of anarchism and socialism. Nothing is clear about these last three concepts, absolutely nothing. And those who think they see clearly with the aid of these concepts are dark souls. Imagine the terrible agonic dialectic of St. Paul applied to these concepts!

Since individuality is the most universal value, there is no way of coming to an understanding in this matter. If the anarchists should want to survive, they would have to establish a state. And the communists must presume upon the idea of individual liberty.

The most radical of individualists tend to found a commune. Hermits join together and found a monastery, that is, a convent of monks, *monachos*, solitary recluses; the recluses must help each other, help bury each other's dead; and they must dedicate themselves to making history, since they do not devote themselves to making children.

Only the hermit approaches the ideal of an individualistic life. I know a Spanish man of science who, nearing sixty, set himself to learn to ride a bicycle, and he told me that it was the most individualistic method of locomotion; to which I replied: "No, the individualistic way of locomotion is to walk alone, barefoot, where there are no roads." In short, individualism is to live alone, naked, in the desert.

Père Hyacinthe, after his break with the Roman Catholic Church, wrote that the Anglo-Saxon race is "the race of the strong, moral family; the race of the free, energetic personality; the race of individualistic Christianity. . . ." The notion that Protestant Christianity, especially Calvinism, is the creed of individualism has been repeated often. But individualist Christianity is only possible in celibacy; Christianity within the family is no longer pure Christianity, but a compromise with the world. To follow Christ, a man must abandon father and mother and brothers and wife and children. And if the continuation of the human race is thereby made impossible, so much the worse for the human race!

A universal monastery, however, a monastery for everyone, is impossible. Hence there are two types of Christian: the Christians of the world, of the century, secular—*saecula* means generations, ages—Christians in civil life, those who raise children in the sight of God; and there are others, the pure Christians, those in orders, the Christians of the cloister, the *monachi*. The former propagate the flesh and with it original sin; the latter propagate the solitary spirit.

But it is possible to carry the world into the cloister, the *saeculum* into the *claustrum*, the age into the order; and, conversely, to harbor the spirit of the cloister in the midst of the world.

Both categories of Christian, when they are of a religious character, live in fundamental contradiction, in agony. The monk who preserves virginity, who withholds the seed of the very flesh he believes must live again, who allows himself to be called *Father*— or if a nun, *Mother*—dreams of the immortality of the soul and of living on in history.

St. Francis of Assisi thought he would be remembered in the conversations of men; but he was not, properly speaking, a solitary, a monk, *monachus*; he was a little brother, a *fratello*, a friar. On the other hand, the Christian in civil life, the citizen, the father of a family, though he lives in history yet asks himself if he does not thereby endanger his soul. And if the worldly man who immures himself—or is rather immured—in a monastery strikes us as tragic, the monk of the spirit, the solitary who perforce must live in the world, is even more tragic.

In the eyes of the Apostolic Roman Church the state of virginity is more perfect in itself than that of matrimony. Even though the Church has made a sacrament of marriage, it is by way of concession to the world, to history. Meanwhile, the men and women virgins of the Lord live in anguish because of their natural instinct toward paternity and maternity. And a frenzied veneration of the Child Jesus, the boy-child God, grips many a nunnery.

Could Christianity—could humanity as a whole, perhaps—ever come to constitute a kind of anthill or beehive? Then we would have fathers and mothers on one side, and sterile workers, neuters, on the other. In the anthill and beehive, the neuter ants and bees (why in Spanish do we make both ants and bees feminine and assume they are females rather than aborted males?), the sexless ants and bees, are those which toil and nurse the offspring of the sexually-driven ants and bees; they are the maternal maiden aunts, or if you prefer, the paternal maiden uncles. With us, it is customarily the fathers and mothers who work to maintain their progeny; it is the proletariat, authors of their progeny, those who bring flesh to life, those who produce—it is they, the producers, who perpetuate material life. But what about spiritual life? Among Catholic peoples it is the monks and nuns, the father-uncles and the mother-aunts, who keep alive the religious tradition and who educate the young. But since they must educate them to live in the world, in the *saeculum*, in their time, to become fathers and mothers of families, educate them for civic and political life, there is an innate contradiction to this education. A bee may be able to teach another bee how to construct a cell, but it can not teach a neuter how to fertilize the queen.

And this innate contradiction in the monastic education given future citizens reached its apex in the Society called "of Jesus." The Jesuits do not like being called either monks or friars. A Benedictine or a Carthusian is a monk; a Franciscan or a Dominican is a friar. But ever since the Jesuits, the better to combat the Reformation, the force which secularized and made primary education general, have devoted themselves to educating the laity, citizens, future fathers of families, other religious orders have followed their example and have become Jesuit-ized. In

the end, they have all come to regard public education as an industry—the pedagogic industry. Instead
of mendicants they become schoolmasters.

And thus Christianity, true Christianity, agonizes
in the hands of these schoolmasters, masters of the
age, of the *saeculum*. Jesuit pedagogy is a deeply anti-
Christian pedagogy. The Jesuits loathe mysticism.
Their doctrine of passive obedience, of the three degrees of obedience as expounded by Ignatius Loyola
in his famous letter to the Fathers and Brothers of
Portugal, is an anti-Christian and fundamentally anti-
civic doctrine. With this kind of obedience, civilization would become impossible; and so even would
progress.

On February 24, 1911, Père Hyacinthe wrote in
his *Journal*:

> Europe is doomed—and to say Europe means Chris-
> tianity. It need not wait on the Yellow Peril, even if
> this peril is coupled to the Black Peril, in order to
> perish, for it bears within itself the two scourges
> which would suffice to kill it: Ultramontanism and
> the Revolution. MENE, TEKEL, UPHARSIN. So
> that all that is left us is to *resist*, without hope of
> overcoming, and to safeguard for an unknown fu-
> ture the twin torches of religion and true civilization.

Napoleon was supposed to have said that a century
after him Europe would have become either Cossack
or Republican. He doubtless had in mind something
akin to what Père Hyacinthe—a Napoleon in his own
way: the latter a child of Rousseau, the former of
Chateaubriand, which comes to the same thing—
when he spoke in the same breath of Ultramontanists
and revolutionaries. But what neither of them foresaw was that the Cossacks would turn Republican
and the Republicans Cossack, that Ultramontanism

would turn revolutionary and revolution Ultramontanist. Neither of the two foresaw Bolshevism or Fas-
cism, nor the chaotic disorder which the agonic
Oswald Spengler attempts to render by the architectonic music of his *Decline of the West* (*Der Untergang des Abendlandes*), which is simply the agony of
Christianity.

But the Yellow Peril? The Black Peril? Peril has
no color. And, what about the Muslim Peril? Insofar
as desert Muslimism must play some role in history,
in the measure in which it must act in a civic and
political manner—and warfare, too, as Treitschke so
aptly said, is politics *par excellence*—it also becomes
Christianized, becomes Christian, which is the same
as saying that it becomes agonic, it agonizes in the
throes of proselytism.

As for progress, it is, of course, a civic, and not a
religious, value.

But what, then, is progress, after all? Does history
have a human or perhaps even a divine finality? Is
history not fulfilled at every instant? For Christ and
for those around Him who believed in the imminent
end of the world, the idea of progress had no meaning. Sanctity knows no progress. It is impossible to
be more saintly today, in the twentieth century, than
in the second or fourth or eleventh century. A Christian can not believe that progress helps in the salvation of his soul. Civic or historic progress is not the
journey of the soul towards God. And herein lies
another agony for Christianity.

The doctrine of progress is the doctrine of
Nietzsche's superman. A Christian, for his part, must
believe that he must become not a superman, but an
immortal, that is, a Christian, man.

Is there any progress after death? This is a question which the Christian who believes in the resurrection of the flesh as well as the immortality of the soul might well put to himself sometime. However, the majority of simple evangelical believers like to picture the other life as one of repose, of peace, of quiet contemplation, an "eternalization of the instant," a fusion of the past and future, of memory and hope in an eternal present. The other life, Glory, is for the majority of simple believers a kind of family monastery, or rather phalanstery.

Dante was the most far-ranging in his depiction of the communities beyond the grave: in Hell, Purgatory, and Paradise; though both the condemned and the elect are depicted as alone, and they scarcely form communities. And if they are shown in community, Dante depicts them from the point of view of a political Ghibelline rather than of a Christian poet. His *Divine Comedy* is a biblical rather than evangelical comedy, a terrible and agonic comedy.

Dante, the great contemner, the same who lavished pity on Francesca da Rimini, felt the greatest disdain for the pope who renounced the papacy, poor Pietro del Murrone, Celestine V, canonized by the Roman Church, "him who from cowardice made the great refusal":

> che fece per viltate il gran rifiuto

And the poet places this pope at the entrance to Hell among those who cannot hope to die, among those who lived without infamy or praise among the neuters, pitiful souls who never struggled and fought and agonized, those whom we must let go by without speaking of them:

> Non ragioniam di lor, ma guarda e passa

"Let us not speak of them, but look, and pass on."

IX. The Faith of Pascal

TO SPEAK IN CONCRETE terms, in terms of
a concrete case, I should like to relate the agony of
Christianity in the soul of Blaise Pascal. To do so I
shall reproduce, with brief additions, what I wrote
concerning the faith of Pascal on the occasion of the
third centenary of his birth, June 19, 1623:

* * *

A reading of the works bequeathed us by Pascal,
especially his *Pensées*, does not invite us to study a
philosophy but to become acquainted with a man,
penetrate the sanctuary of an all-pervading anguish
of soul, of a soul altogether bared to the quick beneath a cilice. Since the student of his work will be
another human being, he runs the risk noted by Pascal himself in his *Pensée* 64: "It is not in Montaigne,
but in myself, that I find what I see in him." Risk,
did we say? No, there is no risk in it. The endless
strength of Pascal lies in the existence of as many
Pascals as there are readers who feel him—and not
merely understand him. And thus he lives in the com-
municants of his anguished faith. I propose, then, to
present to you my Pascal.

Since I am a Spaniard, so doubtless is my Pascal.
Was Pascal not influenced by Spaniards? He cites St.
Teresa on two occasions in his *Pensées* to tell us of
her profound humility, which was her faith. He had
studied two Spaniards, one of them through Mon-

taigne; two Spaniards, or more exactly two Catalans: Sabiude, and Martini, author of *Pugio fidei*. But I, who am a Basque, which is to say doubly Spanish, am able to discern the influence exerted over him by two Basque spirits: the Abbé de Saint-Cyran, the true creator of Port-Royal, and Ignatius Loyola, the founder of the Society of Jesus. How interesting to note that the two extremes, who battled each other so savagely, French Port-Royal Jansenism and Jesuit-ism, both owed their origin to Basques. Perhaps their war, more than civil war, was a war between broth-ers, almost between twin brothers, like the struggle between Jacob and Esau. And this battle between brothers was also waged in the soul of Pascal.

Pascal was touched by the spirit of Loyola through the books of the Jesuits against whom he contended. But then perhaps he saw through these casuists and recognized dullards bent on smothering the original spirit of Ignatius.

Among the letters of Ignatius Loyola—St. Igna-tius—there is the one unforgettable letter, pertinent in any study of Pascal's soul: the one to the Portu-guese Jesuit Fathers and Brothers, written at Rome on March 26, 1553, wherein he establishes the three degrees of obedience. The first degree "consists in car-rying out whatsoever is commanded, and this degree does not merit the name of obedience since it does not attain the value of this virtue unless it is raised to the second degree, which consists in making the will of the Superior one's own, in such manner that there exist not only an effective execution of the command, but affective conformity of wanting and not wanting the same thing. . . . But whoever aspires to total and perfect oblation of self, transcending will, must offer up his understanding (and this constitutes another, the highest, degree of obedience), so that he not only wills with his Superior, but feels with him, subjecting his own judgment to the Superior's, insofar as a devout will can incline one's understanding." For: "whoever is truly obedient must incline himself to feel whatever his Superior feels." In short, he must believe true whatever the Superior declares true. In order to facilitate this obedience, making it rational by means of a methodical scepticism (*scepsis* is the process of rationalizing what is not evident), the Jesuits have invented the "probabilism" against which Pascal rebelled. He rebelled against it because he felt it in himself and sensed its dangers. Is the famous argument of "the wager" anything more than a probabilist argument?

Pascal's rebel reason resisted the third degree of obedience, but he felt drawn to it by his senses. In 1705, Pope Clement XI, in his Bull *Vineam Domini Sabaoth*, declared that in matters condemned by the Church respectful silence was not enough and that only a heartfelt belief in the decisions of the Church as being founded on right and reality would suffice. Had he been living, would Pascal have accepted such a declaration?

Pascal, so far from submissive in himself, unable ever to tame his reason, perhaps persuaded but not ever convinced of Catholic dogma, talked to himself about submission. He told himself that whoever does not submit "for want of knowing the time to surrender," ("manque de savoir où il faut se soumettre") does not grasp the full force of reason (*Pensée* 268). What is this *must, falloir*? He told himself that "Surrender is the right use of reason, which is the essence of real Christianity" (269); that "Reason would never surrender if it did not consider that there are moments when it must" (270). But he also told himself that "the Pope hates and fears the learned, who have not vowed obedience to him" (873), and he ranged himself against the coming dogma of Papal Infallibility (876), final stage in the Jesuit doctrine of obedience, obedience of judgment, basis of Catholic faith.

Pascal strove to submit; he preached submission, preached to himself, as he sought, *en gémissant*, sought without finding, while the eternal silence of infinite space terrified him. His faith was a matter of persuasion, but not of conviction.

His faith? But in what did he believe? Everything depends on what is understood by faith and by belief. " 'Tis the heart, not reason, that feels God. This is Faith: God felt by the heart, not by reason" (278). And elsewhere he speaks of the simple folk who "believe without reasoning." And adds: "God gives them love of Him and hatred of self. He inclines their heart to believe." And therefore: "We shall never believe with a belief that avails and springs from faith, unless God inclines the heart" (284). A belief that avails! Here we are again, face to face with probabilism and the Wager. Availing! Not without reason he writes elsewhere: "If reason were reasonable . . ." (73). The poor mathematician, the "thinking reed" who was Pascal, Blaise Pascal, for whom Jesus "shed those drops of blood" as "I thought of thee in Mine agony," this poor Blaise Pascal sought an availing belief to save him from his reason. And he sought it in submission and in habit: "This will quite naturally bring you to believe, and will calm you . . . will stupefy you [*vous abestira*]. 'But that is just what I fear.' Pray why? What have you to lose?" (233). What have you to lose? Here we have the utilitarian argument, probabilist, Jesuitical, irrationalist. This calculation of probabilities is no more than a rationalization of chance, of the irrational.

Did Pascal believe? He wanted to believe. And the "will to believe," according to William James, another probabilist, is the only kind of faith possible for a man endowed with a knowledge of mathematics, a lucid mind, and a sense of objectivity.

Pascal turned against rational Aristotelian proofs of the existence of God (242) and he noted that "never has a canonical writer had recourse to nature to prove the existence of God" (243); and as regards "the three roads to belief" which he mentions, "reason, habit, and revelation" (245), it suffices to read Pascal with an unprejudiced mind to sense that he did not believe through reason; he was never able, even when he so desired, to believe with his reason; he was never convinced of what he had persuaded himself to believe. And that was his personal tragedy. He sought his salvation through the scepticism he favored against the inner dogmatism he suffered.

In the first text ever dogmatically declared infallible, the canons of the Vatican Council of 1870, anathema was hurled against whoever denies that the existence of God can be rationally and scientifically proven, even when the denier believes in Him. Would not this anathema have damned Pascal? It would not be farfetched to say that Pascal, like many another, did not perhaps believe that God *ex-ists* so much as that He *in-sists*, so that he sought Him in his own heart, though he had no need of Him in his experiments on vacuum or in his scientific work, but needed Him so that he would not feel, for lack of Him, annihilated.

The inner life of Pascal strikes us as a tragedy, one summed up in the words of the Gospel: "Lord,

I believe; help thou mine unbelief" (Mark 9:24).
This sentiment does not, of course, represent belief
precisely, but rather a longing to believe.

The truth to which Pascal refers when he talks of
connaissances de cœur is not rational, objective truth,
and it is not reality, as he well knew. All his effort
was directed toward creating, upon the natural world,
another, supernatural, world. But was he convinced
of the objective reality of this super-nature? Convinced, no; persuaded, perhaps. And he preached to
himself.

What difference is there between Pascal's position
and that of the Pyrrhonists, those Pyrrhonists whom
Pascal so opposed because he felt himself one of
them? There is one difference, and it is this: Pascal
did not resign himself, did not succumb to doubt, submit to negation or *scepsis*; he required dogma and he
sought it by stultifying himself, *en s'abestissant*. And
his logic was not dialectical but polemical. He did not
seek a synthesis of thesis and antithesis; he abided by
contradiction, as did Proudhon, another Pascal in his
own way: "It is the fight alone that gives us pleasure,
not victory" (135). He avoided victory and feared it,
for it might after all be that of his reason over his
faith. "The cruelest war that God can wage against
men in this life is to leave them without the war he
came to bring them" (498). Pascal feared peace.
And he had good reason! He feared finding himself
face-to-face with nature, which is reason.

But can faith in the possibility of rationally demonstrating the existence of God ever be found in a
fully developed man, in a rational being aware of his
reason? And for this kind of man, would the third
degree of obedience *à la* Loyola be acceptable? The

reply might well be: Not without grace. And what then is grace? Another tragic evasion.

When Pascal knelt to entreat the Supreme Being (233), he did so to ask that his reason be made subservient. Did it submit? Pascal wished to submit. And he did not find rest except in death and with death. And today he lives on in such of us who have touched his naked soul with our own naked souls.

* * *

I should add that Pascal, though closely connected with the Port-Royal recluses and a recluse himself, was not a monk; he had taken no vow of celibacy or virginity. Whether or not he died a virgin we do not know; in any case he was a citizen, a civic man and even a political one. For his campaign against the Jesuits was essentially political and civic, and his *Lettres Provinciales* are political. Herein lies another one of the innate contradictions of Pascal, another one of the roots of the agony of Christianity as expressed in him.

The same man who wrote the *Provinciales* wrote the *Pensées*; the two spring from the same source.

Note that they are called *Pensées*, not *Idées*: they are thoughts, not ideas. An idea is something solid, fixed, formulated; a thought is fluid, changeable, free. A thought turns into further thought; an idea collides with another idea. A thought might be defined as an idea in action, or an action in the form of idea; an idea is a dogma. Men of ideas, men taken by ideas, rarely think. The *Pensées* of Pascal go to form a polemic, an agonic polemic. If he had written the apologetics he projected, we would have something quite different from—and quite inferior to—the

Pensées. By their nature the *Pensées* could draw no conclusions: agonic is not apologetic.

I have just read *La Nuit de Gethsémani, essai sur la philosophie de Pascal,* by the Russian writer Lev Shestov, and extract the following: "An *apologia* should defend God before men; and it must necessarily, *bon gré mal gré,* recognize human reason as the court of last appeal. Had he completed his work, Pascal could only have expressed himself in terms acceptable to men and men's reasoning." Perhaps. But meanwhile men accept, *bon gré mal gré,* the *déraisonnements,* the irrational reasons, of Pascal.

To our mind Shestov errs when he says that history is implacable to apostates—Pascal was an apostate from reason—and that no one heeds Pascal even though candles are burned at his shrine. Pascal is indeed heeded, and heeded in agony; Shestov heeds him, and that is why he wrote his splendid study.

"Not Pascal," adds Shestov,

> but Descartes is the one considered to be the father of modern philosophy; and it is not from Pascal but from Descartes we accept truth. For where is truth to be sought unless it be from philosophy? And such is the judgement of history: one admires Pascal and one does not go down his road. He is bypassed. It is a judgement without appeal.

Is that so? But one does not really bypass a road one has traveled with admiration, with love. Dante's *guarda e passa,* look and pass on, is something reserved for the despised, not for the admired, not, that is, for those one loves. And, moreover, is truth really sought in philosophy? What is philosophy? Metaphysics perhaps. But in addition to a metaphysic, there is a *meta-erotic,* which is beyond love, *meta-agonic,* beyond agony and dream.

The *Provinciales* sprang from the same spirit as the *Pensées*, and represent another agonic experience, another treatise full of contradictions. The Christian who in these letters speaks out against the Jesuits senses clearly their human, all-too-human (*par trop humain*), nature, their civic and social side; he senses that without the compromises made possible by their slack morality any ethical life in the world would be impossible; he senses that the Jesuit doctrine of grace, or rather of free will, is the only one that allows of a normal civic life. At the same time he senses that all this is anti-Christian. And thus we see that Augustinian ethics, even as Calvinist and Jansenist, contribute as much as that of the Jesuits to the agony of Christianity.

The truth is that, fundamentally and in spite of appearances, ethics is one thing and religion another. Even within the domain of ethics, or, let us say, morals—*ethics* rings a bit pedantic—being good is not the same as doing good. There are people who die without having transgressed the law—and also without ever having desired any good. On the other hand, the thief who died on the cross alongside Jesus rebuked the other outlaw for blasphemy in asking the Master to save them, if he were the Christ, saying: "Dost not thou fear God, seeing thou art in the same condemnation? And we indeed justly; for we receive the due reward of our deeds: but this man hath done nothing amiss." And then turning to Jesus he said: "Lord, remember me when thou comest in thy kingdom." And Christ answered: "Verily I say unto thee, To-day shalt thou be with me in paradise" (Luke 23:39-43). The thief who repented at the hour of death believed in the kingdom of Christ, in the kingdom of God, which is not of this world, in the resur-

rection of the flesh, and Christ promised him paradise, the biblical garden where our first parents fell.
And a Christian must believe that every other Christian—and even every man—will repent at the hour
of death; that moreover death is, in itself, a form of
repentance and expiation; that death purifies the sinner. Juan Sala y Serrallonga, the bandit celebrated
by the outstanding Catalan poet Juan Maragall, told
the hangman before his death on the gallows in expiation for his gluttony, desire, lust, avarice, wrath,
thieving, killing: "I shall die reciting the *Credo*, but
do not slip the knot around my neck until you have
heard me say, 'I believe in the resurrection of the
body.' "

Was Pascal in the *Provinciales* defending moral
values—the moral values of the police, practically—
against the strictly religious and consolatory values
of the Jesuits? Or did the latter represent an adapt-
able police force of their own equipped with a casuis-
tic morality arrayed against pure religion? One thesis
is as easily sustained as the other. The fact is that
there are two orders of police, two moralities, and
two types of religion. And this doubling is the basic
cause of the agony of Christianity and the agony of
our civilization. The *Pensées* and the *Provinciales*
may seem mutually contradictory, but in truth they
are contradictory in themselves.

"We might assert," writes Shestov, "that if Pascal
had not discovered *l'abîme*, the *abyss*, he would have
remained the Pascal of the *Provinciales*." But in all
truth he discovered the abyss in writing the *Provinciales*, or more accurately, the *Provinciales* came out
of the same abyss as the *Pensées*. In plumbing the
depths of morality he reached religion; digging into

Roman and into Jansenist Catholicism he reached Christianity. For Christianity lies in the depths of Catholicism, and religion in the depths of morality.

Pascal, the man of contradictions and agony, foresaw that Jesuitism, with its doctrine of passive mental obedience, of implicit faith, kills off all struggle, agony, and with it the very life of Christianity. And still it was Pascal who in a moment of agonized despair wrote the famous "cela vous fera croire et vous abestira," "that will make you believe and stultify your reason." Of course a Christian may stultify his own reason, *s'abêtir*—he is allowed to commit rational suicide; what he may not do is *abêtir* someone else—kill someone else's intelligence. And that is what the Jesuits do. Only, in the attempt to stultify, to deaden others, they have stultified and deadened themselves. Treating other men like children, they have themselves become infantile in the saddest sense of that term. So that today there is nothing more puerile than a Jesuit, at least a Spanish Jesuit. All their pretended astuteness is pure legend. Anyone can outwit them, and they will swallow the biggest whopper. In their eyes, living history, today's, the history now taking place, is a species of magical comedy. They are taken in by all kinds of artifice. The likes of Leo Taxil deceived them. In them Christianity does not agonize: it neither struggles nor lives, but is dead and buried. The cult of the Sacred Heart of Jesus, the *hierocardiocracy*, is the sepulcher of Christian religion.

"Do not ask me that, for I am ignorant. Holy Mother Church has doctors who will know the answer." Such is the reply to a certain question in the most popular catechism used in Spain, the one composed by Father Astete, a Jesuit. And the doctors in question, from habitually not teaching certain things to those who have implicit faith, have themselves forgotten and become as ignorant as any implicit believer.

The anticlerical Alain writes in his *Propos sur le christianisme*: "Pascal offers opposition continuously and essentially; an orthodox heretic." An orthodox heretic! Well! An "orthodox heterodox" would involve a fatal contradiction in terms, in which the two counterposed terms would destroy each other, since another (*heteros*) doctrine may be right (*orthos*), for what is other to something else is still integral. But the term heretic is a clearer matter. For a heretic (*haereticus*) is one who chooses a doctrine for himself, one who thinks freely—freely? really?—and one who can freely judge the right doctrine, who can create it, who can create anew the dogma said to be professed by others. Was there not a similar process in the course of Pascal's geometric studies? St. Paul says somewhere (I do not have the reference at hand and my schedule of life does not permit me to look for it) that as regards a certain doctrine he is a heretic. "In this matter I am a heretic," he says flatly. I will not translate his Greek, a common usage in dealing with Gospel texts; but paraphrase his meaning: "In this matter I profess my own private, personal, opinion, not the prevalent one." He implies that on this point he diverges from common sense in favor of a personal, individual sense based on free examination. And who can deny that personal sense or interpretation sometimes discovers principles of common sense; who can deny that heresy may lead to orthodoxy? All orthodoxies began by being heresies. To re-

think commonplaces, to re-create them, to turn ideas
into thoughts is the best way to break free of their
evil spell. And Pascal, the heretic, in thinking
through Catholic *ideas*, those that others were said to
profess, turned their *ideas* into *thoughts*, made dogmas into life truths, and re-created orthodoxy. And
this process was the opposite to that of implicit faith,
the Jesuit "faith of the charcoal burner."

The man who wants to *s'abêtir*, to stultify his reason by his own volition, in pure solitude, will dominate the *bête*, master the brute and rise above it more
truly than he who obeys a superior *perinde ac cadaver*, like a cadaver, in accord with the third degree
of submission, surrendering the intelligence, judging
to be best whatever the superior judges to be best,
and perchance setting himself to watering a walking
stick planted in the monastery orchard because the
prior so ordered. Pure sport, that is, and comic, comic
play on the theme of command and obey, for neither
the one who commands nor the one who obeys believes
that the walking stick will take root, let alone sprout
leaves and flowers and fruit like the budding staff of
the Patriarch St. Joseph. The whole show is a pre-
arranged connivance, an exercise for taming human
pride, without thought that obedience of this kind is
rather an exaltation of pride. For though it is written
that whosoever humbles himself shall be exalted, it
does not say that he will be exalted who humbles himself with an eye to exaltation. And this type of obedience has bred the inflated collective pride—Lucifer-
ian pride—of the Society of Jesus.

Pascal was riled by the small talk of the Jesuits,
by their hairsplitting and pettiness. Not that their
faults are petty! Their *scientia media* irritated him,

and so did their theory of probabilism. And the Jesuits must play at liberty. And so they pronounce: *In
necessariis unitas, in dubiis libertas, in omnia cari-
tas*—In necessity, unity; in doubt, liberty; in all,
charity. And in order the better to play at liberty,
they enlarge the field of doubt, labeling doubtful what
is no such thing. One need only read the *Metaphysics*
of Father Suárez, for example, to behold a man amusing himself quartering a hair longitudinally and then
weaving a braid with the four strands. Or consider
their historical studies: what they call history, for it
rarely extends beyond archeology; they amuse themselves in counting the hairs in the tail of the Sphinx,
in order to avoid looking into its eyes, to avoid its
gaze. Their labor is self-stultification and the stulti-
fication of others.

When a Jesuit—at least a Spanish Jesuit, I repeat—tells you that he has devoted himself to study,
do not believe him. It is as if one of them were to tell
you that he is much traveled, because he has circum-
ambulated the residency garden in a daily ten-mile
treadmill.

Naturally, the solitary man, the true man of solitude that was Pascal, the man who wished to believe
that Jesus shed a drop of his blood for him, Blaise
Pascal, could not come to terms with these militants.

And their science! A medical friend of mine, in his
capacity as physician, went to attend a novice in the
cloistered section of the novitiate at Oña and there, in
one of the galleries, he saw a painting which depicted
the Archangel Michael with the Devil, Satan, at his
feet. And Satan, the rebel angel, held in his hand—
a microscope! A microscope, the symbol of hyper-
analysis!

These people are out to prevent, to stop, the agony of Christianity. And they do so by murder. "Let it stop suffering!" To deliver Christianity from its agony, they administer the fatal opium of their Spiritual Exercises and their education. They will end by making Roman Catholicism into something resembling Tibetan Buddhism.

X. Père Hyacinthe

In the course of compiling this anguished work, I chanced upon three volumes written by Albert Houtin concerning the anguished life of Père Hyacinthe Loyson.

I read, or devoured, these books with ever-growing anguish. Here is one of the greatest tragedies I have ever encountered, comparable to and even more intense than those of Pascal, Lamennais, and Amiel. For here we have the tragedy of a Father. Although in truth we now know that in the case of Amiel, as revealed in the new edition of the *Journal intime*, finally rescued from the Calvinist prude who first edited it, that he was tortured by the agony of virginity, key to the mystery of his anguished life as a poor professor of aesthetics in the Geneva of Calvin and Jean-Jacques.

Père Hyacinthe. *Père*! Father! In this fatherhood lies the quintessence of his tragedy, of the agony of Christianity as manifest in him. He left the Church in order to marry, he married in order to have off-spring, to perpetuate himself in the flesh, to assure the resurrection of his flesh. But let us look at his life story.

Père Hyacinthe, doubtless forgotten nowadays, buried now in history, immured in the immortality of the soul, was in contact with the luminaries of his time: Montalembert, Le Play, Victor Cousin, Père Gratry, Renan, Guizot, Msgr. Isoard, Doellinger,

Dupanloup, Pusey, Cardinal Newman, Strossmayer, Taine, Gladstone, Jules Ferry. He even earned the insults of that mad dog Louis Veuillot.

The innate quality of his soul, as he himself said, was "an inseparable mixture of mysticism and rationalism" (Vol. I, p. 7). He did not leave us any written work to be read; only this life as written down at his direction by Houtin (I, 10). "Lamartine in his early *Méditations poétiques* awakened him to thought, to sensibility, to life at the age of thirteen, and the youth was to develop into manhood, alone, at the foot of the Pyrenees, under the influence of nature, poetry, and religion" (I, 26). Not under the influence of the Gospel, note. And even more than Lamartine, it was Chateaubriand, the great sophist, the great falsifier of the genius of Christianity, who formed him (I, 27); Chateaubriand, who wrote of the loves of Atala and René. In the seminary of Saint-Sulpice he received the "revelation" of the Virgin (I, 52), the Virgin Mother. And with this revelation, the revelation of paternity, came a concern with the civil, historical, political life of the enduring world, with fame and the immortality of the soul: "I pass unnoticed through this life here below, without love and without exerting any influence. When my bones have whitened in the earth, when they have lost their outline and their very dust will have no longer any name among men, what will then remain of me in this world?" (I, 69). He wished to remain in the world because he was of the world and not of the Christian kingdom of God.

He joined the Sulpician order, passed like a fugitive shadow among the Dominicans, then entered a monastery of the Discalced Carmelites, where the profound tragedy began. He struggled against the egotism of the body which he found as odious as the egotism of the individual (I, 110).

And then commenced the temptations of the flesh: "The faithful and enthusiastic practice of celibacy had led me to a false unhealthy state. . . . I am enamored, not of one woman, but of women" (I, 115). But what he craved in the ultimate depths of his being was a child of the flesh in whom he might survive. At the age of thirty-seven, in the small Carmelite monastery of Passy, he dreamed of "the songs of birds and the songs and games of children" (I, 122). When he converted Mrs. Merriman, who was to become his wife, it was he who was wholly converted by her to paternity, to the kingdom of this world. A deceptive mystical alliance was formed between them: not a mystical alliance like the one between St. Francis of Assisi and St. Clare, nor the one between St. Francis de Sales and St. Jeanne de Chantal, nor that between St. Teresa of Jesus with St. John of the Cross. Neither was there a basis of sexuality in Père Hyacinthe's love. He was clearly possessed by a furious drive for paternity, a desire to ensure the survival of the flesh.

Let us leave to one side all his other agonies and concentrate on this particular agony. He first celebrated a mystical espousal of Mrs. Merriman, at the age of forty-five; shortly afterwards, he married her. At forty, he knew no more about women than what they themselves had taught him in confession (II, 9); he did not know them any more than David knew Abishag. Later, when he was old, at eighty-two, he wrote that a man is "but fully a priest in marriage" (II, 122). Priest? *Prêtre?* He meant *père,* a father. And he cried out: "God and Woman!" (II, 123). He meant: God and the survival of the flesh! And that "force superior to my will" which, "with a persistence

that astonishes and at times terrifies me" (II, 81),
and which pushed him into matrimony, was the force
of unsatisfied paternity. That was the nature of his
love. "To attempt to extirpate it would be tantamount
to suicide" (II, 82)—an eternal end! When at the
age of eighty he wrote that "the great vision of God
and of the Eternal City always present in my con-
scious mind and even more in my *subconscious* has
been MY JOY as much as my strength" (II, 350-
51), he did not then realize that his subconscious
was the genius of the species, of which Schopenhauer
the pessimistic bachelor spoke: the genius of the species in search of a faith in the resurrection of the flesh.
He had need of a son. He was not satisfied to let the
dead bury the dead, while those who believed themselves alive engendered more life, and while he himself took refuge in the community of such as believed
in an early end to the world: "Let the Church and the
child be born together for the greater glory and kingdom of our God" (II, 142). He needed to ensure the
perpetuity of the flesh in order to ensure that of the
spirit. He wanted to give physical life to a son in
order to infuse in him a soul (II, 147). He wanted
to make his son a monk, one like himself; he wished
to transmit the monastic state via the blood: "If God
should grant me a son, I shall say to him as I pour
baptismal water on his head, 'Remember one day that
you are of the race of the monks of the West! Be a
monk, a solitary recluse in this world of incredulity
and fanaticism, of superstition and immorality. Be
a monk, consecrated to the God of your father, wor-
shiping Him, as did John the Baptist, in the desert
of the soul and to announce His coming'" (II, 151).
He wished to transmit his solitude, his agony! We
do not know that John the Baptist was a father—he

was so firmly convinced of the approaching end of the world!

He wanted his son to be a monk so that he might inherit his own Christian solitude! But a hereditary monastic state would necessarily be political, and Père Hyacinthe detested politics, which is of the kingdom of this world. And yet he was forced to act politically, for he was a carnal father, and carnal paternity is of the kingdom of this world, and not of the kingdom of God, for it is part of history. The very nepotism of the popes and bishops and priests out to forward the careers of their nephews is altogether of this world and scarcely Christian at all. And much of the pretended religious vocation of parish priests—who are not monks or friars—has been a family or economic matter. "The priest's profession knows no slack." Politics, and nothing but politics!

Still, inheritance is the soundest basis for any firm political action. It constitutes the backbone of the English political aristocracy, educated as they are in the tradition of polity. A young English lord may hear talk of politics in his home from the beginning. In England there are dynasties of conservatives. They wish to perpetuate their race, and they also know that politics is of the world and of the flesh, of the world of inheritance, of the world in which the dead bury their dead, of the world of history.

We hear sometimes that Christ did not found the Church, for the Church is of necessity part of the world of the flesh, and that what he instituted was the Eucharist. But the Eucharist, the sacrament of bread and wine, of bread which is eaten and wine which is drunk, is almost of this world, inasmuch as the bread becomes flesh and the wine blood. And it is all a struggle against death, an agony.

Père Hyacinthe needed a son who would be not only an offspring of love but of his faith (II, 159), one who would inspire in him faith in the resurrection of the flesh. Perhaps he prayed for this son to the Mother of the Creator, repeating the words of the Psalmist: "My soul shall live for him, and *my race shall serve him*" (II, 161). Only read the pages of incandescent faith, deeply despairing, written when his son Paul was born. He wished to turn his home into a monastery (II, 170). And at the same time he was tormented by the thought of the immortality of the soul and of living on in history: "Others in whom I shall live again, children of my blood and children of my word" (II, 269). In his *Testament* he bequeathed his belief and his hope—what he believed he believed and hoped—"to my son, who will be, I hope, the son of my soul more than of my blood" (II, 299), to that son whom he called "the flesh of my flesh, the breath of my soul, and the fruit of my life" (II, 303), to that son whom he saw die: "My beloved son who will perhaps follow me closely into the unfathomable mystery of death; perhaps he will even precede me," as he wrote in his seventy-ninth year (II, 353); and his son preceded him in the mystery, but not without leaving him grandchildren. And Père Hyacinthe, one of the most representative men of the "stupid nineteenth century," did not exploit the death of that son in whom he frantically loved himself. Nor did he in all truth envy his own father; but we should know that the latter, even if he was a distinguished man and even a poet, had not bequeathed to his son a name in history; if Hyacinthe was envious of his father for anything, it was of his condition as father.

Compared to this agony, the agony of ideas was of little consequence. While he was still in the Carmelite monastery, Père Hyacinthe wrote: "I want to be able to live, by God's grace, as if I were to die the next instant. . . . The Church is here, too, in this garden, in this cell" (I, 118); but he did not feel what he wrote. He spoke of the "most scientific and freest needs of the inner life" (I, 144). Scientific needs, indeed! How right the uneducated are when they identify the temptations of knowledge with those of the flesh! And why was Père Hyacinthe shocked at the profoundly Christian sentiment expressed to him by Msgr. Darboy? Darboy told him: "Your error consists of believing that a man must do something in this life. Wisdom consists of doing nothing and enduring." To which the poor Père Hyacinthe added a gloss in his diary: "Such scepticism filled my soul with bitterness and doubt" (I, 308). Scepticism? Pure Christian wisdom, rather! And that was what filled him with doubt.

Poor Père Hyacinthe, who was in truth two men in one person, asked himself: "May a third man not exist to settle the differences between these two? Or will he perhaps emerge only in eternity?" (I, 280). And meanwhile the father, the citizen, thirsting for the resurrection of the body and the immortality of the soul, struggled in him with the Christian, the solitary, the monk.

He left the Church when the infallibility of the Pope was proclaimed; and he also abandoned it to marry and have children. He buried one of the dead, Lamartine, in 1869; he went on to an interview with Pius IX; then mingled with Protestants, Saint-Simonians, Jews, and rationalists in the International and Permanent League for Peace; proposed to join the so-called Old Catholics; founded the National Catholic Church of Geneva and served as its pastor;

then, the Gallican Catholic Church of Paris; traveled around the United States lecturing on religion; applied in old age for a Roman Catholic parish in the East, where priests are allowed to have wives; dreamed of uniting Christians, Jews, and Moslems; and ended the long agony which was his life at eighty-five, a widower bereft of a son, or rather a widower orphaned by his son. In short, an orphan!

And he had to struggle, to agonize, to provide bread for his wife and offspring, bread for his flesh. Some American impresario proposed a lecture tour, with or without fanfare and young ladies to ask for his autograph. For he was news! If newspapers had existed in Judea at the time of Christ, how much worse would have been Christ's agony!

Père Hyacinthe fought against Ultramontanists and rationalists, but he fought above all against himself. Before marrying he wrote the future mother of his child, and, in a sense his own mother: "Doubt lurks in my innermost spirit; it has been lying there since I began to think; but faith lies at the bottom of my soul" (II, 17). What kind of distinction did he draw between "spirit" and "soul"? For the rest, to think is to doubt; to have ideas is something else again. Deism helps one to live, not to die, and the Christian lives to die. "All those men," he wrote at the age of eighty-one, "have accomplished nothing because, though speaking in the name of God, *they had not seen him*. But I who had seen him, I have done nothing either!" (II, 97-98). The Scriptures tell us that he who looks on the face of God must die. And he who does not look—must die as well!

And Père Hyacinthe, while he hated politics, was forced to indulge in political life. While he strove to lend heat to David in his agony, he served Solomon.

The Masses he celebrated after leaving the Roman Catholic Church were essentially political Masses. And in his last days with the Carmelites "he no longer says Mass every day and, when he does so, it is with the same liberties which might be taken by a Protestant who believed in the real presence without worrying about transubstantiation" (I, 294). All of which means nothing at all, or means that our priest did not *celebrate* Mass, did not consecrate the bread and wine, did not pronounce the ritual words upon which, in accord with Roman Catholic doctrine, the miracle depends, independent of the state of the celebrant's soul, inasmuch as the sacrament is *ex opere operato* and not *ex opere operantis*. Or in other words: in order to eschew a sacrilege, he indulged in deception, playing out a comedy, the fiction of a Mass.

Père Hyacinthe fought Ultramontanists and unbelieving rationalists, and concluded that Christianity is a middle way (II, 218). And the truth was that Christianity was agonizing within him.

He also fought the fanatical Pharisees who asked him if it was licit or not to pay tribute to the Empire, or to rebel against the Roman Pontiff and marry to have children of the flesh; and he fought the sceptical Sadducees who asked him whose wife the woman who had married seven brothers and been had by them all would be when they all came back from the dead.

Père Hyacinthe praised the Mormons, believers in the resurrection of the flesh.

And this praise involves a most characteristic aspect of his agony:

1. They have understood that we are approaching the end of a religious economy, that Protestantism is gone as far afield as Romanism, and that the Kingdom of God will come and reign on earth.

But it will not be a kingdom where men live like heavenly angels without marriage and the begetting of children. 2. They have understood that theocracy is the true and right government of human societies. . . . Not for divine society.

Even if Rome has abused the concept of theocracy, that proves nothing against the principle. 3. They have understood that the relation between the sexes forms part of religion. They have erred in the matter of polygamy, but we err even more. The hypocritical polygamy which has become customary in modern Christianity is far more unwholesome and reprehensible than the polygamy practised by the Mormons with religious consecration, and, I do not hesitate to add, incorporating moral safeguards for the women and children. 4. I also praise the Mormons for their respecting the Old Testament. The world of Gentile Christianity has strayed too far from its Israelite cradle. We no longer feel ourselves the offspring and perpetuators of the patriarchs and prophets: we have severed all links with the royal house of David.

And with the royal house of Solomon?—". . . And we have nought but scorn for the priesthood of Aaron" (II, 249).

The poor Father, feeling Christianity agonize in his soul, longed to return to the days when Jesus, the Christ, the Son who was not a father, struggled against Ultramontane Pharisees and rationalist Sadducees. The page written on the Mormons is dated February 28, 1884. On March 16, still in the United States, he wrote: "But now I must return to my French impasse, to be crushed anew between Ultramontanists and sceptics, between revolutionaries and reactionaries! *Deduc me, Domine, in via tua et ingrediar in veritatem tuam!*" (II, 250).

In one passage he says: "Christianity has perhaps been surpassed" (II, 254), a statement uttered in anguish. "I cannot recreate the world within my thought, and if I do recreate it, I do so in words that pass, not in deeds that last!" (II, 269). He was unable to believe in the eternity of the Word, of the Logos, through which everything was created; he chose to believe in the eternity of the Act, of the Flesh, perhaps even of the Letter.

His last years, from his sixty-sixth to his eighty-fifth year, 1893 to 1912, following his withdrawal from active life, were the most tragic of his life, the years of his greatest solitude. His was a robust old age, and, like David, he agonized for years: "I suffer greatly. I am witness to an agony which is dolorous and *dishonorable*" (III, 113). The world always with him! Religious isolation caused him suffering. Like Jacob, he wrestled alone with the angel of the Lord, from sundown until the breaking of the day, and calling out to him, "Tell me . . . thy name!" (Genesis 32:24-29). He felt the presence of two men within him, each one equally sincere and equally religious, the Christian and the monotheist (III, 134), and the fact that he suffered the discord between Christianity and monotheism attests sufficiently to the moral and religious depth of his agony of soul. His son Paul, the son of his flesh, abetted the monotheist in his father against the Christian. Paul was one of the dead who came to bury the dead father. In the end, it is impossible to be a father and a Christian without agony. Christianity is the religion of the Son, not that of the Father, and it is of the Son still virgin. Humanity began in Adam to terminate in Christ. "For the greatest sin of man is ever to have been born," as our Calderón de la Barca says. It is the true original sin.

Père Hyacinthe wrote his son: "Every soul, as you

say, must be left face-to-face with the Eternal, and nobody has the right to judge save God" (III, 140). He believed his own place was no longer with his contemporaries, "but in solitude, awaiting death, or rather the other side of death" (III, 143). What solitude? He remembered the words his son had spoken to him: "My poor father, you have no other Church, at the end of your life, but that of your family!" (III, 147). And he wrote: "I remain alone with Emily . . . and with God" (III, 148). He remained alone with the spirit and with the flesh, with the immortality of the soul and the resurrection of the flesh. Commenting on one of Émile Ollivier's judgments regarding Père Hyacinthe, Baron Seillière said that Père Hyacinthe was "a Rousseau Catholic, not a rational Christian" (III, 418). Apart from the absurd notion of a "rational Christian," the allegation would be in order if Père Hyacinthe indeed derived from Rousseau. But in fact he was heir to Chateaubriand, or at most to Rousseau by way of Chateaubriand. For is not *René* after all a Rousseau Catholic?

Père Hyacinthe wanted to return to the "Aryan hearth and home of pre-Christian times" (III, 176). When his wife—the mother—died, he was eighty-three and still a child. At that time he wrote:

> There is a superior law of the world and of God which prevents the dead from speaking to the living and from manifesting themselves to them in any way whatsoever. The spiritualists' experiments and the mystics' apparitions are a vain attempt to gainsay this law. O silence of the dead! O silence of God! (III, 185).

Pascal, who was never a father, did not ever surpass the dread accent of these words.

"If darkness and silence had prevailed until now in

Sheol, it would be time for a man to appear there and begin the resurrection of the dead" (III, 186).

Why not he? His Emily dead, why should not he be the first to be resurrected from among the dead?

> She who was my life has been taken away from me *forever*, and there is no hope, no consolation in this life. And I am beset with terrible doubts, involuntary doubts, *irrational* doubts, which desolate my heart and mind's imagining. I have a sort of instinctive perception of the nothingness of being, the nothingness of things, the nothingness of people. . . . And yet these doubts are involuntary; but I could not yield to them without renouncing Christian faith and even human nature such as it exists in me. It would constitute a moral suicide, seen doubtless to be followed by actual suicide. For in all truth the game would not be worth the candle, the lugubrious game of a life *sans raison d'être*, a life without solid substance and without consoling hope (III, 187).

These lines were written to his son Paul, the son of his Emily. And to them should be added the observation that doubts are always voluntary inasmuch as they are willful, a product of the will: it is the will which doubts. And the poor Father, in his second childhood, in his second virginity, at eighty-three, strove all the same—like a new Abishag from Shunam—to revive David.

He had written to Renan a few years previously, at seventy-four, before he had experienced the death of his wife, his mother, that he firmly held with "the survival of souls and their final salvation" (III, 371). Later he wrote à propos of Renan: "His intellectual power did not go beyond doubt" (III, 374). And what of his will? He adds: "Renan doubted everything, and what to my mind is infinitely sad is that he did not die of his doubt, but instead lived from it;

he did not suffer from it but rather amused himself with it" (III, 375). Perhaps this judgment is unfair. But he himself, the Father, agonized in his doubt. Renan knew that truth is, at bottom, sad.

Père Hyacinthe depicts himself at fifty-seven in a tragic vision he experienced beside the great Niagara:

> My soul is a torrent flowing down from the mountains, carrying along the water of the years and perhaps of the centuries, falling down ever steeper slopes and down declivities ever more precipitous, hurtling toward a catastrophe as inevitable as it is overwhelming: death and that other abyss lying beyond death, until the creature has found its peaceful course in another order of things and its ultimate repose in the bosom of its God. Always palingenesis. . . . Emily and I will soon encounter it . . . (II, 251).

Not Rousseau, not Chateaubriand (or better, *René*), not Sénancour (that is, *Obermann*), none of them ever spoke in accents more tragic.

Such was the man, such the Father, such the Christian in an agony of Christianity!

XI. Conclusion

I COME TO THE END of this little book because all things must have their end in this world and perhaps in the next. But is there really a conclusion available to me? It depends on what is meant by conclusion. In the sense of finishing, this end is merely a beginning to the theme. In the logical sense this end is no conclusion.

I write this Conclusion outside my fatherland, Spain, which is rent by a most shameful and stupid tyranny, by the tyranny of militaristic imbecility—far from my home, my family, my eight children, but no grandchildren yet. Raging within me is a religious war as well as a civil war. The agony of my country, the death-rattle, echoes the agony of Christianity. I feel politics raised to the height of religion and religion raised to the pitch of politics. I feel the agony of the Spanish Christ, Christ in the death-throes. And I feel the agony of Europe, of the civilization we call Christian, of the Graeco-Latin or Western civilization. Both agonies are one and the same. Christianity and Western civilization destroy each other. Thus they live, killing each other.

Meanwhile, many believe a new religion is born, a religion both Judaic and Tatar in origin, the religion of Bolshevism: a religion whose prophets are Marx and Dostoevsky. But: is not Dostoevsky's religion Christianity? Is not *The Brothers Karamazov* a Gospel?

And people also say that this France where I write these words and whose bread I eat and whose water I drink, water salted from the bones of her dead, that this France is being depopulated and being invaded by outsiders because the hunger for maternity and for paternity has vanished here and because the French no longer believe in the resurrection of the dead. Do they believe, now, in the immortality of the soul, in glory, in history? The tragic agony of the Great War of 1914-18 should have cured many Frenchmen of their faith in glory, *la gloire*.

A short walk from where I write, there burns a continual flame, under the *Arc de l'Étoile*—an arch dedicated to imperial triumph!—the flame lit on the tomb of the Unknown Soldier, whose name will not pass into history. Still, is the epithet *Unknown* not already a name of sorts? Is not Unknown as good a name as Napoleon Bonaparte? Before this tomb, fathers and mothers have knelt to pray, wondering if that unknown one was not their son; Christian fathers and mothers who believe in the resurrection of the body. And perhaps mothers and fathers who were unbelievers, even atheists, have gone to pray there. And, perhaps, Christianity is reborn on this tomb.

The unfortunate Unknown Soldier, who perhaps believed in Christ and the resurrection of the body, or who perhaps was an unbeliever or a rationalist with his faith placed in the immortality of the soul in history or without history, sleeps the last sleep, clothed not so much in earth as in stone, under the prodigious ashlar slabs of a great door which neither opens nor shuts but whereon are graven the letters of the names of Imperial Glory. Glory? *La Gloire?*

A few days ago I was witness to a patriotic ceremony: a civic procession filing by this tomb of the

Unknown Soldier. Alongside his bones, not interred but *enstoned*, stood the President of the Republic of the goddess France, together with his government and a clutch of retired generals disguised as civilians, all of them sheltered under the stones which announce in their lettered names the sanguinary glories of the Empire. And the poor Unknown Soldier was perhaps a youth with his head and heart filled with history, or conversely he was one who hated the whole idea.

After the parade, and after the prime minister of the goddess France and his party retired to their homes, and after the shouts had died down from the nationalists and communists who demonstrated later, some poor believing mother—believing in the virginal maternity of Mary—approached the tomb of the Unknown Son, came up silently and alone, and prayed: "Thy kingdom come!"—the kingdom of God, which is not of this world. And then: "Hail Mary, full of grace, the Lord is with thee! Blessed art thou amongst women and blessed is the fruit of thy womb, Jesus. Holy Mary, Mother of God, pray for us sinners now and at the hour of our death. Amen!" Never was such a prayer uttered on the Acropolis! And with this mother all of Christian France prayed. And the poor Unknown Son, who heard—who can say he did not?—the prayer, had dreamed at the hour of his death that he would return to his resurrected home there on high, in the heaven above his country, in the skies over France, his sweet France, and that the kisses of his mother would warm the centuries of centuries of eternal life in the kiss of light of the Mother of God.

Beside the tomb of the Unknown Frenchman, who is somewhat more hallowed than the average Frenchman, I felt the agony of Christianity in France.

There are moments when we imagine that Europe, the civilized world, is passing through another millennium, that it is now approaching its end, the end of the civilized world, of civilization; we feel like the primitive Christians, the true evangelists, who believed that the end of the world was impending. And there are those who must feel an emotion like the one summed up in the tragic Portuguese expression "Isto da vontade de morrer.—It all makes one want to die."

And now they also want to establish a headquarters for a League of Nations, a United States of Civilization, in Geneva, under the shadow of Calvin and Jean-Jacques; and under the shadow of Amiel, who smiles sadly down—from where?—upon this politicians' masterpiece. And Wilson also smiles wryly down, Woodrow Wilson, another Christian politician, another contradiction made flesh and made spirit; Wilson, the mystic of peace, a contradiction in terms as absolute as the first Moltke, the mystic of war.

The hurricane of madness sweeping over a large part of European civilization seems to be an insanity of the type which medical men call specific in origin. Many of the agitators and dictators who pull the masses hither and yon are early-stage cases of progressive paralysis. They are examples of the suicide of the flesh.

Then there are those who speak of the mystery of iniquity. . . . Let us look again at the ingrained tradition which identifies the scriptural sin of our first forebears, their tasting the fruit off the tree of the knowledge of good and evil, with the sin of the flesh which longs for rebirth. The flesh, however, ceased being preoccupied with rebirth, it was not moved by the hunger and thirst for paternity or maternity, but came to be preoccupied with mere pleasure, pure lust.

The source and fountain of life was poisoned, and with it the source and fountain of knowledge.

In one of the gospels of Hellas, Hesiod's *Works and Days*, a text more religious than Homer, we are told that in the reign of peace, when earth teems with life, when the oak branches are burdened with acorns and the trunk harbors bees, when the wooly ewes give birth to lambs, then "women bear children resembling their parents" ἐοικότα τέκνα γονεῦσιν, which does not seem to mean "legitimate" but, rather, "well-formed" or, even better, "sound."

Once I fell into conversation with an old peasant, a poor mountaineer who lived near Las Hurdes, a region in the center of Spain considered barbarous. I asked him if it was true that people there lived in promiscuity. He asked me what that was. And when I explained, he answered: "Ah, no! Not now! It was different in my youth. When everybody's mouth is clean, everybody can drink out of the same glass. There was no jealousy then. Jealousy came along with those diseases that poison the blood and breed imbeciles and madmen. And it's all wrong to make an imbecile or a crazy child, for such a one will be no good later. No it shouldn't be." He spoke like a sage. And perhaps like a Christian. In any case, he did not talk like one of those husbands in a drama by Calderón de la Barca, one of those husbands tormented by a sense of honor, which is not a Christian sentiment but a pagan one.

Through the words of the laconic old man of the mountains I understood the tragedy of original sin and the tragedy of Christianity and what is meant by the dogma of the Immaculate Conception of the Blessed Virgin Mary. The Mother of God who resurrects the dead must be exempt from original sin.

And through the words of the laconic old man of the mountains I also understood the agony of our civilization. And I thought of Nietzsche.

But is this sin of the flesh the most execrable of sins? Is it the true original sin?

In the eyes of St. Paul, the most execrable sin was that of avarice. And that was because avarice consists in taking the means for the end. But what is meant by "means"? What is meant by "end"? Where does the finality of life lie? And there exists an avarice of the spirit and also an avarice of maternity and paternity.

Kant postulated that the supreme moral law required that we consider our neighbor as an end in himself, not as a means. It was his way of translating "Love thy neighbor as thyself." But Kant was a bachelor, a lay monk, an avaricious miser. Was he a Christian? And perhaps he considered himself an end in himself. Human generation came to an end in him. "Love thy neighbor as thyself." And how is one to love oneself?

And added to this harrowing physical malady was a second, psychic, malady, offspring of spiritual avarice: envy. Envy is the Cainite sin, the sin of Cain, the sin of Judas Iscariot, the sin of Brutus and Cassius, according to Dante. Cain did not kill Abel for reasons of economics, of economic competition, but from envy at the favor Abel found in the eyes of God. And Judas did not sell the Master for the sake of the thirty pieces of silver, but because he was an envious wretch.

I write these lines outside my Spain. But I carry that Spain of mine, my daughter-Spain, the Spain of immortality and the resurrection, with me in this France, in the lap of France, my France, which feeds my flesh and spirit, my resurrection and immortality. And along with the agony of Christianity I feel in me the agony of my Spain and the agony of my France. And I say to Spain and to France and, through them, to all of Christendom and to all of non-Christian humanity as well: "Thy kingdom come. . . . Holy Mary, Mother of God, pray for us sinners now and at the hour of our death." Now, now, which is the hour of our agony.

"Christianity is like cholera which sweeps across a land, carries away a certain number of the elect, and then disappears." Père Hyacinthe heard these words from the mouth of Monsieur Gazier, the last of the Jansenists, who uttered them on the occasion of a symposium-dinner on January 25, 1888. And is not civilization still another malady which carries away its own elect through its madness? Cholera, after all, carries men off quickly. For Monsieur Gazier, Christianity was a disease. Civilization is another. Fundamentally they are both perhaps one and the same disease. And the ill lies in their inner contradiction.

I write these lines, I say, far from my Spain, my mother and my daughter—yes, my daughter, for I am one of her fathers—and while I write them, my Spain agonizes, and Christianity agonizes in her. She wished to extend Catholicism by the sword: she proclaimed a crusade, and now must die by the sword, a poisoned sword. And the agony of my Spain is the agony of my Christianity. And the agony of my Quixotism is the agony of Don Quixote.

A few days ago, at Vera, in the Basque country, a handful of poor deluded souls, whom a military court martial had acquitted, were nevertheless garrotted. They were garrotted because the reign of terror made it necessary. They can consider themselves lucky they were not shot by a firing squad! For when I once observed to the present King of Spain—King he is today, Saturday, December 13, 1924—that we must do away with the death penalty in order to do away with the hangman, he answered me: "But this penalty exists nearly everywhere, in the French Republic, and here, luckily, there is no shedding of blood! . . ." He was comparing the garrot to the guillotine. But Christ agonized and died on the Cross, and He shed blood, redeeming blood, and my Spain agonizes and doubtless will die on the crosspiece of a sword shedding blood . . . redeeming blood, perhaps. Perhaps the blood will wash away the poison.

Christ on the Cross not only shed blood, blood to baptize Longinus, the blind soldier, and make him believe, but "his sweat was as it were great drops of blood falling down to the earth," ὡσεὶ θρόμβοι αἵματος, in His agony on the Mount of Olives. And those blood-like drops were the seeds of agony, the seeds of the agony of Christianity. And Christ grieving sighed: "Not my will, but thine, be done."

O Christ, our Christ, why hast Thou forsaken us?

Paris, December, 1924

II

Essays on Faith

Nicodemus the Pharisee

Gentlemen,

THIS IS THE FIRST time that I speak in this place and the first time in more than eight years, the number of years I have been a professor, that I make a public address. I naturally desire that a certain cordial communion be established among us. The Junta of this cultural association has asked me to give a lecture here. But in my present circumstances, hurrying to return home, I was unable to prepare anything especially for this occasion. Neither did I want, under any circumstance, to come here and improvise whatever might occur to me. There was only one course open to me, therefore, and that was to select something from among my unpublished writings which might prove suitable and read it to you.

There is scarcely any question which does not draw my attention, a fact which perhaps leads me to disperse my forces. Among all known themes, probably economic and religious problems have most aroused my spirit. Religion and economics are the two hinges of human history. The so-called materialist conception of history, the conception of Marx, who saw the economic factor as ultimate *ratio* at the heart of every social process, shows us only one face of reality, the external one; while the other, which we might call the spiritualist conception of life, or better than spiritualist, the affective-ist, which involves everything, is given us by religion. The economic drive provides the incentive and mainspring of life, while the religious provides the motive for life. A motive for living: in other words, everything.

I might say, using a well-known terminology, that the economic is the efficient cause of human progress and the religious is its final cause. And if someone, on hearing me say this, were to pass judgment based on certain convictions—which, like all convictions, I respect—and silently argue that such a final cause does not exist, I would answer that the search for it constitutes the essence of all religion. There is not in reality more than one great problem, and it is this: What is the end purpose of the entire universe? Such is the enigma of the Sphinx; whoever does not resolve it in one way or the other is devoured.

The universe has no purpose, perhaps? Then let us give it one, and such a grant, if it is fulfilled, will be no more than the uncovering of the universal hidden finality. When reason tells me there is no transcendental reality, faith answers that there should be one, and since there should be one, there will be one. For faith, gentlemen, does not so much consist in creating what we have not seen, but in creating what we do not see. And only faith can create.

Faith! How little we meditate with our hearts, rather than with our heads alone, concerning the nature and importance of faith! It can not be a mere intellectual adherence to an abstract principle, to a formula almost without content; nor can it be the affirmation of metaphysical or theological principles. No, it must be an act of abandonment and a heartfelt handing-over of the will, a serene confidence in which nature and the spirit concur in a final end, in which by naturalizing the spirit we render it more intensely spiritual, and in which by spiritualizing nature we render it more intensely natural; faith is a firm confidence that truth dwells within us, that we are its vase and receptacle, and that truth is consolation, a firm confidence that if we act with a pure and simple intention we serve a supreme design, whatever it may be.

I sow seed, gentlemen, according to the grace God grants me, I sow the grain He has placed in my granary, striving to make my sowing a work of prayer, and I sow without looking back, lest what happened to Lot's wife befall me; I sow my grain looking always toward the future, which is the only kingdom of liberty, and I leave it to the earth to fertilize it, and the air, the water and the sun to foster it. Ah, if only in place of growing uneasy about the seed we sow we simply went on sowing it!

But for this work it is necessary that we all commune with each other, communicating with each other through bonds of the heart, and that the inner unsociability—where each one searches out the other's ears rather than his heart and where we are united by the need to chatter and hear others chatter—this inner unsociability, which serves as a basis for the apparent sociability of our race, be broken through once and for all. For here, now, in this nation of orators, who really pours himself out? Who lets his spirit flow in public? Who bares his soul with religious modesty? Does anyone feel any fervor in what he hears roundabout? Do we not find, instead, that the man who makes the words of his mind accord with the song of his heart is made to look ridiculous?

I am a professor, I know the ills of our educational system, and have written something on the subject. And the greatest evil is that even the man who gives his utmost to his task gives, in general, only his intelligence. It is a rare teacher who takes out his breast and gives of his own sustenance; the student never feels the warmth of the teat on his mouth. Our education is an affair of nursing bottles.

This deep damage has been aggravated by an evil transported from across the Pyrenees to consume some of our youth: intellectualism. The most terrible aspect of this intellectualism is that it is of very poor intellect.

Those subject to the disease pretend to be moved by nothing, to take the world as a spectacle, like aesthetes, and you will hear them citing books and authors and theories, and shuffling dry ideas, discoursing on style and beautiful form. Impassivity is their badge.

This intellectualism is a terrible illness which undermines the strength of the most distinguished, of those who consider themselves the flower of the human stock, of those who feign to believe that the millions of simple beings who keep quiet, and pray, and work, are merely there to produce a handful of geniuses and sub-geniuses. In short, these intellectualists are Pharisees in the strict definition of that word.

We have an example of a Pharisee, an intellectual seduced by Hellenic culture, in the Jew Saul, who began by persecuting the simple people and who, once his heart was aroused, spread the good word to the gentiles, bringing them true knowledge of that unknown God to whom they had erected empty altars in Athens, in that Athens where, according to this same Saul, later Paul, the people passed their time discussing the latest novelty, running after whatever was curious.

Our intellectuals, too, spend their time talking about the latest novelty, and making comments on it, smelling the fresh ink of the latest book arrived from Paris, meanwhile suppressing—from a sense of propriety—whatever heartfelt impulses are left to them. The religious problem at length comes to interest them also—as a curiosity. But they do not approach it with simplicity of spirit, they do not abandon themselves, for deep inside themselves they fear it. They do not want to awaken.

I know what intellectualism is; I have suffered from it, and even today, as I strike out against its icy crust, I may still be suffering from it more than I should like. I have known this infirmity, similar in the spiritual order to what in the material order constitutes autophagia: as in an ulcerated stomach, for example, where the epithelium having been destroyed, the organ begins to devour itself. One must cure oneself; and in order to effect a cure, one must have recourse to a lacteal diet on the spiritual plane, one must drink a sedative milk, sweet and calming. It is necessary to return to the milk of one's infancy.

In those moments of obstinate inner struggle, when my heart, beating beneath the ashes of rational thought, was stirred by the substance of every solemn crisis, and I was able to affirm my own personality over and above the personality of the Christian civilization in which we live and from which we live, I would resurrect my childhood and submerge myself in the childhood of our spirit's culture. How? By searching my child's soul and suckling the milk which made us men, and listening to the voice of our social childhood, the voice of the Gospel.

In it I found the story of a typical Pharisee, of an intellectual who longs for consolation in truth and

for truth in consolation; I found the story of Nicodemus, the reticent disciple, who goes to see Jesus at
night and in secret, and who, when Jesus dies, helps
to bury Him, as so many intellectuals, enamored of
His sovereign beauty, would like to bury Him in
analyses and studies and convert Him into an artistic
and literary theme.

I read and re-read the story of Nicodemus and I
meditated upon it. And then I allowed these meditations, meditations from the heart rather than rational
disquisitions, to crystallize into the narrative which I
will read you this evening.

No reason to cry fraud, though. This is not a lecture, nor have I come here presuming to demonstrate
anything at all; I do not aspire to do more than to
suggest in you a state of mind, to touch certain fibers
in your spirit. I do not seek to have you leave here
with new ideas or new data. I would be satisfied if
when you find yourselves alone later, each one in his
house, an echo were to resound in you, however weak
and dulled it might be, like the imperceptible lingering left on the air when the ringing of a bell dies away
in space.

Let no one cry fraud, I say. What you are about
to hear will sound more like a sermon than anything
else. There may be those who will think it improper
to this place. I assure you I am not acting out of a
desire for singularity, but simply in the belief that we
are in need here of an outpouring, and I will pour
myself out as an example.

All I ask is that you hear me with sympathy—
making an effort to hear me, in a state of mind analogous at least to that which moved me, and with a
certain concentration. I know it is asking a good deal;
I know that every man has his own cares and pre-

occupations, thinking, perhaps, of a coming appoint-
ment, of a friend who awaits, of the business one is
engaged in; I know that many have come out of pure
curiosity, like Athenians; I do not know how many
are disposed to hear things that, in general, only
weary or annoy. There will be nothing agreeable
about what you are going to hear.

And believe me, if the sense of form in which the
Greeks were educated, as they contemplated their
bodies in the nude during their Olympic games, contributed so much to the creation of Hellenic culture,
Christian culture will perfect itself only when we educate ourselves to contemplate our souls in the nude
during religious confessions.

I am going, then, to show you the soul of Nicodemus the Pharisee.

The Gospel According to St. John, 3:1-24; 7:45-
53; 19:38-48.
"There was a man of the Pharisees, named Nicodemus, a ruler of the Jews: The same came to Jesus
by night, and said unto him, Rabbi, we know that
thou art a teacher come from God: for no man can
do these miracles that thou doest, except God be with
him."

* * *

The Pharisees are idealist believers in a vague life
superior to the worldly life, and princes among their
followers, who pay them heed and homage. Among
those who guide human thought are not a few who
indulge their spirits in hesitant beliefs in immortality,
impersonal beliefs, floating hopes in a supra-percep-
tible ideal. When they hear the words of Christ,
words of simple reality, without deceitful nebulosity,
they still resist leaving their uncertain religiosity for

the sake of religion; but at length they feel moved from within, when their eyes are filled with heartfelt tears, when the ancient simplicity of their infancy inundates their minds with the deep spiritual waters that continue to rise in them. For we were not children in vain, and the child we carry within us still is the just being who justifies us. But the Pharisees are princes among the Jews, they boast a history and a prestige, and the intimate man, who finally wakes in them, has not sufficient force to shake off the exterior, the outer being which others have made of them. Their prestige chokes their souls. And what nights of anguish for the poor Nicodemus when he considers the chains he must shatter, the nakedness in which he must stand, as he thinks how he must destroy the labor of years, undo the work of his days! It is a sacrifice beyond his strength.

But in the end he can not resist any longer, for the spirit impels him, and one night he stealthily goes to visit Jesus. Avoiding the curious, making his way in secret, after seeing that all the doors had been shut and bolted, in the quiet silence of the night, he will interview the Master alone and tell Him: I know you are divine, for your work could not be human; what do you say to that?

"Jesus answered and said unto him, Verily, verily, I say unto thee, Except a man be born again, he cannot see the kingdom of God."

Nicodemus is prostrate at the feet of the Master, begging Him at night and alone for the nourishment of knowledge. And Jesus tells him he must be reborn to see the kingdom of God, for whose advent thousands of simple tongues clamor.

"How am I to change now," Nicodemus asks himself, "and make myself a new man? I am in debt to my past; more than that, I am only the result of my life. It is impossible to undo what has been done, nor can I be anything but what I have come to be. I can not be saved except through faith. But faith is not a voluntary matter; it is due to grace, and if I do not have it, what shall I do? It would be necessary to make myself someone else; but then I would not be myself. If I could only make myself another! . . . But how am I to make myself another, me, me myself, who am as I am and not otherwise? According to what I am, I see and judge my inner state; it is this very state which judges itself; how to change? To be born anew? Only by being born again as another, no longer me, might I see the kingdom of God; but it would not be I who would be seeing it, but another. . . . How absurd!"

Have you ever meditated in your heart, Nicodemus, on the tremendous mystery of irreversible time? Have you felt the great truth that the past does not return ever, ever, ever, piercing into the marrow of your bones? Have you considered the solemn and unique reality of the present, between the infinity of the past and the infinity of the future, the solemn reality of the eternal present, always present and always fugitive? Have you stopped to gaze on eternity in the bosom of the always fugitive now without past or future? For the eternity you imagine extends from the fathomless shores of the last inaccessible yesterday to the fathomless reaches of the last inaccessible tomorrow, is an eternity dead in its repose, and you must seek the live eternity sustaining the present movement, in the very entrails of the present, of its very substance, like the root of the permanence of the fugitive, seek it in God, for whom yesterday and tomorrow are always today. The meditation of time resting in eternity, of our life flowing over God's eternal life, is something to shake the roots of our soul.

Time is irreversible. If you take one road, you close all the others. If various roads are opened for you, choose one! But remember that as you choose one you renounce the others, and that you can never retrace your footsteps. Think of how each of your acts will remain irreparable, of how there is no power, human or divine, which can stop you from doing what you have already done, and of how the effects of your acts will go on reverberating in future times. You are at the confluence of the immensity of space with the fathomless procession of time; everything that has happened and everything that will happen is reflected in you, and the entire creation concurs in determining you. At the same time, each one of your acts reverberates like the waves of a blow struck in a lake without shores. It is true that your act is one amid an infinity of others, and that it is fused with the others; but keep your eyes on your own deeds and consider the irreparable nature of past action. All your deeds are irreparable. But is your intention, is your soul, irreparable? Your action in time is doubtless irreparable, but is its root in eternity beyond reach? If the past is something more than a simple memory of us, and as long as this something lasts, and ends, and goes to establish itself in the eternal sediment, and there lives, is it irreparable? You yourself, who were born once and for all time, who will die once and for all, are you irretrievable in your eternity? Can you not be born anew there?

* * *

"Nicodemus saith unto him, How can a man be born

when he is old? can he enter the second time into his
mother's womb, and be born?"

I do not see how, Nicodemus says to himself, a rebirth is possible. I am old; my habits, feelings, and
doctrines of today are what make me what I am, are
me. To undo them would be to undo myself. I can not
go back to mother earth, to the unconscious again, to
the crossroads where the roads of life opened out for
me, and be born again.

* * *

"Jesus answered, Verily, verily, I say unto thee, Except a man be born of water and of the Spirit, he cannot enter into the kingdom of God. That which is
born of the flesh is flesh; and that which is born of
the Spirit is spirit. Marvel not that I said unto thee,
Ye must be born again. The wind bloweth where it
listeth, and thou hearest the sound thereof, but canst
not tell whence it cometh, and whither it goeth: so
is every one that is born of the Spirit."

The truth is, Nicodemus, that you gaze only on the
carnal man and not on the spiritual; that you gaze
only on the man of temporary appearances and not
the one who remains in the eternal realities; that you
wander among the superstructure without descending to find the live faith which animates everything;
that you do not go beyond the man who may act in
good faith to search for the one who may be good;
for you do not search beneath the man who acts for
the man who is. It is one thing to do good, as you will
acknowledge that morality demands, and another to
be good, as religion asks of you. You should live
hoarding the past, treasuring your time in eternity,

in growth and not in mere advancement. And how? By striving to be better, more divine today than yesterday. What good works will not make you better as you accumulate them? "Good intention is the life of the spirit." (Richard of St. Victor.) Preserve a good intention, and ask God that good works come of it. If your weakness makes you yield to sin, if temptations overcome you, you will repent as long as you keep your good intentions and your frailty will be forgiven you. But if you wish evil and are filled with perverse intention, even though you do not commit wrong, held back by some fear, or if you are honorable because you dare not sin, your bad intent will poison your soul, though you appear just. Be good, Nicodemus, and do not be content merely with not sinning against anyone, or even with doing good, for if you help another but at the same time murmur in your heart against him or curse him in secret, there will be no benefit in the act, for he who abhors his brother is a homicide (1 John 3:15). Learn to hate sin in the degree that you feel compassion and love for the sinner, for hatred of evil is in inverse ratio to hatred of the agent of evil. Until you reach the state where the sight of the wretch who committed a horrendous crime does not wring from you a loving cry of "Poor brother!" you will not be radically good, a total Christian. The intention is faith, and if faith without works is dead faith, works without faith are also dead works. You are lord of your affections and intentions, in a way that you are not lord of your action and deeds.

In all of us, Nicodemus, there are two men, the temporal man and the eternal, the one who goes forward or backward in changing appearances and the one who grows or declines in immutable reality. From the time of our carnal birth, earthly and temporal, from the time our spirit, then in embryo, was first placed in the matrix of the world, whence we will be born in the parturition of death to spiritual life, celestial and eternal, we receive from the world, as from a placenta, coats or layers which envelop us, coats or layers of passions, of impurities, of iniquities, of egotism; at the same time the spiritual embryo continues to grow, with internal growth, struggling to unfold within itself a life of virtue and divine love. There is a growth from inside out, a growth which proceeds from God, who lives within us, and there is another growth, from outside inward, which proceeds from those layers of alluvium the world deposits around our eternal nucleus in an attempt to drown it in time. Thus do we live separated one from another by crusts of varying thickness through which the fire of divine charity radiates with great difficulty and almost always deformed. Even so, the eternal depths of our soul communicate with the eternal depths of the creation around us, with God, who inhabits everything and vivifies it, and in whom, as in a common sea, we are, we move, we live. When God, who inhabits the innermost recess of everything, displays Himself in your conscience, one with Himself, inhabiting as He does your inmost recess, you will be lost in the immense sea, without temporal consciousness of your own, living in Him within your own sight.

Even through the hard worldly crust which smothers us, the heat of our spirit seeks the divine heat, and sometimes, in the souls of saints, the longing is so intense and lively that the crust is split, and the content of the souls is shed in a bloodbath of burning charity which is warmed in the divine fire. The crusts are worn away, beginning with those deepest within,

tion is subject to the irreversible and irretrievable nature of time. It is not so much in the doing as in the wanting that you should seek for your liberty, for the spirit blows, like the wind, from where it will, and you hear its sound without knowing whence it comes. Intern yourself in holy liberty, take refuge in it from the tyrannies of your soul's crust, and then you will be able to exclaim with the apostle: "The good that I would do I do not; but the evil I would not that I do, wretched of me! Who will free me from this body of death?" If your evil deeds assail you, oppose them with your good intention, and seek in good faith to rid yourself of them.

* * *

"Nicodemus answered and said unto him, How can these things be?"

Everything seems like a mystery or an artifice, Nicodemus tells himself, for he is buried in the pharisee morality and can not penetrate Christian religiosity. Goodness buried beneath bad works is scarcely seen, and Nicodemus perhaps repeats: "Let the devil work the miracle." If we prevent wrong from being done, what matter that we do not act from good intentions? But this view does not satisfy him either, and so he asks how Jesus' words are to be realized.

"Jesus answered and said unto him, Art thou a master of Israel, and knowest not these things? Verily, verily, I say unto thee, We speak that we do know, and testify that we have seen; and ye receive not our witness. If I have told you earthly things, and ye believe not, how shall ye believe, if I tell you of heavenly things? And no man hath ascended up to heaven, but he that came down from heaven, even the Son of man which is in heaven. And as Moses lifted up the serpent in the wilderness, even so must the Son of man be lifted up: That whosoever believeth in him should not perish, but have eternal life. For God so loved the world, that he gave his only begotten Son, that whosoever believeth in him should not perish, but have everlasting life. For God sent not his Son into the world to condemn the world; but that the world through him might be saved. He that believeth in him is not condemned: but he that believeth not is condemned already, because he hath not believed in the name of the only begotten Son of God. And this is the condemnation, that light is come into the world, and men loved darkness rather than light, because their deeds were evil. For every one that doeth evil hateth the light, neither cometh to the light, lest his deeds should be reproved. But he that doeth truth cometh to the light, that his deeds may be made manifest, that they are wrought in God."

And you ask, Nicodemus, how can this be done? You are a master and do not know? You have spent so many years in building your prestige and forming your culture and you do not know this? And instead of being humble in your ignorance when someone comes to tell you the answer you say to yourself: I have not found the secret after delving into the deeps of knowledge, so how is it possible that this vulgar and uninformed man might know? Can ignorance possibly pretend to teach wisdom? They say they have seen all this, that they have seen it with faith. . . . Illusions! Those who are not hypocrites pretend to believe; the deluded strive to believe without achieving it; the remaining believers believe they believe without really achieving a positive faith. But there are doubtless some among them whom the very potency of their illusion converts into seers, and who, carried away by their ardent desire for faith, plunge into the most profound waters of the spirit, where they uncover immense fields, virginal and fertile. Religiosity, thinks Nicodemus, doubtless has roots sunk deep into the very depths of the human spirit, and can lead to such fantastical states that the marrow of truth, closed to mere logical reason, will be penetrated. What can poor ordinary believers, tied to the letter of official, imposed religion, possibly show me? But those among them who penetrate into another world, breaking the crust of the letter, descending to the spirit and breaking with dogma, behold faith pure, and these I can ask how it is all done. And I may very well ask this Jesus with whom I talk alone about His Gospel, this prophet of immense destiny, I may ask Him, stealthily and at night, for the substance of the teaching which He sheds on the poor, simple people in figures and parables.

Look, Nicodemus, when He told you about earthly things you did not believe Him, and how are you going to believe Him if He tells you of celestial things? You want to do without the letter in order to reach the spirit; you want to delve into profound regions scorning the fulfillment of precepts; and as you break into praise of mystical clairvoyance you secretly attack the law. But no one has ascended to heaven except one who descended from there, the Son of Man who is in heaven. Only He who descended from heaven can give you some reflection of those potent intuitions you seek, those fires that light your eternal road. Those seers of love took their visions from God, from Christ, through whom God teaches. They learnt their wisdom along the way of abnegation, of sorrow, of sacrifice, their eyes fixed on the cross.

When the Israelites were wandering in the desert, the people spoke out against God and against Moses for having led them out of Egypt so they might perish in the wilderness, where there was neither bread nor water and where they had grown to loathe the light breadstuff they had. And the Lord sent fiery serpents among the people, and they killed whomever they bit. And the people went to Moses, confessing they had sinned in talking against God and against him, and they asked him to destroy the serpents. Moses prayed, and, in obedience to the Lord, he made a serpent of metal, which he put upon a pole, and whenever anyone who was bitten looked upon it, he was cured (Num. 21).

Wandering in the desert of your world and your knowledge, you have spoken, Nicodemus, almost without knowing it, against God; you have murmured in your heart against Him and against the prophet who led you out of that enchanted Egypt, where you sweetly slept the sleep of slavery, where you did not endure the fright you now feel. You have lost your calm, a strange unease troubles your heart, everything seems bleak, you suffer from spiritual hunger and thirst, and you are weary of the light breadstuff of your desert. It is a terrible thing, in truth, when you come up against that "Vanity of vanities!" and every beauty loses its attractiveness and every impression its savor; when you are possessed by the painful obsession of the desert, which makes us deliberately kill time and plunges us into the sadness where every effort seems useless; when, the appetite for life lost, one lives as from necessity, from routine, from cow-ardice or fear of death. Then, even he who believes he does not believe confesses to God in his heart, per-haps even blaming Him for his evils. And the Lord sends him real ills, gnawing temptations, serpents that kill whomever they bite. Pain acts as a spur, and the man who had no appetite is suddenly hungry, and confesses that he sinned, and asks that the serpent biting him and poisoning him be driven off, and the cross which weighs him down be taken away. And then he sees raised before him the banner of the be-lievers with its Saviour's cross, the imperishable metal cross, the cross of sorrow eternalized, and he is in-vited to gaze upon it with love so he may live again and be cured of the wounds of his own cross. "And as Moses lifted up the serpent in the wilderness, even so must the Son of man be lifted up: That whosoever believeth in him should not perish, but have eternal life."

All those seers who achieved the peace and wisdom you so desire, Nicodemus, made their way along the path of suffering, of sacrifice, and humility, amid bit-ing serpents and oppressive crosses, with their eyes fixed on the cross of the Saviour. They gained their knowledge of love through the study of sorrow. This wisdom is not a spiritual delicacy for the enjoyment of refined palates, for the placating of tastes weary of the desert; it is not a turn of mind reached by intel-lectual lucubrations. These lucubrations are only the road to the Buddhist Nirvana, to nihilism, to the pure phantasmagoria of the spiritual alcoholic, or to an inner sensuality. True wisdom is a vision of love, it is an active wisdom, a faculty one achieves through abnegation and sorrow, through humility above all, with incessant contemplation of the cross raised in the desert so that those who gaze upon it with love will be able to live under the weight of the cross they bear.

Watch out, Nicodemus, lest you turn your pharisaical morality into Christianity, and your vague aspiration into faith; beware you do not fall into false mysticism. All that vision of another life which the Gospel reveals to you, must it not be more than fantasy, mere literature, aesthetics, pure consolation? Does not the vanity of vanities include the very vanquishment of vanity itself? Might not the end of it all be merely to console man for having been born, and may not religion be merely an enhanced or heightened art? "It is terrifying, really terrifying," you say to yourself, and add between the waves of doubt: "It is terrifying, but does that make it false? And why should consolation be true?"

Pray, Nicodemus, pray and ask, and do not be like those who drive these thoughts out of their minds and hearts, and who with the pretext of a lying health say to themselves: I do not want to start thinking of my beliefs, nor examine my faith. . . . Let me live! No, you can not nor should not live like that now; you can not, no, you can not, by the grace of God; you can not, and, by way of a cure, you will be sent crosses, true crosses, and biting serpents, to make you keep your gaze on the cross of eternal sorrow, so that from the abyss of your misery and pain you may give birth to a new life. Yes, only those who suffer can reach an intuition of the truth of the supreme consolation. Only by suffering is real belief achieved. Suffer, then, suffer, and resign yourself to suffering so that you may believe; for it is better to believe contorted in pain than to consume yourself in the inner despair and the overwhelming disgust of the temporal life's flaccidity. Set yourself to thinking of that immense doctrine of a God who descends in the Son to incarnate pain and suffer it, and thus make it divine; think on it, and ask for sorrows so that you may become divine to the extent that you can, and come nearer and nearer the perfection that the Master suggested when he said we should become as perfect as our celestial father is perfect.

God did not send His Son to the world so as to condemn it to the nausea of a reality in vivid contrast to His word's ideality, but sent Him so that the world might be saved through Him. Whosoever does not believe in Him shall be condemned to eternal loathing and nausea, to anguish and to the terror of nothingness.

And why is there no belief, Nicodemus? Why do some rebel against the faith they say is imposed upon them, while others merely feign to believe, still others believe they believe without truly believing, and some assert they want to believe but can not? Why is there no belief, Nicodemus? Or rather, why is there belief? "The light came into the world," Jesus says to you in private, "and men loved darkness rather than light, because their deeds were evil." Here is why they do not believe: because their deeds are evil.

It is not so much, Nicodemus, that the good are good because they believe, nor the wicked bad because of lack of faith, but rather that the good believe because they are good, and because they are not good that the bad do not.

Do you perchance believe that goodness, inner goodness, does not provide a more penetrating and clear light than reason? With his reason, if it is a powerful reason, a man, even if he be bad, can come to comprehend and grasp the temporal world, and reach an understanding of the "reason" of things; but to feel and see the eternal world, to arrive at the truth of everything, and not merely its "reason," is an attribute given only to faith, "the substance of things hoped for" (Heb. 11:1), faith, which goodness draws down upon us, and which goodness upholds upon its immovable foundation. And the intimate substance of goodness, its root, is humility.

Ah, Nicodemus! If you understood the intense light which is goodness, the divine capacity for vision which it furnishes the spirit! In order to see, and see truly, the true and eternal, not merely the rational and passing, it is necessary to rid oneself of impurity and see with the eternal nucleus, with the interior man, free of the worldly crust which obscures, dims, and confuses the true vision. Your masters show you, Nicodemus, that no one can see except whence he stands, from his enforced point of view, through his own eyes, and they do not know that a man can look from God, in whom he is, and that he can see through goodness, which is the interior vision itself, more than the most transparent crystal. Only the good man, not merely the honorable man, truly forgives, for only the good man sees the inmost recesses of the offense and the unique justice of pardon; and because only God is in all ways good, only God forgives entirely. But Jesus Himself, who shows us that only God is good, shows us also that we should be perfect like Him. Our goodness consists in ceaselessly striving for the inaccessible. And that is the highest goodness, which draws faith after it. For if only the truly good man truly believes, only the man who truly believes is truly good. The evildoers, the proud, do not believe: "For every one that doeth evil hateth the light, neither cometh to the light, lest his deeds should be reproved."

Yes, Nicodemus, they hate the light. Observe them well, and you will see that their tolerance will cease as soon as it comes up against real faith; you will see that they will countenance your maintenance of any doctrine, any cult, any fantasy; but they will not stand for your giving yourself over to this Jesus whom you see stealthily at night and of whom they talk as about a poetic fiction. You may believe in all sorts of phantasmagory, you may distract them, amuse them, move them if you can; but do not touch on eternal realities, nor go beyond the pleasing appearances which delight the mind or give rise to soft tears. They do not want to think, or to feel the eternal realities. They hate the light because the light means vigil and it awakes them from their somnambulism, from the dream where they live attempting to convince themselves that they are made of the very substance of dreams. Look and you will see how they stubbornly persist in not meditating on the eternal. At most they will inquire about it, they will attempt to rationalize it, they will analyze it from outside, but they will not meditate on it from within, in their hearts; and if perchance they try to do so, then as soon as they feel a convulsion in the entrails of their souls, they will cry out that it is a sickness and delirium, and will avert their eyes from the subject, which is their cross, and they will go back to living like sound beings, like rational wise men, in the bosom of the dream, in full flight from vigil and the madness of the cross. "But he that doeth truth cometh to the light, that his deeds may be made manifest, that they are wrought in God." Yes, Nicodemus; the man who searches for more than delight and strives to do more than deceive life and death, the man who acts truly and not merely well, the man who feels deeply and hungers for eternity, this man comes to the light without fear of the convulsions or the personal wretchedness which the light uncovers, this man goes to the light so that his works may not seem his but made in God, in whom he lives and is.

* * *

Nicodemus ended his nocturnal and circumspect visit to the Saviour, and with his mind filled with high ideas and profound sentiments once again submerged himself in the world of daily cares. His soul again lived the exterior life, the life of the earthly crust, but always retaining in the hidden depths the fervor of that night. While he followed the course of his affairs, of his pharisaical teachings, of his conversations and dealings, he maintained a silent dialogue in his intimate recesses. And he followed Jesus, who was evangelizing the poor in spirit, followed Him with his eyes, across squares and down streets. Sometimes he might have mingled with the crowds listening to the Master, and if he happened to have been present at the healing of the paralytic whom Jesus asked "Do you want to be cured?" he must have felt a twisting within his own paralytic soul.

As the Feast of Tabernacles approached, Jesus went up from Galilee to Jerusalem, while the Jews sought Him out, disputing whether He were a good man or a deceiver. And in the midst of the feast Jesus taught in the temple doctrine that was not His, but of Him who sent Him, and He did not talk of Himself or seek glory for Himself, but rather for Him who sent Him. And then the Pharisees sent their followers to seize that fomenter of sedition who clamored: "If any man thirst, let him come unto me and drink." A grave discord arose in the populace, for the good men, guided by their goodness, said that Jesus was the Christ, the awaited prophet, and the others, tied to deadly law and to desiccating reason, cited the letter of their law as evidence against the Master. But none dared to lay a hand upon Him. When the officers presented themselves before the chief priests and Pharisees without Jesus, they were asked why they had not brought Him, and the officers answered "Never man spake like this man." Then the Pharisees said: "Are ye also deceived? Have any of the rulers or of the Pharisees believed on him? But this people who knoweth not the law are cursed."

What! Are you going to allow yourselves to be deceived by the illusions of the ill, of hallucinated beings, of women, and children, of ignorant and simple men? Are you going to reduce the dignity of reason and turn deceiving consolation into truth, instead of making reason serve as consolation, as strong spirits should? Has any authentic genius or anyone nourished with the marrow of the lion of knowledge ever believed in Him with sincere faith?

Did the great geniuses, the supreme intelligences, the powerful minds of Christianity do aught but battle without respite to rationalize their faith, to temper contradiction by force of dialectic? Or did they ever do more than overcome dogma through the knowledge of dogma itself? Who believes? The populace, ordinary men, those who do not know the law, those who are ignorant of the irreducible laws which govern the universe, the poor deluded masses who, slaves to appearance, have not penetrated into the august determinism of everything that exists, or who have not absorbed the principle that everything rational is real

and everything real rational. The poor folk are unaware that their beliefs have, like everything else, a
law which rules them, and a rigid process. They believe because they have no other alternative but to
believe. And with their faith they perpetuate fanaticism and hypocrisy and deceitful vulgarity upon the
earth, and hinder the ministers of the wise and of the
distinguished from seizing Jesus and bringing Him
before them so that they may analyze and reduce Him
to His rational reality. They are cursed. . . . So think
the Pharisees.

"Nicodemus saith unto them (he that came to Jesus
by night, being one of them) Doth our law judge any
man, before it hear him, and know what he doeth?"

The internal fire which had warmed the entrails
of Nicodemus' soul ever since the nocturnal visit now
loosened his tongue to such an extent that in the
gathering of the Pharisees, the assemblage of his own
people, he appealed to their law in behalf of Jesus.
In the name of reason you ask, Nicodemus, that Jesus
be heard, that He be truly heard and with a clean
heart, and that what He had done, which is matter
for high understanding, be understood. In the name
of that poor reason, elevated to an idol, you ask, Nicodemus, that what Jesus works in the hearts of all
those wretches who do not understand reason be
understood. Have you meditated, he asks them, on
that word which consoles the crestfallen, lends legs
to the paralytic, gives sight to the blind, fortifies the
weak, and extracts from goodness, buried under the
ignorance of the wretched, splendid light to shine in
the darkness?

"They answered and said unto him, Art thou also
of Galilee? Search and look: for out of Galilee ariseth
no prophet."

"Do you come to us with all this nonsense?" they are saying to Nicodemus. "You are a dreamer like that very Jesus for whom you intercede now; go and study, examine and see if from the regions of dreams there ever came anyone to foresee what reason foresees."

* * *

"And every man went unto his own house."

* * *

Thus concludes this Gospel passage. "Every man went unto his house": every man returned to his business, to his preoccupations, to his domestic affairs, to the hard core of his worldly concerns, and they separated so as to go each man to his house, instead of joining so as to go all together to the common house, that of the Lord.

Nicodemus also went to his house, and submerged himself in his affairs after that public profession, still bearing with him the heat of that nocturnal visit despite the disparaging repulse at the hands of his comrades. Every man went to his house.

Jesus continued His divine career, while Nicodemus doubtlessly followed Him with his sight and his steps across squares and down streets. The scribes and Pharisees brought the adulterous woman to the Master, in order to tempt Him, and they heard from His lips the tremendous sentence that he who was without sin should cast the first stone; and, reproved in their consciences, they left Him alone. And Jesus, who from His divine goodness beheld the essence of sin, pardoned the woman when He was left alone with her, once her accusers had gone away.

Nicodemus must have known all this, and he must have heard words of life from Jesus in streets and

squares, and heard his own companions, the Pharisees, complaining that the prophet had given sight to
the blind man on the sabbath.

When Jesus raised up Lazarus, the Pharisees had
their fill, and said: "If we leave him thus, everyone
will believe in him, and the Romans will come and
will remove our place and nation." For this reason,
which will never be sufficiently meditated, they decided to kill Him. They decided to kill Him so that
the Romans should not eliminate them as a nation,
to kill Him, as they said, for being a traitor.

The feasts of Passover arrived, and people from
everywhere flocked to Jerusalem. And Nicodemus,
aware of the designs of his fellows, must have felt a
rare restlessness in the midst of the bustle and traffic
of the celebrations. The simple multitude received
Jesus in triumph and with palm leaves, as He entered
the city mounted on a donkey.

Underneath the feasting, obscured by the joyous
celebration, the passionate struggle grew more intense. And it seemed as if the Galilean was pleased
to proclaim Himself envoy of God and light of the
world, thus attracting upon the Jewish nation the
suspicious gaze of the Romans. This seditious man
lacking in all prudence seemed ready to provoke
among the masses of celebrants a conflict which
would furnish a pretext for the Romans to abolish
the Jewish nation and hurl it out into the world to
wander.

At length, Jesus saw His hour near and supped
with His people in the last supper of farewell and
communion, and as He finished He spoke to His
Father in front of them all, raising His eyes to heaven,
pronouncing that prayer that can scarcely be read
except on one's knees and with a clean heart, that

prayer in which He asks that as He was in His Father and His Father in Him, so should we all be one in them.

Jesus went out of there toward the brook Cedron; He wrestled with humanity in the olive grove; He was taken by the betrayer and was tried.

And Nicodemus? Nicodemus must have followed from afar, with profound dismay, these first acts in the divine drama, and when the words of Christ to His Father reached him, who was one of the Pharisees, that is, of the *ferishim*, or the distinguished, he doubtless meditated on Christ's prayer that we all become one, the common people and the distinguished, all those of Christ and not of the world, so that once we are one we should be one in God.

In the anthill of the Passover, amid the coming and going of the people driven hither and thither by their affairs, their leisure, or their passions, Nicodemus must have been present before the praetorium and seen the rioting populace ask that Barabbas be released instead of Jesus, and he must have seen Him with a purple robe and a crown of thorns, made a laughing-stock of the crowd who had hailed Him a few days before. "Behold the man!" the procurator said to the populace, and Nicodemus must have said to himself: "There is the man, yes, the man I sought out at night so that he might tell me the truth; there is the man who shook my spiritual entrails now turned into a figure of mockery for this wretched populace!" And then, while the crowd screamed from the square: "Crucify him, crucify him!" Nicodemus no doubt felt, more than love for the Christ derided, a hatred toward the fickle mob which today receives the envoy with palms and tomorrow asks an ignominious cross for Him. And this hatred born of his pharisaical crust, this distinguished man's disgust, drowned the loving feeling of compassion for the prophet, that affection from which an immense pity for the poor blind mob that denied Him and condemned Him would have surged, for love and hatred do not stand together, though the love is felt for the victim and the hatred for the hangman. Perhaps Nicodemus cursed, not the sin in which he was a participant, but the ostensible ministers of it, the blinded populace; he doubtless cursed it with the same tongue with which he blessed Jesus; with that tongue which is a world of injustice and which contaminates the entire body; with that tongue with which we bless God the Father and curse men made in His image and likeness. The pharisaical moralism of his worldly crust suffocated the Christian piety aroused in his bosom on the night of the visit.

Nicodemus followed the dispute between the astute Roman and the aroused Jewish nation. "Behold your King!" said Pilate cunningly, and the people, that same populace which wanted to make Him king when He multiplied the bread, howled: "Crucify him, crucify him!" The procurator, ensconced in the haughty indifference of his skeptical Roman spirit, desired merely to ridicule the prophet, to make Him the laughing-stock of the mob, leaving formal Roman law out of the question, and avoiding condemnation of one he considered righteous; he simply wanted to render Him powerless, and turn the tragedy into a farce. But the populace, religious even in its error, demanded a tragedy and a sacrifice. The skeptical functionary at last gave in; he washed his hands, thinking perhaps that it was all a small matter among Jews, a slight incident compared with the immense majesty of the Empire; and he handed the prophet over to the mob to be crucified.

Nicodemus followed Jesus from a distance as He went to the scaffold, and he cried within himself together with the women who wept as they followed along, and he heard the sentence, "Do not cry for me, but cry for yourselves and for your children." He might have seen, from the walls of the holy city, how at the gates, at "the place of a skull, which is called in the Hebrew Golgotha," they raised Him on the cross between heaven and earth, naked and exposed to the people, a prey to pain. He must have seen how the people demanded not only a death, but an agony, a spectacle. And if he felt hatred again and pharisaical disgust toward the mob, he must at the same time have heard: "Father, forgive them for they know not what they do." And these words would have made him consider his own sins, and would have engendered profound pity for the blind, God-killing crowd. Who knows whether at that moment he did not understand that it was his own sins which were crucifying the Master?

From the walls of the holy city, on that feast day, the poor Nicodemus must have watched how Jesus struggled with death, how He was mocked by the mob, which hounded Him and harried Him like children worrying a poor bat nailed up for their sport. The mockery which the Roman had planned now ended in tragic play.

Then Nicodemus, dissolved by inner tears, a great part of his worldly crust melted by them, and his spirit become like that of a child, a humble child, felt the entire weight of his sins, the heaviness of his own cross, the writhing of his doubts, and he must have fixed his eyes on the cross which loomed up against the stormy sky. He did battle with himself; he trembled; perhaps he broke into a sweat.

He heard the words: "I thirst." Lacking courage to do so, he would yet have liked to run and brought Him cold water. But he felt tied to the city walls.

Once Jesus was dead, Nicodemus went to join the shamefaced disciples of the Master, those who from fear of the Jews visited Him only at night. Among them was Joseph of Arimathea, who had come to ask the procurator for permission to take away the body.

"And there came also Nicodemus, which at the first came to Jesus by night, and brought a mixture of myrrh and aloes, about an hundred pound weight. Then took they the body of Jesus, and wound it in linen cloths with the spices, as the manner of the Jews is to bury. Now in the place where he was crucified there was a garden; and in the garden a new sepulchre, wherein was never man yet laid. There laid they Jesus therefore because of the Jews' preparation day; for the sepulchre was nigh at hand."

He had died, the Master who had filled the heart of Nicodemus with new life on that unforgettable night, the Master who had spoken to him of rebirth and eternal life, He had died! Would all the hope but lately conceived likewise die? Was that lovely doctrine of consolation also condemned to die? Had it been anything more than an illusion? Was it anything more than a lure to retain men in this life?

Jesus had died, and Nicodemus, the secret disciple, went to bury Him, bringing myrrh and aloes. He also enveloped Him in the perfumed balsam of his affection and buried Him in his heart. His enthusiasm, his longing, his love, his knowledge, all were converted into myrrh and aloes with which to anoint the body of the Master in his soul, and he buried Him in his heart, where no one had ever been put before.

But it fell out that on the first day of the week, early in the morning, while it was still dark, Mary Magdalen went to the sepulchre and found the stone taken away from where Joseph of Arimathea and Nicodemus, the reticent disciples, had placed it; and she hurried to find Peter and John, and they, who came running in competition, found the winding sheet and linen clothes lying to one side, and they saw and believed, while Mary remained by the empty tomb to weep. Then Jesus appeared to her. She took Him for the gardener, but when she heard her name called, "Mary!" she answered, "Master!" And it was Mary of Magdala who went to tell the disciples the news that she had seen the Lord and spoken with Him.

What must have gone on in the heart of Nicodemus, the Pharisee, the distinguished Nicodemus, when he learned that the Master who had been buried by him had appeared to the poor Mary Magdalen, the repentant sinner, the one time public woman? What would the reticent disciple think when he learned that the resurrected Master had shown Himself first to the woman who had publicly bathed His feet in tears and dried them with her hair and kissed His feet anointed with unguents in the house of Simon the Pharisee, who was scandalized by the sinful woman's daring? Nicodemus must have then recalled the words of the Master:

"I entered into thine house, thou gavest me no water for my feet: but she hath washed my feet with tears, and wiped them with the hairs of her head. Thou gavest me no kiss: but this woman since the

time I came in hath not ceased to kiss my feet. My
head with oil thou didst not anoint: but this woman
hath anointed my feet with ointment. Wherefore I
say unto thee, Her sins, which are many, are forgiven;
for she loved much: but to whom little is forgiven,
the same loveth little."

And later, when He had told her, "Thy sins are forgiven," the people at table began to ask themselves
"Who is this that forgiveth sins also?" And Jesus had
said to the woman: "Thy faith hath saved thee; go
in peace."

"Whoever loves much, is pardoned much," Nicodemus must have said to himself, and repeated in his
heart: "Thy faith hath saved thee; go in peace."

Then he must have understood that if he wanted
pardon and life he must water with the affections of
his soul, wipe with his powers, kiss with his reason,
and anoint with the unguents of his love—love, the
only necessary feeling—that dead body he carried in
his heart, and that only in this way would He resurrect in him and pardon him for having loved.

And now, gentlemen, each one of us will go to his
house, return to his tasks. May God see to it that
whenever anyone of you in the midst of his comings
and goings remembers my lecture tonight he do so
as a distant song, without words, an evocative song
that awakes in his spiritual entrails a deep preoccupation, an emotion strong enough to tear him away
from the trivial. For that is all I desire; I do not want
to furnish you with ideas, mine or someone else's—
ideas are worth little—but play upon strings that are
usually silent in the psaltery of your hearts.

I have sown my grain, the grain that has been
given me to sow, and I do not want to turn my head

back or see whether the shoot will come up here or there. I leave it to the fecund earth, to the air, the water, and especially the sun, the only Sun.

Let each of you return, then, to your house, and I will go to mine and may we find peace in every one.

Faith

Liv og tro skal smelte sammen.
Life and faith must fuse.
Henrik Ibsen, *Brand*, akt. V

"*Question*: What is faith?
Answer: To believe what we did not see."

Believe what we did not see? No, not believe what we did not see, but rather beget, create what we do not see. Create what we do not see, yes; create it and live it and consume it, and then again to create it and consume it once again, living it anew in order to again create it . . . and thus on and on, or round and round, in a ceaseless vortex of life. And that is living faith, for life is continuous creation and consummation, continually, and, therefore, incessant death. Do you perchance believe that you would be living if you did not die every other moment?

Faith is the consciousness of life in our spirit; few of the living have faith in their living or believe they are alive, assuming one can give the name life to what they are living.

Before and above all else, faith is confidence; whoever has confidence in himself—in himself and not in his ideas—has faith in himself; whoever feels that his life flows, overflows from him, and carries him and leads him on, whoever believes that his life brings him ideas and that life takes them away also has faith.

Not he who wants but he who can has faith, he to whom his own life gives him faith; for faith, if you will, is a vital gift and divine grace. For if you possess an unbreakable faith in carrying out something, the faith which moves mountains, then it is not strictly speaking the faith which gives you the strength to move the mountain, but rather is it the strength pulsating in you that is revealed as faith. Do not then spur on your faith, for that way it will not ever burgeon. Do not probe too deeply. Wish for it with all your heart and all your might, and hope—for hope is already faith. Are you weak? Have confidence in your weakness, confide in it, and conceal yourself, efface yourself, resign yourself; for resignation is also faith.

Do not then seek faith directly and at first hand. Seek out your life, for if you saturate yourself with your own life, faith will come. See to it that your outer man is in concert with your inner self, and hope. Wait and hope, for faith consists in waiting and hoping.

Faith feeds on the ideal, and on the ideal alone, on a concrete, real, live, incarnate, and at the same time unattainable ideal. Faith seeks the impossible, the absolute, the infinite, and the eternal: life at the full. Faith is a matter of communing with the entire universe, working in time for the sake of eternity and without pursuing mean and immediate external effects; working not for History, but for eternity. Faith is preaching at night in the middle of the desert while gazing at the stars where they glitter and trusting they hear you where you speak to their souls like St. Anthony of Padua preaching to the fishes.

Intellectualism is to blame for the notion that faith is believing what we did not see, lending intellectual credence to an abstract, logical principle, instead of trusting in life and abandoning ourselves to it, to life radiating from our own spirits, radiating from people and not ideas. Abandon yourself to your own life, yes, to your own specific life, and not to what is called Life, which is another abstraction, an idol.

You will see how in the order of religion, indeed in the only order of religion which speaks to our souls, souls formed by Christianity, that is, in the Christian order, faith consists in the trust placed by the repentant sinner in the Father of Christ, the only revelation available to us of the living God. This is the only saving faith, the only salvation. From it issue our works and deeds, like water from a spring.

Examine language, for language carries along with it, under pressure of the centuries, the secular sediment which is the richest alluvium of the collective spirit. Scrutinize language. What does it tell you?

We inherit our Spanish word *fe*, faith, along with the concept it envelops, from the Latin *fides*, whence *fidelis*, Spanish *fiel*, loyal, *fidelitas*, Spanish *fidelidad*, loyalty, *confidere*, Spanish *confiar*, hope or confide or trust in, and so forth. The Latin root, *fid*, is the same as the Greek πιθ- (labial for labial, dental for dental) root of the verb πείθειν, to persuade, in the active voice, and πείθεσθαι, to obey, in the middle voice: to obey is the office of love and trust. And from the root πιθ- came πίστις, faith, something very different from γνῶσις, or knowledge. Go to the German and you will find *Glaube*, faith, from Old High German *gilouban*, Gothic *galaubjan*, from the root *liub-*, *lub-*, which suggests the idea of love. But it is in Greek, in the difference between *pistis* and *gnosis*, that the shade of meaning proper to the word faith most clearly emerges.

It was the time when Jesus had just been about the world; the scent of His passing and the living echo of His words still lingered; His disciples were still imbued with the memory of Him; it suffused them like a sun setting on a weary earth amidst blooded clouds; the communities of Christians were still young and they awaited the coming at any time of the Kingdom of the Son of God and of the Son of Man; the person and life of the Divine Master was the magnetic North of their longing and desire; the teachings of the Master could not be appreciated except in His presence, and His works could not be understood except through His life, for they were inseparable from Him; these Christians were altogether transfused with true faith, of the kind which is indistinguishable from love and hope and which is called *pistis*, πίστις, faith or trust, religious rather than theological faith, pure faith, faith still free of dogma. They lived the life of faith; they lived on hope in the future; they awaited the kingdom of eternal life, and they lived it. Each individual Christian gave his hope the imaginative or intellective shape which suited him best, even if it was within the bounds of the common hopes, so that the *concepts* formed of Jesus and His work were varied. Among the so-called Apostolic Fathers it is not uncommon to find differing notions, usually not very well defined, regarding one and the same object of the faith of hope. The Fathers even enjoyed the holy right to contradict themselves. The embryonic outline of the tendencies which would become the long procession of heresies could already be traced in that boiling mass of longings and aspirations. There was scarcely any distinction between the heretics and the orthodox, or rather, heresy was orthodox, since every doctrine chosen and formed by everyone fell within the precincts of belief, which in those days was a matter of lively hope. Hence, the word heresy itself comes from this choosing, for *haeresis*, αἵρεσις, means "election." *Pistis*, incandescent faith, lent a profoundly unifying tone to all that immensely rich and palpitating variety of future diversity, just as today a *pistis* informs the contending Christian confessions.

In the measure that the white heat of faith abated and as religion adjusted itself to the world, the molten mass of belief became encrusted with a superficial layer, more and more impervious to the atmosphere and cut off from the necessary supply of circulating air. And thereby the fatal separation between religious life and common life took place, when in truth the second should be no more than a form of the first. Cores of solidification and of crystallization began to appear here and there. The early *pistis* began to be replaced by *gnosis*, γνῶσις, knowledge, belief rather than actual faith: doctrine and not hope. The teaching was put about that life consists in knowledge; the practical ends of religion turned into theoretical and philosophical principles, and religion became a metaphysics which was supposed to have been revealed.

Sects, schools, dissidence, and dogma were born. Bit by bit the creed developed and, on the day that the so-called Symbol of the Faith was raised in all its precise neatness, *gnosis* triumphed. On that day an orthodox gnosticism was established. It was a gnosticism born of slow adaptation rather than one of the common variety of gnosticisms as such; it was a gnosticism resulting from a fast and premature Hellenization of the Bible. Thenceforward, faith would become a matter, for many, of believing in what they had not seen, of abiding by formulas: *gnosis* instead of *pistis*,

pistis being trust in the kingdom of eternal life and belief in what one did not see. And thus passes youth.

Movements analogous to those which united those original Christian communities are to be seen among us even now. Today, the young of spirit are joined in a common hope in the advent of the kingdom of man. A true faith moves people these days, *pistis santa*, trust in the ideal, which is always in the future—a refuge in the future—faith in utopia. Many people believe and trust in the new millennium, in a coming redemption, in a future life of fraternal and equitable liberty. This ideal will never come to pass. It will eternally be in the future. In that way it will be able to conserve its precious quality of being ideal. For it is the ideal which arouses us, moves us. The early coming of Christ, likewise, did not come to pass, for Christ's kingdom is not of this world. But, just as Christ came, and comes, to the soul of each and every believer in Him, to anyone who believes with true faith, so shall future man reign in the soul of each one of the faithful. We shall all thus live in the future, while the accumulated sum of so much private and intense travail will leave a memorable and meaningful impress upon daily life.

For, in all truth, is this man of the future, this super-man of whom everyone dreams, in any way different from the perfect Christian who, like a butterfly-to-be, sleeps in contemporary Christian larvae or chrysalises? When this super-man breaks out of the Gnostic cocoon in which he is enveloped and emerges from the mystic obscurity wherein he is able to abhor the world, God's world, and even perhaps disown life, everyday life, will this man of the future be in any wise different from the perfect Christian? At that point nature will equal grace. At that point the somber medieval concepts—suitable for slaves or slaveowners—which have throttled the simple, luminous, and human Gospel will be burst asunder. Then the anchorite will withdraw into his own spirit in order thence to penetrate life, and then give himself to common life and live the life that all men live. For only in works of love towards others is the love of God sustained.

And what, after all, is Christian faith? Either it is trust in Christ or it is nothing: in the historical Person and in the historical revelation of His life, whichever one chooses. This trust is felt by many who claim to deny Christ: they would discover it for themselves if they plumbed themselves but a little. This faith is a faith in Christ, in the divinity of Christ, in the divinity of man as revealed by Christ, in which we are, in which we move, and live in God; it is a faith which does not stem from His ideas, but from Him; a faith not based on a doctrine which might be representative, but a faith grounded in the historic Person, in the spirit in which He lived and loved. Ideas do not live or love. Christian faith is based not on the Christ of the theologians, but on the Christ of the Gospel in whom we behold and through whom we are drawn to the living, *irrational*, super-rational or infra-rational God, the God of the heart, the cor-dial God, the God of the religious imperative and not the abstract Supreme Concept of the theologians, not the motionless Prime Mover of the Stagirite with its cortege of arguments in physics, cosmology, teleology, ethics, and so forth. God in our spirits is Spirit and not Idea, love and not dogma, life and not logic.

Anything short of a yielding of the heart to that trust of life is not faith, even though it be belief. All belief, in the long run, becomes a *credo quia absurd-um*; either it ends in the suicide—from despair—of intellectualism, or it becomes the terrible "faith of the charcoal-maker."

The terrible faith of the charcoal-maker! Why, what is the *reductio* of the faith of the charcoal-maker?

> What do you believe?
> Whatever our Holy Mother Church believes and teaches.
> And what does our Holy Mother Church believe and teach?
> What I believe.

And the vicious circle goes on! And good and vicious it is! The Book of the Seven Seals is handed over tightly sealed, and the order is issued: "Believe these contents!" Whereupon the answer is "I believe them." But does the believer believe in the contents? Does he know what the book says? There is something here very much like the attitude behind "Whatever you say," "If you say so," and then the signature on the dotted line! No need to think: and that's a saving! That's all there is to it.

Such faith is no more than an act of submission to a worldly, a mundane, authority. It is a way of making faith into a merely mundane affair. It is not a matter of trust in God through Christ, but a submission to a hierarchical and juridical institution.

True, only one faith can be maintained in any one Church. In any one Church: but what is a Church? A Church is the congregation of the faithful, of all those who believe and trust. And the most ample Church is Humanity.

But behold what happened! The attempt was made to wed the two most incompatible elements possible:

the Gospel to Roman law, the glad tidings of love and liberty to the *ita ius esto*, the spirit to dogma. And thus they clipped the wings of Hebrew prophecy, which called for love, not immolation, and they loaded religion with the ballast of Justinian edicts and pagan *sacra*. They have put out the flame of religion with their lustral water. And over the scorched earth they have raised up the Stagirite, with his windmill logic, his syllogisms, his entelechy, his "patient" and "agent" understanding, and all his categories and categorems, eaten away by a horde of wretched ideophages who reduced the human heart to a heap of analyzed dust. And then there sprouted in the shadow of mortal Canon Law, decadent Theology (daughter, rather than mother, of Canon Law), a brilliant Hellenic fantasy spun around Gospel themes, later bound around with legalisms in the Roman spirit, the spirit of soldiers and praetors, of discipline and codes, formed along the lines of *adversus hostem aeterna auctoritas* and of the *ita ius esto*. In the end *auctoritas* was the only *ius* exercised *adversus hostes*, against the faithful as a whole, who were turned into *hostes*, into enemies. For, in effect, *man* is the enemy, the evil-doer. And the law had to be used against man, inasmuch as man is, by nature, rebellious and proud. Poor man!

And everything became a matter of Shibboleths!

"What's that about Shibboleths?" you may well ask.

Turn to Chapter 12 of the Book of Judges, and you will find the explanation. Here it is:

The men of Ephraim warred against the men of Gilead, and Jephthah gathered together the men of Gilead and fought against Ephraim: "And the Gilead-ites took the passages of Jordan before the Ephraimites: and it was so, that when those Ephraimites which were escaped said, Let me go over; that the men of Gilead said unto him, Art thou an Ephraimite? If he said, Nay; Then said they unto him, Say now Shibboleth: and he said Sibboleth: for he could not frame to pronounce it right. Then they took him, and slew him at the passages of Jordan: and there fell at that time of the Ephraimites forty and two thousand."

So we are told in verses 5 and 6 of Chapter 12 of the Book of Judges. In Spanish terms, it is as if the men of Castilla la Vieja were to war against those of Castilla la Nueva, and then when some of the latter attempted to cross the Guadarrama Mountains they were to be asked "Are you a Madrileño?" and replying in the negative were told "Then say *pollo*," whereupon they would naturally reply by saying *"poyo"* because they could not pronounce the Castilian for "chicken" any other way. Whereupon, their throats would be cut at the Guadarrama Mountain passes.

The word *shibboleth* has remained in use, especially in English, a language much influenced in its formation, like the people who speak it, by a biblical inheritance, and now the word means the sign and seal of some party or sect, an exclusivist test-word, in short.

The word has not passed into Spanish, but, as for the concept . . . we are loaded with shibboleths, or *sibboleths*, if you prefer, adapted to our language, for all the signs and seals, shibboleths on all sides. "Jesuit!" yells one man, and thinks he has said something. "Krausist," yells another, and feels relieved. Shibboleths, shibboleths everywhere, shibboleths to cover the lack of faith. "Say *pollo*," and the opponent says, *"Poyo."* "What," says the first, "you say *poyo*! *Poyo*? I'll cut your throat! You must be an Ephraimite!"

From out of dire and daily battle, with infinite travail and anguish, with desperate longing and despairing joy, out of the soul of a community, there sprouted the flower of dogma. It flowered from a plant burgeoning with vitality, a well-rooted plant with sprouts and leaves and sap. And the community transmitted through its greenest shoots the select flower which was destined to give fruit or, rather, in which the plant was destined to grow to fruition. And thus it came about; but on giving fruit, the flower died, as is inevitable. And the faithful gathered up the faded petals and deposited them in a shrine, where they keep them under a bell-glass, venerating thus the faded petals of a dead flower.

And these faded petals, like flowers pressed between the leaves of a prayer-book in remembrance of some past love, have turned into shibboleths. And when some Ephraimite chances along and goes to look at the bell-glass in the shrine, a Gileadite is there to suggest he smell the faded petals, the pressed flower from the liturgical herbarium, smell it through the glass of the case. The temple guard may well ask then "What does it smell like?"; and if the Ephraimite is truthful he will answer, according to whether or not his olfactory sense is sharp, either "It doesn't smell like anything," or "It smells of death!" Thereupon the Gileadite will cry out "I'll cut your throat!"

That's it! Cut his throat! Off with his head—morally! Brand him with the iron! Bring down on him the ever-present and ubiquitous Inquisition! So a pressed flower doesn't smell like a flower, doesn't it? This man simply has no sense of smell! The wretch! Yes, he's a wretch, all right, worthy of pity; but a

menace all the same to everyone, because this kind of
infernal catarrh is infectious and will spread and ruin
our pituitaries and all faithful Gileadites will lose
their sense of smell, and if that happens, what in heav-
en's name will become of the tribe of Gilead? Without
a sense of smell the tribe will fall victim to poison, for
the sense of smell is the sentinel placed at the entrance
to the mouth, and without it the sense of taste is useless. Bring the sword, the sword of Jephthah, quick,
and off with his head! Off with his head before he
infects us with his infernal catarrh and we lose our
sense of smell and can no longer smell the mysterious
flower, and life turns sour!

Yes, we must avoid, at all costs, losing our sense
of smell, avoid what is known as loss of the spiritual
sense of smell (which in all truth would amount to
gaining or regaining it). We must not allow the
herbarium's dried flower to seem to smell of death, or
even of drouth, and avoid going out into the countryside to pick the flowers that grow in the sun and bear
fruit and die. A flower only fructifies when it dies,
just as the grain gives forth a new plant only by dying. By dying? No, by re-birth. And, what shall we
say of whatever is not an incessant rebirth, what shall
we call it?

* * *

Hello waxed ecstatic over the singing of the Creed.
It can be sung, of course, but is it not reduced to
words, words for music, perhaps, mere melopoeia,
melodica. *Qui ex Patre Filioque procedit . . .* ! This
Filioque is the result washed up by oceans of ink, it
represents a supreme effort of ingenuity, legions of
syllogisms and mountains of invective. And how does
it intensify the life of whoever repeats it today? Why
has it been omitted from the popular vernacular

Creed, the one taught at school, from the *Credo ad usum servi pecoris*, while it remains in the other one, the liturgical, the one set to music for singing? In what manner is the singer or listener of the sung Creed made more divine? How is his heart raised? What light does that *Filioque* shed to inspire him to ascend to *Amor*?

Still, it will not do to condemn any faith when it is simple and spontaneous, even when it is forced to express itself in forms which serve to deform it. All faith is sacred. Even the faith of fetishism, which animates, consoles, fortifies, encourages, and performs miracles.

Consider the wonder-working wood statue, rough log miracle-worker, carved out with hatchet-blows by some farmer perhaps: generations of villagers have deposited their cares, their longings, their anguish at its feet, and there they have revivified their imagination for the future. The image is surrounded with ex votos: worn crutches, locks of hair, yellowed shifts, faded ribbons, primitive paintings, wax limbs grown twisted. Go and visit Notre Dame des Victoires in Paris, for an example. That church is a cemetery of fetishism. The dry skeleton of the structure reeks of fetishism. The usually extemporaneous ex votos have here become regularized into inscriptions in red letters on white marble. The temple resembles a wall newspaper, complete with squibs and personal announcements. It also recalls those partisan declarations accompanied by a list of supporting names published in party newspapers. Or niches inscribed with names in a mausoleum. And one notes the boneyard stench. Here we have fetishism according to rule, subject to double entry bookkeeping, with its ledger, scribe, and cash-book. Yes, most particularly a cash-book! The system was later improved upon and there is, elsewhere, an experimental laboratory, for miracles.

Shortly after my visit to Notre Dame des Victoires with its vast walls of advertisements, I chanced to visit a small undistinguished chapel in a village of my native Basque country, a little church hidden among the mist-covered mountains. To the right of the entrance stood the rustic baptismal font, a great stone basin where the holy water is poured over the heads of the children of the villagers while the luxuriant chestnut trees pour rainwater down over the ferns and heather and gorse. The front part of the nave, with its wooden floor, serves as a cemetery for the remains of country people who worked and died in peace. Black cloths thick with wax drippings litter the floor, along with copypaper filled with the calligraphy exercises of the grandchildren, perhaps, of the buried dead; pieces of newspaper, one bearing an advertisement for Singer sewing machines, and shreds of wallpaper are spread under irregular chunks of wood into which rolled wax tapers are stuck. Not long ago the yellow beeswax was vital substance flowing in flowers and now is consumed to make a melancholy light for the dead. Among the dead kneel the humble village housewives, soundlessly weeping and faltering out their prayers, their heads shrouded in black shawls bordered with fringe, their faces hidden behind handkerchiefs in the light of the also weeping candles. Now what does that woman there think of the *Filioque*? She may have contemplated the wax visage of the *Dolorosa* wrapped in a black mantle on the left-hand altar, or the image of St. Anthony in that painting filled with shadows under a mottled gold sky, or the effigy of St. John in the desert; she may have studied the inevitable prints on each side of the main altar, or the rough-hewn, dark, Spanish Virgin on the Gospel side, with the lively eyes and serious mien and embroidered cloak and long hair flowing free, holding the frolic-some Child who is also dressed in embroidered clothes, both Mother and Son wearing crowns; or she may have considered the French Virgin in the side chapel with her tight-fitting white dress laced with blue ribbons, her hands joined together, her face re-calling a painted lily, her eyes cast heavenward; she may have looked over at that St. Elizabeth on her deathbed, with St. Joseph and the Virgin beside her, each one looking in a different direction; or she may have let her gaze linger on that oaken Christ illumi-nated by the faint light filtering through the red cur-tains. No matter, and in any case: whatever does *filioque* mean to a village woman of Alzola?

The country church boasts a portico, a covered colonnade with rustic beams to keep the sun off the stone benches; nearby stands the great wall, the *frontón*, against which Basque *pelota* is played, iron bands marking the field of play. The village plaza includes a long stone semicircular bench and two great rocks by way of table under a stand of walnut trees. The river is visible in the near distance, the stones of the riverbed standing out here and there to whiten in the sun, or breaking the riverflow in other places. Ducks waddle by the washing stones. Bridge and houses are reflected in the calmer lengths of the stream; their image is topped by the peaks of the mountains in the background. This landscape's vast temple is decorated with the green of the mountains, dark green where the chestnuts grow, light green where the cornfields run; by way of incense, a light breeze runs through this temple of the open air, stirring the poplars, the walnuts, and the chestnuts. And for the humble village woman of Alzola, coming out of her humble church, the church where she learned to pray, into the vast temple of the mountains, what for her is the meaning of *filioque*? But, does she have faith?

Yes, she has faith, she trusts. She is sincere, she lives simply, she does not search out subtleties; she knows no dogma, she has her faith, her own faith.

It is the lie that kills, not error. Lies, liars tremble at the thought of finding themselves out, at the thought of coming face to face with themselves. There are people who, dimly realizing that they live on lies, avoid looking too deeply into anything. They chant: "I don't want to think about it!" You don't want to think about it? Then you *are* lost!

That in which you don't believe is already a lie: for could that in which you do not believe be any kind of a truth for you? Whoever teaches one of those proclaimed truths, and does not believe in it, lies.

Truth! And "What is Truth?" asked Pilate and did not stay for answer, turning his back on Christ without waiting for answer, turning his back on truth. For Christ had said: "I am the truth," and He said it of Himself—not of His doctrine. You say He did no such thing? Why, He tells us the same thing every hour of the day.

Faith is, above all else, sincerity, tolerance and mercy.

Sincerity! It is a holy longing to bare one's soul, to tell the truth always and everywhere, wherever it may be, most especially and all the better precisely where it would seem most intemperate and indiscreet in the eyes of the officially prudent! It is the holy longing to bring our spirit out into the open, into the open air of the whole world, there to expose it to new currents.

Tolerance! That means a lively understanding of the relativity of all knowledge, of all *gnosis* and all belief. For it is only through the development and unfolding of each one of us in his own world of ideas and feelings that we will arrive at a harmonious unity of faith in a rich variety of belief. Tolerance! Tolerance is a daughter of the profound conviction that there are no good or bad ideas, and that it is only one's intentions, one's faith, and not doctrines, not dogma, which justify all acts!

Mercy! Charity is not something different from faith, but a form of faith, an amplification of one's trust in man. Every one of the faithful must exorcize the diabolic satisfaction felt by *honorable folk*, by the so-called just—in terms of the law—by men of order, when some delinquent is given the death sentence; by their reaction they clearly express, through the person of the hangman, the criminal instincts which they thus share with the unfortunate hanged man!

Sincerity: to seek out the ideal and oppose it to the reality. Tolerance: towards all the diversity of belief within the area of the common trust. Mercy: towards the victims of the past and those who will not be coerced by the present. Such is faith.

Have faith; above all have faith in faith itself. For if lovers are made stronger by love of love itself, so will the faithful be more powerful from faith in faith itself, from trust in the all-powerful force of trust in itself.

What is Truth?

CHAPTER 18 OF JOHN'S Gospel recounts how Jesus was brought a prisoner before Pilate, the intellectual Roman praetor, and how Pilate took Jesus aside and asked Him if He was King of the Jews. When Jesus answered that His kingdom was not of this world, and that He had been born to bear witness to the truth, Pilate then asked: "What is truth?" And without stopping for answer, he went out to tell the Jews he could find no fault in that man.

Even before the birth of Christ the intellectuals who governed or tried to govern the nations were asking "What is truth?" and, without stopping for answer, would go about settling the affairs entrusted them on the basis of lies. And now that Christ died in witness of the truth, the Pilates ask in passing "What is truth?" and then wash their hands once more in a holy water of lies.

What is truth? I pick up the first philosophical book that comes to hand, one we used as text in the university when I took my two courses in metaphysics and which possesses the invaluable advantage for our purposes of being outlandish in all three dimensions; it is totally lacking in any originality, and faithfully mirrors the abyss of vulgarity, imbecility, and dotage into which the doctrine we call Thomism has fallen. The book in question bears the full title of *Filosofía elemental escrita por el excelentísimo señor don Fray Zeferino González, obispo de Córdoba* (thus the title page of the second edition). The author is among those who have written the greatest rubbish ever penned in Spain. I open this detestable book with which my teachers cobwebbed my mind at sixteen, and in the first clause of the second chapter of the second section of Book One I read that truth is divided into *metaphysical*, *logical*, and *moral*.

They were quick to dismember truth, that is, derange it for us. But let us press on and see what else this book—a typical book of its kind, written by one of our most representative men—has to tell us about truth:

"Metaphysical truth *is the objective reality of things insofar as these, by means of their essence, correspond to the typical idea of the same pre-existing* ab aeterno *in the divine intelligence*." Let us avoid this muddle without going into the question of whether things are not already, in themselves, these very same typical ideas pre-existing in the divine intelligence.

And let us not get involved in finding out what is meant by the statement that things correspond to the divine idea *by means of their essence*; nor how the essence is to be distinguished from the things themselves for which it acts as medium. All this intellectual swill is what was served up to us in our youth.

"Logical truth . . . *may be defined as the conformity or equation between the intelligence as knower and the thing known*." These words are no more than a paraphrase, in heavy-handed Spanish, of St. Thomas' well-known definition, "adaequatio intellectus et rei." Let us leave off, then. This idea has earned a thousand critiques.

"Moral truth *is the conformity or equation between external language and internal subjective judgment*."

As we take leave of Fray Zeferino, let us concede that the real truth, the radical truth, is this last truth, the one he calls moral. From it originates the other truth, logical truth.

The contrary of logical truth is called error, and the contrary of moral truth is called the lie. And it is obvious that one can be truthful, can say what one thinks, and be in error, and that one can state a logical truth and be lying.

And now I submit that error is born of the lie.

More than once before I have said, and I intend to keep on saying it, that the error in which one believes is worth more than the reality in which one does not believe. It is not error, but the lie that is the death of the soul.

Man lies and learns to lie from other men. We learn to lie from social intercourse, and since man sees the world through human eyes, he humanizes everything. He humanizes nature, attributing to it human qualities and purposes; and since man says one thing and means or thinks another, we suppose that nature also thinks or feels in one way and presents itself to us in another; we suppose that nature is lying to us. And hence our errors, errors which come from endowing nature and reality with a hidden intention altogether lacking in them.

"What does snow mean, or lightning, or crystallization, or parthenogenesis, or atavism?" we ask ourselves. They mean to say no more than what they say they mean, since nature does not lie.

If men were always truthful, if we never lied either by omission or by commission, if we neither falsified the truth nor concealed it, it would never occur to anyone to speak of the conformity between external language and internal judgment, for then language and judgment would be one and the same. If we did not lie, either in word or in silence, there would be no distinction possible between the substance of our thought and its form; nor would the word be merely the garment of an idea, but would be the idea itself externalized. Speaking would be merely thinking aloud, thinking to others. And then, applying this image to nature, we would understand and feel— feeling is rather more deeply seated than understanding—that there is no distinction whatsoever between reality and what appears to us to be reality, and that nature speaks to us in thinking or thinks in speaking to us.

But the fact is that by some subtle magic, in some mysterious way, nature lies to liars.

I am convinced that if absolute veracity were to reign among men and over all their relationships, if the lie were to come to an end, error would disappear and truth would reveal itself bit by bit.

The only perfect homage that can be rendered to God is the homage of truth. The kingdom of God, whose advent is mechanically exhorted every day by millions of tongues defiled by lies, is none other than the kingdom of truth.

Forget the reform of all vice, of all weakness; submit to the scourge of arrogance, wrath, envy, gluttony, lust, and avarice; but resolve never to lie either by omission or by commission; resolve not only not to lie, but also not to conceal truth; resolve to tell the truth always and on every occasion, but especially when it is most prejudicial to yourself and seems most inopportune in the eyes of the prudent, of the world in general; act in this wise and you will be saved, and all those deadly sins will leave no mark on your soul.

Are you a slave to arrogance, or envy, or lust, or
to avarice? Then don't try to conceal it. Don't be a
hypocrite—either with the hypocrisy of the official
hypocrite, or with the hypocrisy of the cynic, who
tries to deceive us with the truth, lying to us by citing
reality.

We are told that in the confession of sins forgive-
ness depends on contrition, or, in its absence, on attri-
tion. No! The essential thing is to confess them, make
them public, tell the truth. The Gospel (v. Luke 23:
39-41) does not make it clear whether the malefac-
tor crucified with Christ was repentant or not when
he rebuked his comrade and confessed his guilt—but
he received Christ's promise of paradise. He declared,
true enough, that he deserved his punishment; but a
criminal can declare that the punishment he receives
is justified, and still not feel repentant for his crime.
He spoke to his comrade of the fear of God, but the
essential point is that he confessed his guilt aloud.
He did not lie either by word or by silence.

Some people are outraged when you speak to them
of the reign of absolute truth, of truth whether opportune or inopportune, and they imagine that one could
not live in such a world. I was discussing all this with
a highly intelligent woman one day, and said that just
as paganism culminated in the revelation of the nude
body, in the sculptured nude body, so Christianity
should culminate in the nude soul. She replied: "Good
Lord! How awful! If it were not for clothing, how
would the humpbacked, the lame, the crippled, the
ungainly, all those who have something to hide, ever
get through life?" And I answered: "Much better
than they do now, madame! The humpback looks
worse dressed than naked: his suit only exaggerates

his hump and makes us think it greater than it really is. Were our eyes to become accustomed to nudity, we would begin to comprehend bodily deformities. I am sure that among savages wearing only loincloths the humpback stands out less than he does among us." "That's because among savages there are scarcely any humpbacks," she retorted. "There aren't any because they go naked," I said. She said: "It's because they do away with them as soon as they are born." Perhaps that is even better.

* * *

I frequently hear people interpreting Shakespeare's "Words, words, words" to mean that what we need is deeds and not words. And these are people who call themselves Christians and who should know that according to the fourth Gospel, "In the beginning was the Word, and the Word was with God, and the Word was God," and that all things were made with the Word, and without it was not any thing made that was made, and in the Word was life, and the life was the light of men (John 1:1-5). These people call themselves Christians and should know that when, in the house of Simon the Pharisee, Jesus forgave the woman who had sinned, He was not indulging in any *action*, either symbolic or non-symbolic; He made no sign with His hand held high; He did not so much as touch her with His hand, as He did the leper when He told him "I will; be thou clean" (Matt. 8:2-4). He simply told her: "Thy sins are forgiven; thy faith hath saved thee; go in peace" (Luke 7:36-50). He cleansed her of her sin with His word, and with His word alone. The Gospels tell us that He also cast out devils with the word (Matt. 8:16). And it is the word we need: the word which casts out devils.

Jesus did not baptize, He did not confirm, He did not celebrate Mass, He did not celebrate marriage, He did not give extreme unction, but always administered the holy sacrament of the word. The word, when it is the true word, the word of truth—and the word of Jesus was the word of absolute truth, so that He was the incarnation of His word—is the creative force that raises man above brute, inhuman nature. Man is what he is because of the word.

"Give us deeds, not words!" cry the slaves to the lie, never noticing that what we call deeds are usually nothing more than words or that the word is a more fertile form of deed. They call a published law a deed. But what is a published law but the written word?

Still another Gospel passage evidences all the power of Christ's word. When Jesus was on His way to heal the centurion's servant, the centurion sent a message to say that Jesus should not trouble Himself, that he was unworthy to receive Him under his roof, but that He should merely "say a word and my servant shall be healed," for he, a man of authority himself, need only tell a soldier to come, and he came, or tell him to go, and he went. Jesus marveled at what He heard, and, turning to those who followed Him, said: "I have not found so great faith, no, not in Israel" (Luke 7:1-9). And the faith of the centurion, the faith whereby he gained the healing of his servant, was faith in the word, a faith almost dissipated in Israel.

Words! Words! Words! What more could we wish for, if they were words of truth, of opportune or inopportune truth? What more could we wish for, if the words were the very thought of the speaker, whether or not his thought was consistent with reality?

In the assembly hall of our Parliament, that cathedral of the Lie, we have more than once heard resounding those pestilential blasphemies which go: "You can't say that sort of thing here!" or "A statement like that can't be taken calmly!" But the only thing that should not be said, there or anywhere, is the lie, and the lie is the only thing that should not be taken calmly. Everything else can be said there and everywhere, and taken calmly, and when what is said is in error, when it is mistaken, it should be corrected calmly also.

This very day, reading a newspaper report on the parliamentary session of the day before yesterday, I find that when a republican deputy said he and his comrades were not Catholics, murmurs were heard, those stupid inarticulate murmurs that serve as self-expression for the mindless mob. And yet most of the murmurers or mumblers were not Catholics either, for the simple reason that the majority of the deputies in this Parliament are not Catholic—and that goes for the professional Catholics as well. They may stand as Catholics in their role of deputies, but there is some doubt that they are Catholics in their role as men. Many men are Catholics only in their role of office-holders, or journalists, or servants, or sons, or husbands, or fathers. There are newspapers which call themselves Catholic, when they are pushed to it, and on which not a single member of the staff is Catholic.

Strictly speaking, in Spain today, to be a Catholic, in the vast majority of cases, scarcely means more than not to be anything else. A Catholic is a man who, having been baptized, does not publicly abjure what is assumed, by a social fiction, to be his faith; he does not think about it one way or the other, either to profess it or reject it, either to take up another faith, or even to seek one.

And over this awful quagmire of lies and coward-ice, we hear ring out from time to time the words: "Deeds! Deeds! Deeds! No more words!" And the supreme deed, the grand deed, the fruitful deed, the redeeming deed, would be for everyone to tell his truth. With no more action than this, we would vault the abyss opening at our feet.

* * *

And there are still wretched beings who, not daring to defend the lie, the noisome lie, attempt to pass it off as an illusion, and tell us all about the power of that illusion and about the solace to be found in con-scious self-deception.

No: art and the lie are antipodes; the lie is the maximum anti-aesthetic. And the lie is of no consola-tion whatever, while the consoling illusion is no lie.

There is a savage phrase attributed to Voltaire, the one which goes: "If God did not exist, it would be necessary to invent Him." A God thus invented, a deceit for oneself and others, would not even be a non-God, but would be an anti-God, an absolute Devil. And that Devil is the only one that exists: the God invented by those who do not in their hearts believe in Him.

"And what is it to believe in God?" the Pontius Pilates will ask at this point. Putting aside logical faith, which is parallel to so-called logical truth, and cleaving to moral faith, which corresponds to moral truth, I shall assert that to believe in God is to want God to exist, to long for it with all one's soul. Who-ever can not conceive the essence of God through his intelligence, and considers the notion a hypothesis which explains nothing, and holds the alleged proofs of His existence to be mere sophisms, but who in his own heart nevertheless desires that God exist, and comes to an understanding as to a way of life with Him, granting a personality to the Supreme Ideal, that man believes in God much more than the man who is logically convinced that a God exists but who in no way takes Him into account or does so only to justify his cult of the lie.

* * *

One day I was reproved by a zealous Catholic for what he called my subjectivism, and he said that I confused faith with imagination. He insisted on making me understand—by means of the hoariest of arguments, all of which I had learned by memory— the difference between what he called (and here he departed from the canons of his school) subjective and objective faith.

I replied in all calm: "Don't weary yourself, my friend, in repeating all the old arguments. I know perfectly well what you are getting at. Don't weary yourself with syllogistic arguments and formal ratioc- inations. Your kind of faith is dying, strung up by syllogism. The cancer in your Church is rationalism, that very rationalism against which you are always clamoring. You have tried to make religion into a phi- losophy. Every one of those dreadful, arid sermons by some Jesuit belaboring the coryphaei of modern impiety, in speeches larded with endless use of 'thus it is' and 'therefore' and 'thereupon it is clearly dem- onstrated' and other logical figures of speech in the same style, every one of those unfortunate preachings constitutes a new blow against true faith. And in these anti-religious sermons it is the custom to lie brazenly, attributing to those dubbed irreverent all manner of beliefs they never advanced, or criticizing their doctrines without any but the airiest notions—as the preachers are well aware—of what they are. And this last activity is plainly to lie.

"I already know," I went on, "that basically you are a materialist, even though you may not realize it, not because you believe only in matter, but because you require material proof of anything. Like the ancient Jews, you need signs in order to believe; you need to take truth in your two hands, in your mouth, and with your feet. I already know you think yourself lost if the proofs of the existence of God given in the textbooks turn out to prove nothing of the sort. And yet, my friend, I have never found any such proofs in the Gospels, nor have I ever found any of those awful Aristotelian 'thuses' and 'therefores' and the like. Whenever one of your kind encounters the glare of the Sphinx, and when the gimlet of doubt—of sacred doubt, mother of true faith—starts to bore into your heart, you turn your back, turn your back on the Sphinx, and shake off doubt by a process of spiritual mechanics, and tell yourself: 'Come now, it's best not to think of these things!' In short, you hand yourself over to the lie. For that process is no more than surrendering to the lie.

"There are people, my friend, who consider suicide not just a crime as grievous as murder, but much worse. They believe that a person who kills himself is more culpable before God than one who kills another. There are people who maintain—and not from ingeniousness, though they give that impression—that suicide combines all the grievous circumstances of homicide. I do not know, nor does it strike me as possible to know for a certainty about this, but I do believe that to lie to oneself is worse than to lie to others. And there are people who live a continual inner lie, as they struggle to stifle the truth surging within them.

"An unfortunate friend of mine, who was going through an intense religious crisis, went to confession one day in the hope of finding relief, if not a cure. He told me afterwards that the good father confessor had said to him: 'Do you think that the rest of us aren't assailed by these same doubts? Put them aside, don't think about them!' And I told him: 'Welcome them! Don't think of anything else!' My friend went on to tell me that the priest had advised him to put his mind to something else, to take good care of himself, to eat well, to get a lot of sleep; and that if his spiritual anguish pressed him to the wall, he should come to him again for consultation, but not forget to seek medical advice as well. 'That terrible confessor is nothing but a hardhearted materialist,' I said. My friend took the advice I gave, and today he finds more deepseated peace, more solace and more faith amid all his anxiety, restlessness, and unease than others find by abdicating truth."

My interlocutor asked me: "How to find the truth?" And I answered: "By speaking it always." He asked: "But what about external, objective, logical truth, what we call Truth?" And I said: "You need only speak the truth, the inner truth, the subjective truth, the moral truth, what you believe to be the truth, always and in all circumstances, whether it be opportune or inopportune!"

What we call reality, that is, objective or logical truth, is merely the prize awarded to sincerity and veracity. Nature would have no secrets whatsoever for anyone who was absolutely and always truthful and sincere. Blessed are the pure in heart, for they shall see God! Purity of heart is truthfulness, and truth is God.

*   *   *

Thousands and thousands of times it has been said that most arguments are arguments over words, and that often men fight for the same cause though the different contenders give it different names. The fact is rather that these arguments are mostly over lies, and that it is over lies that men fight. Instead of saying: "I want this, and want it because I want it, without knowing why I want it," or, if the reason for wanting it is known, then saying so truthfully, instead of either course, man invents a lie to justify his desire, and fights to uphold his lie. And in most cases there would be no battle at all if the truth prevailed.

There are people who claim to fight not so much for the deed as for the creed, not for might but for right; but if the might of the deed were clear, there would be no need for the right of the creed. If someone says to me: "I am going to take this away from you because it belongs to me by virtue of the fact that you gave it to me or promised it to me or took it from me in the first place," then I will defend what I believe to be mine, and will go so far as to fight for it and cry out: "I did not give it to you!" or "I did not promise it to you!" or "I did not take it from you at all!" On the other hand, were my adversary to state, clearly and simply: "I am taking this away from you because I want it for myself and besides I am stronger than you, I have more might," then I will turn to those around us and say: "This man is stronger than I am, and, since he is stronger than I am, he takes from me what is mine." And I will allow him to take it without a struggle.

It's no use saying that man is basely egotistical and defends his possessions with justice or without it. No; the urge for justice and truth boasts deeper roots than does the urge to self-interest and the lie.

I harbor the belief that all, absolutely every one, of the evils we take to be the cause of our miseries— egotism, the drive for predominance, the desire for glory, contempt for others—all would vanish if we were truthful. If the man who appears to despise his fellows did not mistrust his contempt in such wise that he must disguise and falsify it, we should all come to see—and he himself with us—that his contempt was a contradiction and that in showing contempt for others he was showing contempt for himself.

I believe, too, that among the best citizens, those most useful to their country and their fellow-countrymen, and most capable of good acts, are those known for their arrogance, those who do not conceal a belief in their own superiority and are heard to complain in one way or another whenever their compatriots do not show the appreciation they feel is their due. It is one thing to consider whether or not any one man deserves the distinctive consideration these superior types feel to be their due or whether in fact any such superiority really exists, and quite another to admit the actual existence of people who believe themselves superior and who do not deign hypocritically to conceal their feelings. Such people may be mistaken, but they are not liars.

When I was fourteen and a member of the Congregation of St. Aloysius Gonzaga, I heard an episode in the life of this saint read aloud, telling of how he thought he was the greatest of sinners because he had stolen a bit of gunpowder from his father's soldiers in order to fire his toy cannon and because he had senselessly repeated a blasphemous oath he had overheard from the same soldiers, and I well remember that this self-indictment, far from proving edifying to me, struck me as totally unedifying. Unable to believe that anyone could consider himself the greatest of sinners because of such pecadillos, I felt the whole affair was a way of lying to himself in order to give himself importance as a sinner. The certain fact is that I was never stirred, even in the first flush of my most fervent youthful Catholicism, by this professional Jesuit saint. In the guise he is presented to us—though I am pleased to suppose he must have been quite otherwise—he resembles a little doll constructed according to the design of a perfect model of Jesuit youth: i.e., a perfect Mont Blanc of prudery. I am not surprised that a man as serious, and as sincerely and deeply religious in spirit as William James, after considering St. Aloysius Gonzaga in his *The Varieties of Religious Experience* (1902), should have concluded: "But when the intellect, as in this Louis, is originally no larger than a pin's head, and cherishes ideas of God of corresponding smallness, the result, notwithstanding the heroism put forth, is on the whole repulsive."

I can already almost hear some devotee of the saint crying out: "You can't say that sort of thing! A statement like that can't be taken calmly!" And yet, when a statement like that is made, as it is made by James and made by me, without any intention of giving offense to anyone and solely from a desire to speak the truth, it should be said and it should be taken calmly by all who love the truth, whether or not they believe the statement to be altogether accurate.

Whenever someone, without any desire to annoy or wound the sensibilities of his fellows, states an opinion which happens not to be in agreement with that of his listener, it is truly repugnant to hear the latter exclaim: "You're hurting my feelings!" On the contrary—for my part at least and that of some others—the man who wounds my sensibilities of love for the truth is the man who sets out to agree with what I think though he himself thinks quite otherwise.

Consider, now, a priest in the Church which calls itself the sole depository of Christian truth: he will not tolerate certain heretical propositions to be enunciated in his presence; and, if they are publicly stated, he will exclaim that his religious sensibilities are being wounded. And yet, consider what happens if this same priest is summoned to hear the confession of a dying unbeliever. When he arrives, the unbeliever can no longer see, or hear, or understand, or, if he can see, hear, or understand, he refuses to confess; or, if he does confess, he declares his sins, what he considers to be his sins, but says nothing about his creed and his faith, nor does he declare that his creed and his faith are not those of the Church. And the priest, who feels that his religious sensibilities are wounded when the truth is plainly spoken, gives him absolution. And then the unbeliever is given a funeral and buried in hallowed ground, and he is said to have died in the bosom of the Church. "Because, at the very end, when these atheists stare into the Abyss . . . !" And the dreadful lie about last-minute conversions flourishes and is spread about like a curse.

* * *

"If one were to tell the truth all the time, life would become impossible." Who was it uttered this blasphemy? Who is the truncated spirit who sustains and spreads the word that whoever tries to be always truthful will always be crushed? What is the meaning of the "life" which would "become impossible"? What does it mean to be "crushed"?

In all orders, death is the lie, and truth is life. And if truth were to lead us to death, it would be better to die by truth, to die of life, rather than to live by the lie, to live dying.

In the innermost order, in the most deep-seated order, in the order of religion, the summation of all the wretchedness of this poor country of ours, mired in all class of lies, is the lie that perpetuates itself, the lie that Spain is Catholic. No! Conscious Spain, the Spain of the governing classes, the Spain of those who think and rule, that Spain is not Catholic. Even the majority of those who publicly profess to be Catholics and scale the heights of high preferment are not really Catholics. And just so long as this lie is not eradicated, Spain will not ever be Christian.

The murmur set up by murmuring or murmurous deputies, the racket that bursts out whenever some other deputy merely confesses that he is not a communicant in the official Church, should be reserved for the occasion when a deputy, a cabinet minister preferably, one of those who obviously believe neither in God nor in the Devil, comes up with a public confession that he is a sincere Catholic, as sometimes happens. Those outbursts of murmuring should be kept for the time when some mock saint of the parliamentary lie, in the course of inveighing against so-called clericalism, finds it suitable to make certain reservations, and then—so that he not be mistaken for an anti-Catholic when he is merely non-Catholic—adds that he himself is a submissive son of the Church.

In Spain not even many of those who believe themselves to be Catholics and who hear Mass every Sunday and on holy days of obligation, who receive communion once a year and eat no meat during Lent, are truly Catholic: for they turn their backs on the Sphinx's gaze and they do not care to ponder what they are pleased to call their creed.

To content oneself with so-called implicit faith in the knowledge that it is only such and that there exists another faith which is explicit; to hold to the formula of "I believe what Holy Mother Church believes and teaches," while failing—from weakmindedness or, worse, from fear that no such faith exists— to examine what it is that the Church teaches and believes: that is the greatest lie of all.

"The thing is we can't all be theologians," a friend replied when I mentioned these points. "Theologians only murder faith," was my retort. In the field of medicine, my doctor's knowledge can cure me, even if I do not know the whereabouts of my liver; but in the field of religion, my confessor's faith can scarcely save me. In the life of the soul only my truth saves me, and my truth is not the truth I do not know, though this be the truth of others. So long as I do not understand the concept of the Holy Ghost's proceeding from the Father and the Son—and not from the Father alone—and do not appreciate the difference it may make to my spiritual life whether it be one way or the other, or neither of the two, what good is it for me to listen to the phrase "qui ex Patre Filioque procedit" sung during Mass, in Latin and to the music of Palestrina? All impediments are harmful, and a fruitless weed is an impediment, as are all unfruitful brambles, all ideas, or, even more, every phrase which does not answer to some feeling, every word that does not evoke a warm and luminous concept.

You there who call yourself a submissive and faithful son of the Catholic Church and say you believe what she believes and teaches, what do you do today that you would not do, or what do you not do that you would do, if you believed that the Holy Ghost proceeds from the Father alone—and not from the Father and the Son—or if you believed that It proceeds from neither? That kind of belief, I say to you, is no belief at all.

You describe the Church as the depository of the truths of your faith. The truths that are not deposited in your own soul are not truths of your faith, and are of no use to you at all. Your faith is what you believe in full consciousness of your belief, not what your Church believes. In itself your Church can not believe anything, for it has no personal consciousness. It is a social institution, not a fusion of souls.

* * *

Well then, in sum: what is truth? Truth is whatever is believed heart and soul. And what does it mean to believe something with heart and soul? It means to act in accordance with this belief.

To find the truth, one must first believe in it, believe in the truth with heart and soul. And to believe in it means to believe in what one believes to be the truth always and in all circumstances, but most especially whenever it appears most inopportune to speak the truth.

And the word is the deed, the most profound deed, the most creative deed—whenever the word is the true word.

Blessed are the pure in heart, for they shall see God! Tell your truth always, and God will tell you His. And you shall see God and die. For the Scriptures say that whosoever sees God shall die. And that is the best that can happen in a world of lies: to die of seeing the Truth.

The Secret of Life

IT HAS BEEN SOME TIME now, my dearest friend, that my heart has been asking me to write you. Neither it nor I knew what my subject would be, for it was merely a very vehement desire to speak confidentially with you and not with another.

You have often heard me say that each new friend whom we gain in the course of our life perfects and enriches us more by what he causes us to discover in ourselves, than by what he gives of himself. In each one of us there are certain loose ends of the spirit, corners of the soul, hiding places of the mind which lie inert and inactive, and we may die without ever having discovered them, for lack of the persons who might commune in spirit with us and who thanks to this communion reveal them to us. All of us carry in us potential ideas and sentiments which will pass from potency to act only if the person who will arouse us comes along. Each man bears within him a Lazarus who needs only a Christ to resurrect him, and woe betide those poor Lazaruses who come to the end of their career of perceptible love and sorrow under the sun without ever having encountered a Christ to say to them: "Arise!"

And just as there are areas of our soul which flower and give fruit only beneath the gaze of some spirit come from the eternal region to which they belong in time, just so, when that gaze is hidden from us by absence, these areas long for that magical gaze like the earth longing for the sun so that it may give out flowering plants and fruit. And the fields of my spirit, which ceased to be deserts as soon as I met you and you had made them fertile, have been for some time now wanting to produce. And this is the reason I have been wanting to write you, without being sure about what.

You, who are accustomed to my inversions of sense and to my personal vision, which often leads me to see causes where others see effects, and effects where they see causes, will not be surprised at what I am about to write to you. On more than one occasion you have told me that I tend to see spiritual things much in the manner that we would see material things if the film in a projector was run backwards, from the end toward the beginning, or as if a phonograph record were made to turn the wrong way. Perhaps this is true, and perhaps I suffer from a disturbance in my sense of time and my feeling for logical sequence. But the fact is, it frequently seems to me that the conclusions men arrive at are really premises, and the other way around.

All this is by way of telling you that in my moments of idle dreaming, when I let my imagination deceive itself, believing that it is free from tyrannous logic, I hit upon the idea that it is not the different positions the earth takes with respect to the sun, depending on the curve of its ecliptic and the point at which it finds itself in its annual course, that determine the seasons of the year and with them the flowering of spring, the ripening of summer, the harvest of autumn, and the sleep of winter, but that rather it is the flowering, ripening, harvest, and sleep that determine the positions taken by the earth. It strikes my fancy that it is the need the earth feels to yield flowers—now in one place, now in another—which makes it show first one face and then another to the sun.

Perhaps something similar happens with our friendships. It is not exactly because chance brought you close to me, and we knew and understood one another at once, that this spiritual earth of mine which you made fertile by your affectionate and sympathetic words was awakened to life, but it was rather the need these fields of mine felt to produce the seeds bursting to sprout that made me discover and detain you from among the thousands of men who pass by.

Today I feel a need for you, a need for your presence. Today I feel a need to talk to you, to communicate to you the thoughts that are struggling to emerge. Since you are far away, so far away, I write them out to you.

And that is because today, as never before, I am grieved by the mystery.

You know that we all carry the mystery in our souls, and that we bear it like a terrible and precious tumor, whence sprouts our life and whence our death will also sprout. We live for it, and without it we never would have lived. It is our punishment and our consolation.

You will remember our good friend Alfredo, a writer of a deeply melancholy disposition, a melancholy which seems to drip from every page of his writings like a slow, persistent rain. He once told me he could not resign himself to the defeat of metaphysics, the metaphysics he had believed in as a youth; when I told you about it, I added on my own account: "He is wounded by the mystery."

The mystery sometimes seems to be asleep or benumbed in us; we do not feel it; but then, of a sudden, without our always being able to determine why, it awakes in us, it seems to become irritated and to hurt us, and it goes so far as to make us feverish and spurs our poor hearts into a gallop. Just as the exacerbation of certain tumors seems to depend on atmospheric conditions, in a like way it seems that the exacerbation of the mystery within the mystery of our soul depends on the state of the spiritual environment of the society which surrounds us.

For each of us, the mystery is a secret. God plants a secret in the soul of each man, the deeper the more He loves the man; that is, the more of a man He makes him. In order to plant the mystery in us He works our soul with the sharp spade of tribulation. In carefree persons the secret of their lives is very close to the surface, and there is always the danger that it will not take root, and that failing to root it will yield neither flowers nor fruit.

I know that at this point you will recall, as I do, the first parable of the Gospel according to Matthew, the parable of the sower, in Chapter 13. He went forth to sow, and some of the seeds fell by the way-side, and the birds came and ate them up; part of them fell in stony places, where they had not much earth, and they took, but as there was little earth, the sun burned them, and they withered away for want of roots; and some fell among thorns, and grew but were choked; and other seeds fell in good ground and gave fruit, some a hundredfold, some sixtyfold, and some thirtyfold. And thus does it come about with the secret of every man's life.

For some men, the secret of their lives is spilled outside, on the road, and the birds eat it; for others, the seed falls in stony hearts unscarred and untouched by sorrow, and it sprouts, but is burned by the sun; for still others, the seed is choked by a thousand amusements and diversions; and only for a very few does it work in and take root, so that the roots form a stalk, and the stalk flowers, and produces fruit at last.

And take into account that this seed, this secret of life, buried in the soul, is unseen by everyone and is untouched by the sun. We see the plant, and the sight of it makes us rub our eyes and ease them with the greenness of the foliage; we give our sense of smell a treat with the aroma of the flowers; we please our palates with the flavor of the fruits, and at the same time they are our nourishment. But we neither see, nor smell, nor taste the seed of the plant which was planted in the earth.

Whenever you and I have talked of the duty of sincerity, you have always replied that there are thoughts and feelings which we must not reveal, but rather guard with care and zeal. I argued the matter with you and with a certain aggressive vehemence opposed your reservations, maintaining the need to denude the soul and to make public confession. But then I meditated further and have come to the conclusion that you were right, after all, and that it is precisely the duty of sincerity that requires us to veil the depths of our soul.

And it is the duty of sincerity that orders us to hide and conceal the innermost depths of our soul, for if we were to reveal them, others would see them in a false light, and we would lie. The man who says *yes* in the knowledge that *no* is to be understood lies, even though *yes* is the truth.

We must keep our soul naked, that is true; but naked does not mean cut wide open or with scars showing. The more sincere the soul, the more zealously does it guard and protect the mysteries of life.

It is also true that in moments when the heart is anguished, when we are in dire need of spiritual air to breathe, we tear at our heart so that air may penetrate its depths; but the sun reaches the depths at the same time as the air and its dry light kills the seeds sown there, and the roots wither, and they die without having produced either flowers or fruit.

The roots of our feelings and thoughts do not need light, but water, water under ground, dark, silent water; a water which seeps in and soaks and does not run off, the water of solitude. What needs air and light is the foliage of our feelings and thoughts, the part of them we put out into the world; and once we send it into the world, it belongs to the world.

In order to express a feeling or thought that sprouts from the roots of our soul, we must express it in the language of the world, clothing it in the foliage of the world, taking from the world, from society, the elements which lend consistency, body, and greenness to this foliage, just as a plant takes the elements which make up its leafage from the elements of the air. But the inner source, the ultimate and invisible substance, is at the roots.

The language which I use to dress my feelings and ideas is the language of the society in which I live, it is the language of those whom I address; the very images, the concepts into which I pour the sap, are the images and concepts of those who hear me. But that sap, that vivifying liquid which rises from the roots up into the fruit, that invisible fluid, that is mine. And it is this sap which gives my fruits, which gives your fruits, which gives the fruits of all men, the taste they have.

Certain insipid fruits taste like nothing at all, they leave no lingering aftertaste, they are like tasteless hothouse products; the fact is that these fruits do not come from any seed, but from a slip, from a graft perhaps. They are spiritual fruits which do not proceed from any of life's secrets, from the mystery of any tribulation.

There are souls which have their roots in the air. Unlucky souls! There are souls which boast no roots at all. More than unlucky souls!

* * *

Under the visible and noisy world in which we move, beneath the world we talk about, there is another world, invisible and silent, where we take our ease, a world of which we do not talk. And if it were possible to turn the world around or turn it upside down, bringing the dark into the light and putting the light into the shadows, making the soundless resound and silencing what is vocal, we would all understand and see what a poor thing is that entity we call law, and we would see wherein liberty lies, and how far away it is from where we seek it.

Liberty lies in the mystery. Liberty is buried and grows inward, not outward.

It is said, and perhaps even believed, that liberty consists in allowing the plant to grow freely, in not surrounding it with props, nor trellises, nor any hindrances whatever; in not pruning it, and making it take this or that form; in leaving it to sprout in whatever manner it chooses, without compulsion, and bear its buds, and leaves, and flowers. But liberty is not in the foliage, but in the roots, and no purpose is served in leaving the top of the tree free and the way to heaven wide open, if the roots, as they grow, come up against hard, impenetrable rock, dry and arid, or meet dead soil. Still, if the roots are powerful and lively, if they are driven by a hunger for life, if they come from vigorous seed, they will split the hardest rocks and pass through them and they will distill moisture from the most compact granite.

A spiritual tree with numerous deep roots will produce delicious fruit, however rough and hostile the surroundings may be. And the roots are the secret of the soul.

Oftentimes humanity is astounded by the singular force which is revealed in a work of seemingly pure intelligence, by the fullness of thought that bursts forth on all sides, in a treatise on algebra, or physiology, or comparative grammar, or something similar. There are books of science that, though they contain new principles, new truths, laws discovered by their author, will grow old, we all know, as soon as these truths, laws, and principles are incorporated into science, form part of its wealth, and appear in the teaching manuals where it is expounded. A book of science can make an important new contribution to the field, and still be perfectly impersonal. But there are other books of scientific exposition, and of scientific exposition alone, which contain, apart from the novelty and truth of their principles, an argument, a tone, an animating hidden spirit, a *quid mirificum*, something mysterious that makes them lasting and a source of learning even after the principles expounded belong to the common domain, or after these have been rectified or perhaps even rejected. And these works of immortal science, immortal because their life does not depend on the life of the science which they served, are works that well up from the secret of life, and have their roots in some mystery of tribulation.

The great thoughts spring from the heart, as has been said, and this is doubtless true even for those thoughts which seem most alien and farthest from the needs and longings of the heart. Who knows what "cordial" roots, what heartfelt roots, were struck in the generous and great soul of Isaac Newton, that soul filled with piety, by the discovery of the binomial theorem to which we give his name?

For many fervent spirits, science has been a refuge in which they have taken cover in the course of great inner torments, and many of the greatest and most fruitful discoveries are owed to the mysteries of the heart. And these elevated and noble spirits gave us the fruits of their secret without revealing the secret itself, and they were absolutely sincere with us and showed us the truth.

A tree is known by its fruits; but its fruits are not its roots, though they proceed from them.

Many luminous theories, many suggestive hypotheses, many happy discoveries, are the offspring of profound tribulation, of heartfelt sorrow.

You will recall, my dear friend, the times we have spoken of the profound currents of passion which circulate beneath Spinoza's *Ethics* or Kant's *Critique of Practical Reason*, and of how these two imperishable works are what they are because they sprang from the hearts of their authors and not from their heads. For the man who knows how to read and feel beneath the dry formulas of the Jew of Amsterdam, there is much more passion in the depths of the propositions he expounds in algebraic style, much more warmth of spirit, a much more intimate fire, than in the majority of the resplendent outbursts of those who pass for men of feeling. Flames are not the only or even the principal sign of fire; on the contrary, the most lasting and intense fires do not ordinarily give off flame.

Every one of the propositions of the Spinozan *Ethics* is like a diamond: hard, schematically crystallized, cold, cut in fine sharp edges. But just as in the case of a diamond, a very strong and intense fire must have been necessary to produce it. Ordinary fire turns regular coal into live embers and, once burned, only ashes remain. But to produce a diamond a fire such as no longer exists on the face of the earth was necessary, a fire such as now exists perhaps only in the bowels of the earth, out of reach of the enveloping air. Our external fires, which flame outwards and batten on our air, light up and warm our surroundings for a moment only, and they do not leave behind as fruit of their blaze anything more than ember and ash. Only the hidden inner fire, which does not shine outwardly or receive any air, is capable of producing lasting diamonds, harder than any stones that could strike them.

Do you remember that friend of ours who went off to distant lands, never to return, and of whom we have never heard again? All of us were attracted and surprised by his unusual sweetness, his eternal and mysterious smile, the unalterable serenity of his judgment, the moderation of all his opinions, his perfect dominion over his feelings. When we argued with each other, his words fell upon a fiery issue like refreshing dew; our arguments, dried out and parched by hot obstinacy, grew green again, and greenly became reconciled with each other. When we reproached him for being a skeptic, he would smile mysteriously and say: "No, it's not that I doubt everything, it's that I believe everything." And that phrase "I believe everything" sounded to our ears like the bottomless well of an impotency, of an inability to believe anything at all. And oftentimes, when we said good night to each other, we would ask: "But does that man believe in anything?"

You will also recall that we went so far as to take him for a species of aesthete, for a disillusioned man who, cured of all illusion, considered the world a spectacle and amused himself, as he waited for death, in watching men and things pass by, in watching them all die.

One day we noticed that his voice trembled and that it had another tone, different than usual, as if his heart held his vocal cords in a firm grip; at the same time a strange reflection shone in his eyes, ordinarily devoid of light. It was the day on which he protested against the charge, which someone had made against him, that his sole aim was self-amusement. All of us, his friends, remained pensive and uneasy, the depths of our hearts stirred up, after listening to him say that he detested amusement, and go on to speak of the tragic seriousness of life.

When the poor man went off to those distant lands from which he has not returned and where he has been lost to us, the veil of his secret was somewhat drawn aside for us, sufficiently so for us to see there was a secret, but not enough for us to detect what it was. We discovered he was a man with a secret, though we could get no notion of what it was. All of us who made conjectures on the matter were terribly deceived, and those who thought they had reached the bottom of the mystery were even more totally mistaken. We could reach one conclusion, and it was that the more evidence we obtained as to what might have afflicted him, the farther we were from a knowledge of his tribulation; and this fact imposed itself upon us with overwhelming logic.

When he left us, he told us all the following: "I

am going to bury myself in primitive nature. I am fleeing from myself, because I am afraid of myself. I am fleeing from society because, without wanting it to happen, I am constantly being hurt, and I am afraid the day will come when, without wanting it either, I will do some hurt to society." And he took his leave of us with dry eyes, but with a voice which betrayed the same tone as when he protested that he did not take life for an amusement. And he went away. And we have never heard from him again. He went and took his secret with him. Will it die with him?

No, I do not believe that the secret of his life, the mystery of his heart, dies with a man, though he fail to reveal it to us during the course of his life. A secret is a father force, eternal, fertile; and those secret feelings which seek souls in which to be embodied, after having failed to bear fruit in the soul in which they were embodied, continue to seek. For each soul there is an idea which corresponds to it and which is like its formula, and souls and ideas engage in a continual search for each other. There are souls who go through life without having found their proper idea, and they are the majority; and there are ideas that, manifesting themselves in soul after soul, nevertheless do not find their proper souls, those which would reveal them in all their perfection.

And here, once again, we come up against the terrible mystery of time, the most terrible of all mysteries, the father of them all. And the fact is that souls and ideas come into the world either too early or too late; so that when a soul is born, its idea has already fled, or a soul dies before the advent of its idea.

It must have been a terrible torment for a man to have been born into the thirteenth century with the soul of a twentieth-century man; but it is no lesser torture to be forced to live in our century with a thirteenth-century soul. In that early century, the mysterious and terrible infirmity of the convents was *acedia*, that lack of appetite for the spiritual life, a life which, nevertheless, could not be put aside. Whoever reads the mystics attentively will hear in his heart that deep tone which sounds like a sob muffled in the breast, unable to break forth, and which cries inwardly. But today we suffer from an acedia toward the life of the world, a lack of appetite for society and civilization, and there are souls that feel nostalgia for the medieval monastery. I say the *medieval* monastery, and not simply the monastery, for today's monastery is as different from what it was in the thirteenth century as that century was from ours. And I personally believe that the medieval souls who dwell among us today are those who feel the greatest repugnance for the cloisters of the twentieth century. It has been said of that man of the secret, of that mysterious Dane who lived in a continual inner despair, of Kierkegaard, that he felt nostalgia for the cloister of the Middle Ages.

We all carry our life's secret within us: some closer to the surface of the soul, others more deeply buried, and the majority of men so far within that they never reach or discover it. And if they ever catch a glimpse of it, they turn their gaze outwards in fright; not wanting to know any more about it, they give themselves over to diversion, to losing themselves.

"And what of those who do not even catch a glimpse of their secret?" you will ask me. "Those who go through life with simple-minded confidence, serene and innocent, exposing their innermost souls to the air and the light?" For such people, my dear friend, everything is secret; they live submerged and soaked in it; mystery envelops them. They are like children who see everything. Do you think a child of six does not have his mystery, even though he may not know it? Yes, he has his secret, and his soul sleeps unconscious of it; but from within, from out of his unconsciousness, it vivifies his life. I do not remember a more tragic and mysterious spectacle than that of a poor little girl who was crying her eyes out beside the body, still warm, of a puppy that had been her most precious toy, a live toy.

We all carry around our secret, whether we know it or not, and there is an occult inner world where all the secrets harmonize and are in concert, however much they are unaware of each other in this exterior and manifest world. And if such is not the case, how do you explain such mysterious voices of silence as come to us from deeper than the soul, from deeper than its roots?

*   *   *

Have you ever noticed the strange spectacle of two people disputing: each one expounds his opinion of things, and meanwhile each of them is merely endeavoring to lay bare the other's soul? What interests each one is not what the other thinks, but what he is; not what his opinions are, but who he is. And it is quite frequent that two people conversing, seemingly in great intimacy and on terms of closest friendship, will talk about everything except the matter that most disquiets and preoccupies both. A certain idea, a certain feeling, will dominate them and link them, and yet they will speak of anything except that common idea or feeling which unites them. They are joined together by a secret, and they mutually avoid it, for that is the best way for them to continue to be united by it.

Frequently, when we listen to a conversation between two intimate friends, who are joined by strong and indestructible bonds, we are surprised by things we do not understand or by the tone of the conversation, which seems totally different from what they are saying. The fact is that they are talking of one thing and thinking of something very different; they are conversing on a superficial and obvious theme, and communing in deep secret. There is a common secret which one of them never has revealed to the other.

Nothing joins men more than a secret. Whoever guesses your secret need only look at you, and you will be forced to become his friend. And you will seek refuge in him; and it will be in him that you most carefully conceal your secret. Why reveal it to him, when he has already guessed it? It will be useless to reveal it also to the man who does not guess it, for he will not understand it rightly, and above all, he will not believe in it as it is.

There are people who seem to say and tell all, and they are the very ones who conceal the most. They talk and confess themselves merely to hide their secret more deeply, for they fear silence, which is the most terrifyingly revealing state that can be imagined. Sincerity is drowned in words. The secret, the true secret, is ineffable, and as soon as we deck it out in language, it not only does not cease to be a secret but it is more of a secret than ever.

*   *   *

It is not ordinarily given to us to understand the special secret of our neighbor, his personal anguish, his inner tribulation, the sorrow that torments him or the hidden joy he can not reveal, the passion that consumes or exalts him, the yearning which his heart follows; but what we can know is the common root to the secrets of all men, the secret of our respective secrets, the secret of humanity. It takes different forms in each soul, and these forms are secret, but its ultimate and eternal substance is always the same.

And the secret of human life, the universal secret, the root secret from which all other secrets spring, is the longing for more life, the furious and insatiable desire to be everything else without ever ceasing to be ourselves, to take possession of the entire universe without letting the universe take possession of us and absorb us; it is the desire to be someone else without ceasing to be myself, and continue being myself at the same time I am someone else; it is, in a word, the appetite for divinity, the hunger for God.

The law afflicts and aggrieves us, and when we try to break the law, we do so impelled by a higher or a lower law which afflicts or aggrieves us even more than the first law, and the satisfaction of one longing is only the seed for an ever greater and more imperious longing.

"If I could live another life, and do what I can not do today!" you say. And if you could lead another life and do what you can not do today, you would then—since you then could not lead the life you do lead or do the things you do today—long for your own life and for your present deeds. For what you want is that life, and this one, and the other, and all of them. When the Jews left Egypt, they longed for the Land of Promise, and, once there, they sighed for Egypt. And the truth was they wanted both places at the same time, and man wants all lands and all the centuries, and to live in all of space and all of time, in infinity and eternity.

The motive force of life is the longing to survive in time and space; human beings begin to live when they want to be other beings than they are and still continue to be themselves. And everything that does not live is only food for what lives.

One more question remains, and it is: does not the whole, the totality, the Universe, itself long to be more than it is, to be more than the whole, to be more than Universe? Does not the Universe have its own secret?

Let us stop here.

The Portico of The Temple:
A Rambling Dialogue Between
Román and Sabino, Two Friends

ROMÁN: We've invented nothing, you say? And
what difference does that make? That way we've
saved ourselves the effort of having had to invent,
and our spirit has stayed fresher and more
exuberant.

SABINO: On the contrary. It is constant effort which
maintains freshness and exuberance of spirit. A
talent that is not used turns soft, and languishes,
and grows emaciated. . . .

ROMÁN: You mean not employed in inventing those
things? . . .

SABINO: Or any others . . .

ROMÁN: Ah! And who told you we've not invented
other things?

SABINO: Useless things!

ROMÁN: And who is to judge their usefulness? Don't
fool yourself: if we don't invent those things, it's
because we haven't felt the need for them.

SABINO: But as soon as others invent them, we take
them over, we appropriate them and make use of
them, never fear!

ROMÁN: In that case, let the others invent, and we
will take advantage of their inventions. For I expect that you will be convinced, just as I am, that

electric light gives as much illumination here as in the lands where it was invented.

SABINO: Perhaps better light.

ROMÁN: I would not attempt to go that far. . . .

SABINO: But the others, exercising their inventiveness in inventing such things, condition themselves and put themselves in a position to go on inventing, while we . . .

ROMÁN: While we store up energy.

SABINO: What for?

ROMÁN: To continue living; which is no small matter.

SABINO: The fact is that science possesses not only a practical or applied value for life through the workings of industry, but it possesses also an ideal and pure value. . . .

ROMÁN: Yes; it is the vestibule to knowledge, inasmuch as by virtue of it we form a concept of the Universe and of our place and value in it. Science is the portico of philosophy, isn't that so?

SABINO: Without any doubt whatever.

ROMÁN: But supposing, my good friend, that the temple of wisdom boasted some back door cleverly concealed in the thickness of the walls; a back door through which one might gain entrance without the need for a vestibule or porch of any kind?

SABINO: Perhaps the search for location of this hidden door would prove more difficult than to go in through the vestibule and to wait there for the main door to be opened.

ROMÁN: No doubt it would be more work for us, but work suited to our faculties. What for one is most difficult proves to be easiest for another, and vice versa. Besides, if we insist on gaining entrance to the dwelling of wisdom through the vestibule of science, we run the risk of remaining there all our life long, waiting for the door to be opened; and frankly, my friend, if we are forced to stay outside, the best place to be is in the open air, beneath the sky and the stars, where the air strikes us from every quarter and without any rebound.

SABINO: All that is merely an excuse for laziness, a pretext for idleness.

ROMÁN: Idleness, you say? Look, hand me that book on your right there. That one, the *Sermons of Fray Alonso de Cabrera*, which has just been published in the "Nueva Biblioteca de Autores Españoles." Give it to me. Here it is; in the first sermon of the Considerations for Septuagesima Sunday, upon that text of St. Matthew (20:6): "Why stand ye here all the day idle?" Listen to the good Dominican father defending the friars and monks from the reproach that they earn their keep by singing, and idle their way through the year; he recalls the definition made by St. Thomas, his brother in religion, that idleness stands in opposition to any order so disposed as to attain its proper end. As we might expect, he then says that the idle are all those who are employed in achieving ends not conducive to their proper end, which is to save themselves. "If your concerns, business affairs, and worries cause you to draw away from God, then you are idle, you are lazy, you are a vagabond," he says.

SABINO: And do you approve of that? You?

ROMÁN: I neither approve nor disapprove. I say only that there are many who gain access to the temple porch, not in expectation of entering one day,

but merely to take refuge from the weather, because they can stand neither the touch of the sun's
rays nor the free embrace of the fresh air. I say
only that for many people the cultivation of science is no more than a narcotic of life. I say only
that the delirium with which men and peoples
hand themselves over to what they have decided
to call civilization is merely a consequence of
feeling desperate at being unable to enjoy the
fruits of what we call barbarism.

SABINO: But what about the rear door, the escape
door?

ROMÁN: This is not to be found until one has washed
one's eyes with tears that have welled up from
the bottom of one's heart. "Love is born," says
the Idiot in his *Contemplations*, "like the tears
that fall from one's eyes on one's chest, for love
is born of the intelligence and falls into the heart
through faith." But I think that it happens the
other way around. All the great works of faith
have been daughters of true, that is, painful, love.
Whenever you find wisdom in a work of science,
you need have no doubt but that it was dictated
by some passion, a painful passion, and one much
deeper than that miserable curiosity to ascertain
the "how" of things. "You will be as gods, know-
ers of the science of good and evil," the serpent
tempted Adam and Eve when these two languished in the fatal felicity of Paradise, free from
all pain.

SABINO: Applying all this to our own country, what
do you make of it? How does it apply to our state?
Since you speak of the portico of the temple with
such pernicious and unjust disdain, show us then
the door you talk about, the one through which

one enters directly, without having to wait in the antechamber.

ROMÁN: One man can not show this door to another man, but only, at most, inspire him with a desire to look for it himself. Matters of intimate personal experience are not to be transmitted between men. We pass banknotes or ideas between us, but not the benefits they confer. Only a few days ago I read, in a book by Bernard Shaw, the aphorism: "He who can, does. He who cannot, teaches."

SABINO: You're like the Krausists: everything goes into propaedeutics and prolegomena.

ROMÁN: Notice and observe that those people who here in Spain most had it in for the Krausists thirty or forty years ago because they spent their time in preliminaries have spent their own time in making indexes, epilogues, catalogues, and tables of errata. One is as bad as the other. They have installed themselves not in the portico of the temple, but in the corral, where they busy themselves gathering, ordering, and classifying scraps and leavings.

SABINO: That's all very well, but you open-air chaps, what do you do?

ROMÁN: We are the solitary ones, and all solitaries understand one another even without talking, or seeing one another, or even knowing each other. In my own solitude I am accompanied by the solitude of all other solitaries. There is a great deal of talk about solidarity, and we are told that those who inhabit the portico of the temple and have set up their shops and stands there feel great solidarity for each other. No doubt each stand owner sends the shopper to his neighbor's shop, because they have all their goods divided into specialties and each has his limitation, and thus each one praises the other's merchandise. I am acquainted with the repulsive brotherhood among the merchants of the portico; but I can assure you that in the depths of their hearts they are not any more united than we who wander, without following a fixed course, around the outside of the temple, beneath the open sky, trusting that some grief or anguish will open up the back door, the escape door, the hidden door for us. And at night, when the merchants, after closing their shops, sleep among their goods, they do not sleep well, believe me, for it is then, in the silence, that they know one another.

SABINO: And supposing one day the great doors of the temple are opened wide for them? For after all, they wait humbly.

ROMÁN: Humbly? Some humility! If they were humble they would be saved. But don't you know well enough how these hawkers and peddlers despise, or pretend to despise, the very men who manufacture the trifles they themselves sell? Humbly? If they were humble, the doors to the temple would be opened to them.

SABINO: And suppose they are opened?

ROMÁN: They won't go in, you can be sure of it, they won't go in. Their hearts are so bound up with the trinkets in their shops and stands, each one of them is so satisfied to be a specialist in rings, or in balls, or in perfumed soap, or in whistles, or in second-hand books, that they will not quit their places of business to go into the temple and see the face of God. They are misers, nothing more than misers. And besides, what are they going to do in the temple when even those who once knew have forgotten how to sing? In the temple there is no crying out of wares, but singing. If they did enter in, the Son of the Lord would drive them out with a whip. Let them sell books of psalms in the portico, and let them collate the various editions, and let them study and correct them, let them polish and publish them, but let them not go in to sing. Good Heavens! What has the one calling to do with the other?

SABINO: And yet . . .

ROMÁN: And yet that old Kempis you see there on my table, with his clean naked text, in an ordinary edition, made for battle, has given me more alleviation and consolation than was afforded the man who made a critical edition, preceded by a very learned introduction and followed by erudite notes, all of them totally foolish. That kind of activity is nothing more than a morbid concupiscence of knowledge.

SABINO: And what else would you have men do?

ROMÁN: What else? Fall into despair and tell us of their desperation, or take hope and tell us of their hopes. Sing!

SABINO: Not all birds were born to sing.

ROMÁN: Well, let those who were not born out of song not sing. But neither should they caw. Let them not act the magpie.

My Religion

A FRIEND WRITES me from Chile, telling me he has talked to people there who after reading my writing ask: "Now what, in short, is the religion of this Señor Unamuno?" A similar question has been put to me here on more than one occasion. So I shall try, not to answer it—something quite beyond me—but rather to pose the question in a better light.

Individuals, like nations, given over to spiritual sloth—and spiritual sloth is compatible with fecund activity of an economic and other like order—tend toward dogmatism, whether they are aware of it or not, whether they want it or not, intending it or not intending it. Spiritual sloth avoids a critical or skeptical position.

Skeptical, I say, and I use the word skepticism in its etymological and philosophical sense: a skeptic does not mean one who doubts, but one who investigates or searches, in contradistinction to one who affirms and thinks to have ascertained. There are men who delve into the heart of a problem and there are men who give us formulas, well-constructed or not, as a solution.

As regards pure philosophic speculation, it is precipitate to ask for ready-made solutions when one has merely put forth the statement of a problem. When a long calculation has been incorrectly worked out, the erasure of the work done and a new beginning signify no small advance. When a house threatens to

209

fall into ruin or becomes totally uninhabitable, the first step is to demolish it, and there is no reason to demand that one build another in its place. It would be quite conceivable to build anew using materials from the old dwelling, but that comes after the old has been first demolished. In the interim, the inhabitants can stay in a hut, if there is no other house available, or sleep in the open field.

And it is also necessary not to lose sight of the fact that in order to live our life we rarely need wait for definitive scientific solutions. Men have lived and continue to live on the basis of very frail hypotheses and explanations, and even without any at all. In punishing a delinquent, men do not come to an agreement as to whether or not he exercised free will, just as in sneezing one does not reflect on the damage that may be caused by the tiny obstacle in the throat which causes the sneeze.

Those men who maintain that they would be evildoers if they did not believe in hell's punishment are, I believe in all honor to them, mistaken. If they left off believing in sanctions beyond the tomb, they would not for that reason act any the worse, but would instead seek another ideal justification for their conduct. The good man who believes in a transcendent order is not so much good because he believes in this order but believes in it because he is good. I am sure that this proposition will seem obscure or farfetched to questioners with slothful spirits.

"All right, but what, in short, is your religion?" I will be asked. And I will reply: "My religion is to seek the truth in life and life in the truth, even though I know I will not find it while I live. My religion is to struggle incessantly and tirelessly with the mystery; my religion is to wrestle with God, from the break of dawn until the fall of night, as they say Jacob wrestled with Him. I can not compromise with the concept of the Inconceivable, nor with the notion that "you will not get beyond this point." I reject the eternal *ignorabimus*, the we-shall-not-know. In any case I want to climb the inaccessible."

"Be perfect, as your Father in heaven is perfect," Christ said to us, and such an ideal of perfection is doubtless unattainable. But He placed the unattainable before us to be our aim and goal. And He did this, the theologians tell us, through grace. For my part I wish to fight my battle without thought of victory. Are there not armies and even nations who march out to sure defeat? Do we not render homage to those who let themselves be killed in battle rather than surrender? This is my religion.

Those people who ask about my religion want me to supply them with a dogma, a solution in which the spirit can rest in its sloth. They scarcely want even that, but merely desire to classify me and put me into one of those pigeonholes where they place spirits, so they can say of me: "He is a Lutheran, a Calvinist, a Catholic, an atheist, a rationalist, a mystic," or some other similar denomination, whose clear meaning they do not understand, but which allows them to give up further thought. And I do not wish to be pigeonholed, because I, Miguel de Unamuno, like any other man who aspires to full consciousness, am a unique species. "There are not sicknesses, but only sick men," certain doctors will tell us, and I say that there are no opinions, but merely men with opinions.

As regards religion, there is scarcely a single point I have resolved rationally, and since I have not, I can not communicate any of these points logically, for only what is rational is logical and transmissible. I do have, in my affections, in my heart, in my feelings, a strong tendency toward Christianity, without abiding by any special dogmas of this or that Christian confession. I consider any man who invokes the name of Christ with respect and love a Christian, and I feel repugnance for the orthodox, whether Catholics or Protestants (the latter are usually as uncompromising as the former), who deny Christianity to those who do not interpret the Gospel as they do. I know a Protestant Christian who denies that the Unitarians are Christians.

I confess sincerely that the supposed rational proofs—ontological, cosmological, ethical, etc.—of God's existence do not demonstrate anything as far as I am concerned: all the reasons given for God's existence seem to me to be reasons based on paralogisms and a begging of the question. In this matter I am with Kant. In speaking of the matter I regret I can not speak to the shoemakers in shoemaking terms.

No one has succeeded in convincing me rationally of God's existence, but neither have they convinced me of His non-existence. The reasoning of atheists strikes me as being even more superficial and futile than that of their opponents. And if I believe in God, or at least believe I believe in Him, it is because, more than anything else, I want God to exist, and then because His existence is revealed to me in my heart, in the Gospel, and through Christ and History. In any case, it is a matter of the heart.

All of which means that I am not convinced of His existence the way I am convinced that two and two make four.

If it were a matter which did not involve my peace of mind and a consolation for having been born, I would probably not pay any attention to the problem; but inasmuch as my entire inner life and the well-spring of all my action are involved, I can not satisfy myself by saying: I neither know nor can know. I do not know: that is certain, and perhaps I can never know. But I "want" to know. I want to, and that is enough.

And I will spend my life wrestling with the mystery, even though there is no hope of penetrating it, for the struggle itself is my sustenance and my consolation. Yes, my consolation. I have accustomed myself to extracting hope from despair itself. And simpletons and the simpleminded need not shout: "Paradox!"

I can not conceive of a cultured man without this preoccupation, and I expect very little from the culture—culture is not the same as civilization—of those who live without any interest in the metaphysics of the religious problem and study it only in its social or political aspect. I expect very little, in the way of enriching the spiritual treasure of the human race, from those men or those nations who, from mental sloth, from superficiality, from scientificism, or from whatever, dissociate themselves from the deep, eternal concerns of the heart, from its restlessness. I expect nothing from those who say: "One ought not to think about that!" I expect even less from those who believe in a heaven and a hell of the type we believed in as children, and even less again from those who affirm with the gravity of the stupid: "All that is merely a matter of fables and myths; whoever dies is buried, and there's an end to it." I expect great things only from those who do not know, but who do not resign themselves to not knowing, from those who struggle without cease for the truth and put their hearts into the struggle even more than into the victory.

The greater part of my work has always been to disquiet my neighbors, to stir up the sediment of their hearts, to sow anguish in them, if possible. I said as much before, in my *Life of Don Quixote and Sancho*, which is my most extensive confession on this head. Let them search as I search, let them struggle as I do, and between us all we will secretly snatch a hair from God's beard, and at the very least the struggle will make us more manly, men of more spirit.

To carry out this struggle—this religious struggle—in nations like those which speak Spanish, nations consumed by sloth and superficiality of spirit, fallen asleep in the routine of Catholic dogmatism or the dogmatism of free thought, I have had on occasion to appear immodest or indecorous; at other times, hard and aggressive; and at still other times, complicated and paradoxical. The habit had already been lost, in our mean literature, of shrieking from the bottom of the heart, of clamoring, of forgetting oneself. The shriek was almost unknown. Writers feared to fall into ridicule. They were inhibited in the same way as a person who swallows an affront in the middle of the street because he fears seeing his hat knocked to the ground or himself in the hands of a policeman. That has not been my case. When I have felt like crying out, I have cried out. I have never been held back by decorum. And this is a quality never forgiven me by my fellow writers, so prudent, so correct, so disciplined, even when they preached impropriety and indiscipline. Our literary anarchists have taken care, more than anything else, of style and syntax. And when they sing discords, they sing in tune; their discords tend to be in harmony.

When I have felt pain I have cried out, and I have cried out in public. The psalms which make up my *Poems* are no more than cries from the heart, with which I have sought to make vibrant the hurt cords, the pained strings, of other men's hearts. If they do not possess any such cords, or if the cords are so rigid that they do not vibrate, my cry will not resound there, and they will declare that my verse is not poetry, and they will set themselves to examining it acoustically. It would also be possible to examine acoustically the cry uttered by a man who saw his son suddenly fall dead; a person without a heart or without children would do just that.

The psalms of my *Poems*, together with various other compositions to be found there, are my religion, my religion in song, sung rather than expressed logically and reasonably. And I sing it, for better or worse, with the voice and ear God gave me, for I can not reason it out. Whoever sees only ratiocination and logic, method and exegesis, rather than life in my verse—because they can find neither fauns, nor dryads, nor sylphs, nor water lilies, nor absinthe (that is, wormwood), nor glaucous eyes, nor any other more or less modernist nonsense—is beyond the sound of my cry, and I will not touch his heart with a violin bow or with a hammer.

I flee, I repeat, as from a plague, the thought that I might be classified, and I wish to die listening to the slothful of spirit asking, as they pause to hear me: "And this fellow, what is he?" Stupid liberals or progressives will take me for a reactionary, perhaps even a mystic, without knowing, of course, what the terms mean, and stupid conservatives and reactionaries will consider me a species of spiritual anarchist; both groups will think that I am a poor man bent on being different and passing myself off as original, with bats in the belfry. But no one should pay any attention to what fools and dolts think of him, whether they be progressives or conservatives, liberals or reactionaries.

Since man is a stubborn animal, and averse to illumination, who will fall right back into his old habits and go over the same ground again after hours of listening to a sermon, the questioners and curious who chance to read these words of mine will ask me again: "All right, now, but what solutions do you offer?" And I, in conclusion, will tell them that if they want solutions, to step over to the stand across the street, for I do not carry any such line of goods. My endeavor has been, still is, and will always be to make those who read me think and meditate on fundamentals. I have always sought to agitate and, at most, to suggest rather than instruct. If I start to sell bread, it will not be bread, but yeast and leavening.

I have friends, good friends, who advise me to leave off this labor and to retire to construct what they call an objective work, "something definitive," they say, "something constructive, something lasting." They mean something dogmatic. I declare myself incapable of such a task and I demand my liberty, my holy liberty, even to the point of being able to contradict myself, if necessary. I do not know whether anything I have done or will do in the future will remain for years or for centuries after my death; but I know that if the shoreless sea is struck, troubled with one blow, the concentric waves will spread without cease, though in weakening circles. To agitate is after all something. If, thanks to agitation, another man follows and constructs something lasting, my work will last in his.

It is a work of supreme mercy to awaken the sleeping and shake the indolent, and it is a work of supreme religious piety to search for the truth on all sides, and to uncover fraud, folly, and stupidity wherever they may be found.

My good friend the Chilean now knows, then, what he must answer whoever asks about my religion. However, if the questioner happens to be one of those dolts who think that I must bear a grudge against a nation or a country because I have spoken the truth plainly to one of its impulsive sons, the best thing is to make no answer at all.

The Vertical of Le Dantec

For a long time to come I do not expect to have the opportunity to read a more comic and at the same time typically representative book than the one before me, a book by Félix Le Dantec, who teaches courses at the Sorbonne, on the subject of Atheism: *L'Athéisme*.

And it is not that I am scandalized by M. Le Dantec's atheism. Far from it! He is free to be an atheist—and he and God can come to some understanding! Nor do I wish to speak of his atheism, which is like the atheism of a parcel of other atheists, and doubtless very respectable as well. I want, rather, to speak of the scientificism of this formidable biologist, M. Le Dantec, who is not lacking—and why should he lack?—admirers. But let us leave all judgments until after we have made our investigation.

I began reading this book as a distraction and a means of killing time. Everything went well as long as the author was explaining how he is an atheist, and how he could not but be an atheist, and how he is an atheist from birth, almost *ab ovo*, by a kind of biological determinism. All of which is very diverting, and perhaps indisputable. But then, mind you, on reaching page twenty-seven, I come upon this paragraph: "Descartes, who was a mathematician, knew, nevertheless, that certain quantities can develop indefinitely without ever passing a given limit, or, if one prefers, that certain curves have a horizontal asymptote." "A horizontal asymptote!" I said to myself. I thought I had read it wrongly. Horizontal asymptote!

I invite anyone who knows mathematics to show me how a horizontal asymptote differs from a vertical one, or from an oblique one. The book from which the formidable M. Le Dantec studied his analytical geometry must have carried an illustration of some branch of a hyperbola with its asymptote represented horizontally in relation to the reader's normal position. He need only have given the book a quarter turn and there he would have had the asymptote represented vertically.

But that is not the amusing point. The amusing point is that this publicist of biology, professor at the Sorbonne, formidable atheist and even more formidable scientificist (which does not mean man of science, not by any means) is ignorant—yes, ignorant—of the fact that the ideas of horizontality and of verticality, just as the notions of up, down, forward, behind, to the left, to the right, are not geometric notions or ideas and that geometry has no need of them. These notions might rather be called physiological: they indicate relation to the spectator. Any child, even if he is not a biologist, or an atheist, or a determinist, or has not studied at the Sorbonne, knows that whatever lies on our right, will, if we merely make a half-turn, lie on our left.

"But that is precisely what Le Dantec mentions later on!" someone who has read him might exclaim. And I will answer: "No, that is not what he says. M. Le Dantec assumes the mass of mortals to possess some notions it does not possess: M. Le Dantec is one of those pedants who claim that cold does not exist." Let us take a look.

"Would you say," asks the atheist, "that color exists, that sound exists?" And I reply: "Of course, for I see the one and hear the other." And he says: "I tell you that color results from the encounter between certain circumambient conditions and a living being capable of receiving impressions, so that there must be two factors for color to exist, thus: a particular state of what physicists call the ether, plus a man who sees. Now then, we have such an absolute idea of color that we are unable to imagine color not existing, even though all living beings were to be destroyed." Is it possible to imagine more vulgar superficiality? You may call the objective or external cause of color by any name you please, and you can believe in the ether more than in what you see about you, or than in God—for ether is no less hypothetical than He— but the sensation of color always exists and that sensation is as real, and even as objective, as the supposed ether. For am I not an object and is not whatever takes place in me an object? And in the same way that the cause of color could continue though all living beings were destroyed, so would color continue. To say the opposite would be equivalent to affirming that if consciousness were to be destroyed—assuming that its total and absolute destruction were possible, something of which I know nought—everything reflected in consciousness would also be destroyed. Who knows what external reality is really like, external reality in itself, outside and apart from our representation of it? The formidable atheistic biologist has not gone through Kant; his scientificism is unphilosophic to the utmost degree, that is, of the most unimaginable grossness.

Le Dantec's folly—for it is no more than a folly— is of the same species as that other folly about cold's not existing, and is part of the gratuitous supposition that the populace thinks that cold is something objective, absolutely independent of us, and opposed to something else called heat. And nothing of the sort is true. The populace—that is, the un-scientificist and un-atheistic populace—supposes nothing of the sort. They limit themselves to saying that it is cold, when they feel cold and, when they feel the heat, to saying that it is hot. They are right—and we must not slander the populace. So cold results from the lessening of such and such molecular movements, or whatever? Very well: what difference does it make? It is the same as if I said that ice does not exist, that it is no more than frozen water. But we must follow on with Le Dantec, for now comes the good part.

Now he brings up his incomparable example of the vertical. Listen closely! He speaks of—the absolute vertical! Absolute? What is this? I do not know and I do not think Le Dantec does either. Let us first examine what we mean by vertical. By vertical we mean the line of plumb, the line of a weight when it falls. It is not, therefore, a geometric notion, but a physical one or, rather, a physiological one. Vertical indicates a relation to the normal position of the spectator, when he is standing. It is something that one senses. And we all call the trajectory of a weight falling without an obstacle a vertical, and similarly all its parallels in space. And this is the fact, neither more nor less. But let us return to Le Dantec.

"I have an innate idea of this vertical," he tells us. Innate? Then this formidable biologist believes in innate ideas. It is just as well we know that. But what must he understand by an innate idea? He himself foresees the difficulty and tells us that if we do not care to dispute the matter, if this idea is not innate, that is, if it does not come to him by inheritance from an accepted error accredited, then it was born in him, naturally, as a result of the erroneous but general agreement concerning the flat surface of the earth. Good Lord, what a lot of stuff! (I beg pardon for invoking the Lord in this case.) What could the idea of verticality have to do with whether or not the earth is flat or round? The good Le Dantec doubtless believes that for the populace the idea of verticality comes from the notion of horizontality, and that we consider the vertical to be that which is perpendicular to a horizontal plane. Pedantry, pedantry, pedantry!

Be the earth round, as it seems it is, or be it flat, the line of plumb will always be, for each one of us, vertical, and the horizontal will always be the plane and the lines of this plane perpendicular to the vertical or which form a right angle with it; any plane, such as the plane of a billiard table, where the level plane indicates it, will always be horizontal. And that horizontal plane is an ideal plane. The ideal plane of the sea, the one it would form if it were perfectly and absolutely calm, is that of a curved surface taken otherwise. But we possess not only the idea but also the sense of a plane surface, tangential to the point of the terrestrial curve at which we find ourselves, and this we call horizontal.

And this idea is as real and as objective as any strictly geometric idea whatever.

"Doubtless there are people," writes the formidable biologist, "who do not conceive of an absolute vertical, just as there are atheists." But the vertical is something sensed, M. Le Dantec, something we feel!

And God, too, is sensed. The trouble is that M. Le Dantec does not know very well what a vertical is, and knows even less well what God is. For what emerges from his book is that he has not the remotest idea of the nature of what many of us who still believe in Him call God.

"True enough," he goes on, "the idea of the absolute vertical is mathematically absurd; there are as many verticals as there are points on the surface of the Earth. . . ." Obviously! There is a vertical for each observer, plus all the lines, which are infinite, parallel to it. And is that the reason it is not absolute? And what is the meaning of this absolute? By using this procedure I would commit myself to demonstrating that nothing real is absolute. Everything, then, is relative. Agreed; but what of relativity itself? Is it not also relative? Are we not being led along by these pedantic scientificists playing with words?

But the really thick part follows after the points of suspension above: "The vertical of my antipode is opposite to mine." Marvelous! The formidable biologist apparently divides verticals into those which go from top to bottom and verticals which go from bottom to top. Now I know, thanks to this delightful atheist, that I have in my house *two* contrary staircases: the stairs by which I ascend and those by which I descend.

To which any Le Dantec whosoever, even though of a lesser rank, may be able to retort that the staircase in my house is something real, concrete, tangible and visible, while the vertical or the line of trajectory of a weight falling without interference is only an ideal line. So much the better for my argument. A weight falls from top to bottom, of course, but the ideal line which it traverses neither rises nor falls, nor does it go from top to bottom or from bottom to top.

I am almost ashamed, my readers, to offer these explications, and I would not do so if I did not know the havoc wreaked by scientificism, especially among those who do not possess a solid scientific education and those who have not trained their minds in a serious and austere philosophy, in that perennial philosophy alluded to by Leibnitz, I think it was, and which lives on, always expanding, along with the idea of God, through the centuries. And it is painful to see people fleeing in spirit from the fruitful travail of the encounter with this perennial philosophy and hanging on to some frog-dissecter who talks of horizontal asymptotes, and who talks in that fashion merely as a way of going against God and against the eternal verities of humanity. Counterposed to the famous *odium theologicum* there is an *odium antitheologicum* or *contratheologicum*. But let us return to Le Dantec.

On page 31 of his book, he tells us: "Even if we allow that we could prove that there is no God, just as we have proved that there is no absolute vertical . . . ," which strikes me as similar to what Jesuit preachers—a species of Le Dantecs of the opposing side—always say after they have launched a thesis: "It remains, therefore, clearly proven that. . . ." They add this sentence just in case their audience has not been taken in; and they are like the notorious painter who wrote at the bottom of an ill-drawn monster: "This is a rooster."

I have decided not to pursue the central thesis of atheism in the work of the formidable biologist, discoverer of horizontal asymptotes. Since I would have to begin by saying that Monsieur Le Dantec scarcely has a notion of what enlightened believers mean by God, what would be the use? If only he had been content to say "I just don't know what they mean by God" (for that is the truth: he does not), he could have saved himself writing the book. The formidable biologist does not know what God is, but he does know, on the other hand, that "moral conscience is more developed among bees and ants than it is among men, judging from the perfect order of their social life, at least" (page 34). There is a story that when a disciple of Pliny's heard his master say that the elephant can see grass growing, he exclaimed: "Either Pliny has been an elephant, or some elephant has spoken to Pliny." And the formidable Le Dantec, who deduces from the perfect order (?) of the social life of bees and ants that they possess a more highly developed moral conscience than man—as he might deduce from the movements of the planets that they knew the laws of Copernicus—this same discoverer of the two verticals, of the vertical that ascends and the one that descends, tells us a little farther on (on page 56) that his believing brothers "denied ants, such tiny beings, the very idea of God." Now who would ever think of either denying or imputing to ants this idea or any other idea whatsoever? Such gratuitous imputations fill this book by the horizontal biologist, who imagines a kind of fantastic believer or takes into account merely the innocent and ignorant countryfolk of his native Brittany. He is very careful to tell us that he is a Breton, a countryman of Chateaubriand, of Lamennais, of Renan. . . .

What an extravagant notion he has of believers! "Praying is the most important occupation of believers," he tells us a little later, and he follows this formidable assertion with a few lines in which he clearly demonstrates he has no concept of what prayer is or of what it means to any kind of believer except perhaps his village-countryfolk, above whose field of vision he has not risen, despite all his biology.

It would be best to leave off considering all that follows in his book, including his personal belief that tigers have no idea of God, and other pleasantries of that type. Why go on?

Our popular libraries are nowadays full of these formidable scientificists. Not long ago, in an article as prolix as Le Dantec, Señor Morote disclosed to us that neither the idea of time nor the idea of cold existed inasmuch as they are anti-scientific! Since it is not possible to believe that our fecund publicist meant to say what he said, that is, that the "idea" of time or the "idea" of cold does not exist, for we speak of them, I assume therefore that he meant to say that neither cold nor time exists, which is even more amusing and *Le-Dantec-esque*. The Italian Futurist Marinetti already killed off time and space in a celebrated manifesto—a most amusing document also—some time ago, when he wrote: "Time and Space died yesterday." Now if they will only kill off logic, we will be free of the three tyrants of the spirit, for the fact that we can not be in two places at the same time, the fact that we can not live yesterday, today, and tomorrow, the fact that we can not deduce from a principle the conclusion most to our liking, that is: the fact that we can not be infinite, eternal, and absolutely free is pretty hard to swallow. And yet, logic can not be killed off, and for a very good reason.

Is all this merely a ridiculous pleasantry? No, all this is sad, very sad. Beneath this non-scientific scientificism, beneath this garrulous and vulgar pedantry, clearly lies an *odium antitheologicum*, no less poisonous than an *odium theologicum*—in truth, the very same thing, one and the other.

All this nonsense which wears the disguise of science only serves to poison pitiful spirits anxious for knowledge and serves also to encourage base passions. And all these horizontal biologists, whether they be Le Dantec or Haeckel (though Haeckel is somewhat more serious, he is not much more so, and neither is he any less ignorant of what he strives to efface, as evidenced by his archi-superficial book *The Riddle of the Universe*), form a kind of international association of freemasonry, with customs posts on the frontiers; they translate and champion one another, and connive at suppressing any knowledge of serious thinkers, of those who work in good faith and are free of sectarianism and of raging— either theological raging or anti-theological raging— of those who abide by the perennial philosophy. And there are people who grow ecstatic over Haeckel and yet scarcely know of Darwin, who admire Le Dantec without having duly studied Claude Bernard. Of course neither Darwin nor Claude Bernard ever purported, as far as I know, to prove that there is no God, or that there is one.

These scientificists turned philosophers and theologians—or anti-theologians, which amounts to the same thing—are creating a scientificist and horizontal public, more public and vulgar than ever before. For the simple and carefree populace say that it is cold whenever they feel cold, and that time flies, and they do not indulge in philosophies concerning what cold and time may or not be objectively, while the new mob, the populace adulterated by terrible reading matter badly digested, believe they believe in the

227

ether more than in their own senses and they swallow any old thing, more or less horizontal, of any biologist whoever, so long as it confirms their prejudices and superstitions, equally or even more superstitious than those of the populace as such, and without the excuse the latter have.

How guileless this mob adulterated by scientificism! From time to time I receive a letter from some unknown scientificist reader in which he fires away at me in a dozen-page letter using the most worn and overworked commonplaces of science and the cheapest of philosophies. They must think: "It's not possible that this man can think and say the things he does, unless he simply doesn't know all I've got to tell him." For there are people so ingenuous that, when they find someone who does not think the way they do on some specific point, they immediately assume that it must be because these others are not equally in possession of the data and knowledge they themselves possess on the point in question, and it never occurs to them that those who differ from them know all those facts and have all that data and knowledge, and more besides. And if they ever do have a suspicion that such is the case, they immediately ask one to illustrate the matter, as if it were possible to set up a whole course of study. Theorem 121 is based on 120, which is based on the one before that, and thus successively, and there are times when it would be necessary to explain all 120 theorems. Then there are people who write complete doctrinal theses, and others of us who write single essays with the main aim of stating and suggesting problems rather than of developing them.

In conclusion it would be well to point out that if there is a biology, and a physiology, and a geometry, and a sociology, there is also a theology, as much a science in its method as any science whatsoever. And to add that it is just as absurd for some Le Dantec or other to take it upon himself to write about atheism without having duly acknowledged theology as it would be for a theologian to set about commenting on germinative plasma or biological inheritance without having paid due obeisance to biology.

I will have more than enough occasion, unfortunately, to return to this same theme, one of my favorites. And all horizontalists—biologists or non-biologists—are free to say that I am no more than a sly and retrograde reactionary, a Jesuit in disguise—since they even know how the ants think . . . !

Rebekah

"AND ISAAC WAS forty years old when he took Rebekah to wife, the daughter of Bethuel the Syrian of Padan-aram, the sister of Laban the Syrian. And Isaac intreated the Lord for his wife, because she was barren: and the Lord was intreated of him, and Rebekah his wife conceived. And the children struggled together within her; and she said, If it be so, why am I thus? And she went to enquire of the Lord. And the Lord said unto her, Two nations are in thy womb, and two manner of people shall be separated from thy bowels; and the elder shall serve the younger. And when her days to be delivered were fulfilled, behold, there were twins in her womb. And the first came out red, all over like an hairy garment; and they called his name Esau. And after that came his brother out, and his hand took hold on Esau's heel; and his name was called Jacob."

Thus Genesis, chapter 25, after the previous chapter had told us how Abraham had dispatched "his eldest servant of his house" to Mesopotamia to bring back a wife for his son Isaac, and how the servant found her in the city of Nahor, "by a well of water at the time of the evening, even the time . . . the daughters of the men of the city come out to draw water," and when he said "Let down thy pitcher, I pray thee, that I may drink," Rebekah, daughter of Bethuel, son of Milcah, the wife of Nahor, Abraham's brother, answered "Drink my lord," and then gave water to his camels. And the old servant took her to Abraham, his master, to give to Isaac, Abraham's son.

And Ernest Renan, ex-future Catholic priest, in the study he devoted to Lamennais, the inflamed ex-Catholic priest—Bretons both of them, though Renan had Gascon blood as well—wrote:

> In the apologist who turns apostate, the priest who inflicts a grievous injury by his testament upon the dogma which he has served, we have a phenomenon in which the mysteries of belief appear, so to say, naked. I know not whether the world has seen since Tertullian such a striking example of the kind which Lamennais reserved for our epoch. Never have greater passions aroused greater storms in a greater soul; never has the painful birth of a new world evoked more eloquent cries of pain. It was like the woman in the Bible in whose womb two nations— one elect, the other reprobate—clashed with each other, and she experienced within her feverish breast the battles of centuries. Each convulsion of these heroic men who bear in their heart the wound of their time, each one of their cries, each one of their sorrows, should all be noted, for they are symptoms of the agitation of Humanity. The hidden restlessness which mediocrity nullifies and which calculated interest dissimulates are manifest in these men in all their brutal and exposed truth.

Renan, the Breton with Gascon blood, the blood which also coursed through the veins of Montaigne, Renan was a spectator of the tragicomedy of life, and he said that everything we witness and experience is a spectacle put on by the great *choregos* of the Universe and that we should contribute to the most faithful performance of this play. Was this Renan perchance clearly aware of the meaning of what he wrote

about the tragic Breton priest who experienced the
battle of twin ideas—twins, but deadly enemies—
battling for birth and life in his soul?

Imagine a nation, like Rebekah, experiencing in
its soul the battle of brothers. And yet this is as nothing compared to an individual consciousness reflect-
ing the collective consciousness, the spiritual bosom
of a man who epitomizes the soul of his people and
experiences the prenatal, uterine struggle of Esau
with Jacob, the twin who takes hold on Esau's heel
as if prepared to supplant him, first by deceit and
then by violence.

And if Rebekah could have witnessed the solemn
struggle between Jacob and the angel of the Lord
from the fall of night until the breaking of the day
when, flushed with anguish, he called on the angel to
tell his name, how then would this poor mother, who
when a virgin went to the well for water and gave
drink to pilgrims and camels, how would she have
been able to explain to herself the terrible contained
struggle, the combat between the twins in her womb?

And why did they fight? Was it in order to see who
would emerge first, since they both could not, without an absurd contradiction, emerge together? It was
Esau who emerged first, all red and hairy, and after
him, as if in a subject role, his hand taking hold on
Esau's heel, came Jacob. But in the end, the first-
born sold his birthright to the second-born in ex-
change for a mess of pottage; and then old Isaac,
gone blind, blessed Jacob thinking he was Esau. And
this story is repeated in the history of ideas.

First-born ideas, all red and hairy, their heels
clutched firmly by the hands of the ideas that follow
them—those ideas which fight at night with the angel
of the Lord, demanding to know his name—these

first-born ideas, strong huntsmen, grow faint one day and sell themselves for a mess of pottage.

But the tragedy does not lie with the ideas, but with Rebekah. The tragedy lies in the soul of the conceiver.

How easily do they speak of contradictions, those who have never given birth to enemy twins, or perhaps have not given birth to anything at all, or perhaps can not give birth to anything at all!

Manzoni, in his immortal ode to the fifth of May, the day on which the Unique Napoleon died, chants to us how two centuries, armed each against the other, submitted themselves to him as if awaiting their fate, and Napoleon, falling silent, sat between them as arbiter.

> Due secoli
> l'un contro l'altro armato
> somessi a lui si volsero
> come aspettando il fato;
> ei fé silenzio ed, arbitro
> s'assise in mezzo a lor.

But what if those two centuries, armed the one against the other, had penetrated Napoleon's soul and, instead of submitting themselves to him, had set themselves to battling? But no: Napoleonic souls have little, very little, almost nothing, of the Rebekah about them. They are not battlefields, but rather the rulers over battlefields. And thus their range of action is always, no matter how extensive it may appear, scarcely profound.

The Napoleons pass with the air of conquerors, devastating nations, and then, after their defeat, are cast away on some islet or other in the vast solitude of the ocean; and the Tertullians pass wearing an air of defeat, and they, too, are cast away. But where . . . ?

And the centuries pass and when a human soul goes out to find itself, to touch itself, to feel itself, to be itself, it does not go to look at itself in the mirror held up by the eagle which soared over the battlefield, but rather in the mirror of the battlefield itself, of the other soul which was a battlefield, the womb of Rebekah, bearer of twins at war.

Esau, the first-born, conceived a hatred of Jacob, his brother, and thought to kill him; but Rebekah, their mother, who heard of his words, called Jacob, her youngest son, and told him to flee, until his brother's fury should turn away. And the poor mother said: "Why should I be deprived also of you both in one day?" And Rebekah was weary of her life because of the daughters of Heth, whom Jacob might espouse. Poor Rebekah! Poor Rebekah, who trembled at the thought of fratricide between her sons! She would have one son dead and the other a murderer! The maternal soul, which conceives twin and contradictory ideas, wants all its offspring to live, wants them alive, and not some of them dead and others murderers. Let them struggle, as they did in her womb before birth, but let them not kill each other! Let them all live!

And it is worthwhile reading the psalm-like plaints of the Breton prophet in his *Words of a Believer*. Believer? It is worth hearing what the sharp ex-seminarian has to say about the beliefs of his countryman. This study by Renan of Lamennais, though not one of his best works, is one of the most instructive books I know. It is worth listening to Sara when she pities, actually pities, Rebekah.

Spin from Your Entrails!

> Carking care is my feudal castle. It is built like an eagle's nest upon the peak of a mountain lost in the clouds. No one can take it by storm. From this abode I dart down into the world of reality to seize my prey; but I do not remain down there, I bear my quarry aloft to my stronghold. My booty is a picture I weave into the tapestries of my palace.
>
> Kierkegaard, *Diapsalmata*

THIS SELFSAME TRAGIC Kierkegaard tells us that the spider, when suspended over the abyss, gropes in the void around it. And that enormous Yankee poet Walt Whitman returned to this image, so thoroughly impregnated with symbolic sense. And we would like now to return to the same image once again.

In 1843 Kierkegaard wrote: "What portends? what will the future bring? I do not know, I have no presentiment. When a spider hurls itself down from some fixed point, consistently with its nature, it always sees before it only an empty space wherein it can find no foothold however much it sprawls."

In 1870 Walt Whitman was saying:

A noiseless patient spider,
I mark'd where on a little promontory it stood
    isolated,
Mark'd how to explore the vacant vast surrounding,
It launched forth filament, filament, filament, out of
    itself,
Ever unreeling them, ever tirelessly speeding them.

235

And you O my soul where you stand,
Surrounded, detached, in measureless oceans of
    space,
Ceaselessly musing, venturing, throwing, seeking
    the spheres to connect them,
Till the bridge you will need be form'd, till the
    ductile anchor hold,
Till the gossamer thread you fling catch somewhere,
    O my soul.

And now, at the beginning of another spring, when
people are frightened of the future, which is worse
than trembling at the thought of Death or in the face
of Life; when some want the dream of civil life—
which is History—to be enacted according to the
book and the program; when people ask themselves
in terror, "What will tomorrow bring? What will
happen tomorrow, dear God? What is our fate? What
awaits us?"; when those who speak thus shudder before the leap in the darkness, then we recall Kierkegaard's spider, and Walt Whitman's spider—which
are one and the same spider.

The leap into the depths of darkness? That leap is
feared by those who do not carry with them the rope
of salvation. When one is about to descend into an
unexplored chasm, best take along a lamp; but even
more important, a rope, a lifeline. When Don Quixote
went to let himself down into the marvelous Cave of
Montesinos, he took with him "near a hundred fathom
of cord," with which they later "bound the knight
very fast," though he said: "We have been very care-
less in neglecting to provide a little bell, to be tied
with me to this rope; by the tinkling of which you
might hear me still descending, and know that I was
alive"; but even without a bell, "the scholar and
Sancho, giving him rope, let him down to the bottom
of the fearful cavern."

But in order to make the descent—though why not the ascent?—into the marvelous Cave of the Darksome Future, in order to make the leap into the darkness which is almost upon us, coming thick over our heads and from under our feet, no outside rope whatsoever will serve, even if it be outsize and "near a hundred fathom." Like the spider, our soul must draw the rope, our thread of Ariadne, out of itself, from its own entrails. Everyone, each one, must draw from himself the guide rope, the saving rope, spin it from out of one's entrails. Each one must, if he wants to be saved, spin from his own entrails, weave from his own living entrails, suffused as they are with anguish, despair, and faith.

The most tragic fact about Kierkegaard's spider and Walt Whitman's spider was not that they were surrounded by the void, with no place to set foot, not that they see before them only an empty space wherein they can find no foothold however much they sprawl, but rather that the thread by which they hang must be formed and spun from out of their own entrails, that it is part of their entrails and not a rope outside themselves upon which they must take hold.

Poor humankind, who, in order to let themselves down into the marvelous Cave of the Future, of the New World, of the unknown tomorrow, need a rope, a program! "And who is to govern us?" they ask in terror. "And with what laws? And with what kind of government? What program do these revolutionaries have? How will they organize the future society? What will they substitute for private property? What will they put in place of inheritance? What will they do about my job?" And so on, *ad infinitum*. They end by calling for rope and a little bell to signal for help whenever they should find themselves suffused with the terror of death. And they want a lamp to see in the darkness. They are unaware that a lamp serves no purpose when one cannot see within oneself. Moreover, it behooves us to act like the female glow-worm, which generates light from within, from its own entrails produces the small light which serves, more than to illuminate its way, to illuminate itself, so that its male companion may see it.

My poor friend, terrified at the leap into the depths of tomorrow's darkness, at the social chaos which you foresee, at a future without a political program! Turn yourself into a glow-worm, become a spider! Strike fire from your entrails, strike them hard and strong, until the sparks fly; weave and spin without let. Only one who has been hard and implacable with himself and goes on to spin and weave from his entrails a thread for the exploration of the void, only one who has beaten his soul into metal sheets and rolled it into spindles in the search for his wherefore, for the Soul of the Universe, only he can fearlessly hurl himself into the abyss of the future's deepest darkness. What would be the worst that could happen to him? That the spinning of his entrails not hold and give way? Even so!

Look, my friend, let come what may! It can not be more empty or abysmal than the past. . . . "But what will the future bring us?" you say. And what does the past bring us? What sense does all history up to this point make? Any at all? Vacuity of vacuities; all is vacuity. We already know yesterday's vacuity: let the morrow's come! The day after tomorrow will also become old stuff. Within a century, long before, the society being prepared for us now by the New Social Era specialists will be seen to have become as stupid, as empty, as absurd as yesterday's society. For everyone? For everyone no! For everyone except the man who lets himself down into it with a hold upon the thread of his entrails. Because for that man there is no other world but the one along his thread. The true path of life for the symbolic spider is along the thread of his entrails.

Spin out from your entrails, therefore, my soul, and let come what may! More empty space, more void. . . .

Notes

Epigraph: St. Teresa of Jesus: Teresa Sánchez de Cepeda y Ahumada (1515-82), great Spanish mystic and author of many works. The quotation (in Spanish "Muero porque no muero") is from her poem which begins "Vivo sin vivir en mí . . ." and which is a spiritual gloss—*versión a lo divino*—on a secular love song. This device was cultivated by other Spanish poets of the Golden Age, including St. Teresa's friend St. John of the Cross (San Juan de la Cruz) who also glossed a variant of these lines.

Introduction: In the 1930 Prologue to the Spanish edition of *La Agonía del cristianismo* (printed below as a note), Unamuno tells us that the book was written in Paris at the end of 1924 and was turned over to Jean Cassou who translated it into French for publication. It was then translated into German, Italian, and English, and only in 1931 did it appear in Spanish, the language in which it was written.

*The 1930 Prologue to the Spanish edition
(published in 1931) of* La Agonía del cristianismo

This book was written in Paris when I was an émigré there, a refugee at the end of 1924, and at the height of the Spanish Pretorian, military dictatorship; when I wrote it I was in a strange state of mind, prey to a veritable spiritual fever, to a nightmare of waiting, a state I have tried to describe in my book *How To Make a Novel.* And it was written on request, as I explain in the introduction.

Since I wrote the book for translation into French and for a general, and more particularly a French, audience, I did not take any special care to adapt my language to the idiom and taste of a Spanish public. It never occurred to me, furthermore, that it would appear, as it is now appearing, in Spanish. I handed over my handwritten sheets, full of addenda, to the translator, my close friend Jean Cassou, who is as Spanish as he is French, and who then turned my words into a vigorous French with a marked Spanish flavor, which has contributed to the success of the book, since the text retains the incandescence with which I wrote it. Later the little work was translated into German, Italian, and English. And now it finally appears in the language in which it was composed.

Composed? There are those who might say that the book, strictly speaking, is lacking in "composition." It may indeed be lacking in structure, but I do not agree that it lacks life. For I wrote it, as I have said, almost feverishly, and poured into it not only thoughts and feelings that for years—for so many years!—had worked themselves into my soul, but also those caused by the misfortunes of my country, and those caused by what I happened to be reading at the time. Not a little of what you read in this book is a reaction to the French political situation of the time. Still, I have not felt inclined to delete certain anachronistic allusions which belong to another time and place.

This little book reproduces, in a more concrete form and, because spontaneous, in a denser and more passionate mold, a good deal of what I expounded in my *Tragic Sense of Life*. And I must still keep going over and over and around the same themes, or go round and round myself as they say St. Lawrence did as he roasted on the spit of his martyrdom.

Is this book a monologue? That is what some of my . . . critics, I shall call them, say about me: that I write only monologues. I might call them monodialogues, or perhaps, better yet, autodialogues, that is, dialogues with myself. For an autodialogue is not a monologue. Whoever indulges in dialogue, whoever converses with himself, dividing himself into two or three or more, or into a whole nation, does not necessarily engage in monologue. Only dogmatists make monologues, even when they seem to be engaging in a dialogue, as in the case of the catechism, where the questions and answers are given. But skeptics, agonists, polemicists—we do not engage in monologues. I feel too deeply within my spiritual entrails the struggle, the religious and civil struggle, agony, to be able to live on monologues. Job was a man of contradiction, and so were Paul and Augustine, and so was Pascal, and so, I believe, am I.

Some time after this little book had been written and then published in French, in February of this year 1930, I thought the time had come to return to Spain, and I did so. And here I am in Spain, in the heart of my fatherland ready to resume my civil campaigns—or if you like, my politics. And as I plunge into them, I feel the resurgence of my anguish, or better still, my eternal religious grief, and in the heat of my political pronouncements, I hear that voice which whispers "And after all, what is the point of all this? What is it all for?" And to silence that voice or the source of that voice, I continue addressing those who believe in progress, in secular endeavor, in justice, simply to convince myself that such efforts are of value.

But I have no wish to continue in this vein, and not simply because I am afraid I will again be called a pessimist, an accusation I do not mind at all. I know well enough all that has been done in the world of the spirit by that which simpletons and the poor in spirit call pessimism; and I know well enough what religion and politics owe to those who have sought consolation in struggle for its own sake, even without hope—and even against hope—of victory.

And I do not wish to conclude this prologue without pointing out that one of the reasons this little book has earned its flattering success is that it re-states the true sense, the original and etymological sense, of the word "agony," which is struggle. And because of that re-affirmation, people will not mistake an "agonizer" for a dying or moribund person. One can die without agony and one can live—live for many, many years—with agony and on the strength of it. A true agonizer is an agonist, sometimes a pro-tagonist, other times an antagonist.

And now, oh my Spanish-speaking reader, I bid you good-bye until such time as we meet again in autodialogue; I commit you to your agony, and myself to my own, and may God bless our agony in each one of us.

3. *The military tyranny*: The reference is to the dictatorship (1923-30) of General Miguel Primo de Rivera. Because of Unamuno's opposition to the suspension of constitutional rights and the invective he hurled at the leaders of the coup d'état, he was exiled to the island of Fuerteventura, Canaries, where he arrived on March 10, 1924.

I was taken off the island by a French sailing vessel: M. Henry Dumay, director of the leftist French newspaper *Le Quotidien*, arranged Unamuno's "escape" from Fuerteventura on the schooner *L'Aiglon* on July 9, a few days after the Spanish authorities had decided to rescind the order of exile. On July 11, Unamuno arrived at Las Palmas where he was joined by his eldest son and the latter's wife; ten days later he boarded a Dutch ship for Cherbourg where he landed July 27. On the next day Unamuno arrived in Paris where he lived at a pension located at 2 rue La Pérouse. Thirteen months later, in August of 1925, Unamuno moved to Hendaye where he spent the rest of his exile until February 30, 1930, when, barely two weeks after the fall of Primo de Rivera, he crossed the frontier back to Irún.

4. *Count Joseph de Maistre*: (1754-1821), author of the *Soirées de Saint-Pétersbourg* and *Du Pape*, advocate of absolute monarchy and of a sovereign and infallible papacy. He is much quoted in the Maurras book treated in the next note.

the 1903 program of L'Action Française: from Maurras's book *Enquête sur la Monarchie, suivie de Une Campagne royaliste au Figaro et Si le coup de Force est possible* (Paris, 1924), p. 384, note 2. The *Action Française* (1908-44) was a daily founded by Maurras, Jacques Bainville, and Léon Daudet, and dedicated to anti-democratic, pro-monarchist, and ultramontane Catholic principles. Charles Maurras (1868-1952), a brilliant writer and polemicist, was sentenced in 1945 to life imprisonment for collaboration with the Germans.

5. *"You can no longer deceive anybody"*: The entire quotation is from Père Hyacinthe's journal, dated 16 mars 1892, in Albert Houtin, *Le Père Hyacinthe*,

prêtre solitaire, 1893-1912 (Paris, 1924), pp. 371-72.

"I am the way . . .": Luke 14: 6.

6. *Loyson*: The letter is in Albert Houtin (1924), pp. 234-35. Unamuno leaves out the words "of too personal a nature" right after "too many letters."

10. *so is Christ*: Unamuno appends one of his rare notes at this point: " 'Jesus will be in agony until the end of the world; we must not fall asleep during all that time.' Thus wrote Pascal in *Le Mystère de Jésus*. And he wrote it in agony. For not to sleep is to dream awake, to dream an agony, to agonize."

in another work: in *The Tragic Sense of Life*. Cf. Vol. 4 in this series, p. 17.

12. *In the* Journal *of Pére Hyacinthe*: Cf. Albert Houtin, *Le Père Hyacinthe, réformateur catholique 1869-1893* (Paris, 1922), pp. 160-61. The child referred to farther on is the son, Paul, born to Père Hyacinthe on October 19, 1873.

Frei Tomé de Jesus: (1529-82), Portuguese friar who accompanied his king, D. Sebastião, on the latter's ill-fated invasion of North Africa, was captured, and died in prison. There he wrote *Os Trabalhos de Jesus* (*The Sufferings of Jesus*), published posthumously, the first part in 1602, the second in 1609.

14. *The oracular suffix* ismo *of* cristianismo: cf. the *isme* of French *christianisme*, or the *esimo* of the Italian *Christianesimo*.

Though St. Peter . . . in himself: Unamuno's parenthetical reference in the text is "(*v.* Couchoud, "On the Apocalypse of Paul," in *Le mystère de Jésus*, Chap. II)." Actually it is Chap. II of the "Deuxième Partie" called "Le Mystère." The book (F. Rieder, Paris, 1926) is one of the series called *Christianisme*, "cahiers publiés sous la direction de P.-L. Couchoud," for which Unamuno wrote the original version of his *Agony*, translated into French by Jean Cassou as *L'Agonie du christianisme*.

16. *Lev Shestov . . . Pascal*: the book to which Unamuno refers and from which he will later quote at some length is *La Nuit de Gethsémani, essai sur la philosophie de Pascal* (Les Cahiers Verts, publiés sous la direction de Daniel Halévy, Paris, Bernard Grasset, 1923).

Lev Isakovitch Shestov (Schwarzman), (1866-1938, Kiev-Paris), exile from Soviet Russia; considered by Sciacca (*La filosofia oggi*, 1950) an early Christian existentialist, and by Ferrater Mora (*Diccionario de filosofía*, 1958) a theocentric religious thinker concerned with Kierkegaard's main preoccupations (and thus not anthropocentric and subjective enough in temper for existentialism). Shestov held that reason, instead of freeing man, oppresses him, for it locks him up in a cubicle which he tends to identify with the universe; reason must be disassembled, part by part; philosophy, too, is deceiving, for it gives us the illusion of freedom; creative faith stands against the "eternal values" and "universal ethical norms," Jerusalem against Athens. Shestov's works in translation from the Russian include *Athènes et Jérusalem* (1938) and *All Things are Possible* (1920). *La Nuit de Gethsémani*, translated as *Gethsemane Night; Pascal's Philosophy*, is included in Shestov's *In Job's Balances*, translated by Camilla Coventry and C. A. Macartney (London, 1932), pp. 274-326.

whenever I have encountered in some book a man rather than a philosopher: Unamuno is here paraphrasing and developing Pascal's famous *Pen-*

sée 29: "When we see a natural style, we are astonished and delighted; for we expected to see an author, and we find a man."

Kierkegaard: Søren (1813-55), Danish philosopher whom Unamuno started reading in Danish in 1900 and who exercised an enormous influence on his thought. Unamuno never ceased thinking of Kierkegaard as his spiritual brother and Walter Lowrie says in his *Kierkegaard*, i (New York, 1962), p. 8: "Don Miguel de Unamuno was a Catholic deeply affected by S.K. who has done much to spread his influence throughout the Spanish world. *The Tragic Sense of Life* is not expressly an interpretation of S.K. but a very free rendering of his thought through the medium of a liberal but austere Catholic thinker. S.K., who wanted no disciples, would surely have been pleased with such independent discipleship as this." The fourteen volumes of Kierkegaard, in Danish, to be found in Unamuno's library attest to the profound impact the Dane had on the Spaniard, especially in *The Tragic Sense of Life*.

17. *Non ridere . . . intelligere*: From *Tractatus Politicus*, Ch. I, Sect. 4. The entire statement runs as follows in English: "And that I might investigate the subject-matter of this science with the same freedom of spirit as we generally use for mathematics, I have laboured carefully, not to mock, lament, or execrate, but to understand human actions . . ." (*A Political Treatise*, in *The Chief Works of Benedict de Spinoza*, tr. and Introd. R.H.M. Elwes, N.Y., 1951, i, p. 288).

20. *religio quae non religat*: a religion that does not bind.

Le Mystère de Jésus: p. 37.

21. *"the revelation of the revelation"*: quoted in Houtin (1922), p. 280.

23. *Apocalypse*: The Revelation of St. John the Divine 10:8-11. The command is in verse 9: "And I went unto the angel, and said unto him, Give me the little book, And he said unto me, Take it, and eat it up; and it shall make thy belly bitter, but it shall be in thy mouth sweet as honey."

25. *La Sibylle*: the entire title is *La Sibylle, trois essais sur la religion antique et le christianisme* (Paris, 1924), p. 46. This book, written by Tadeusz Zielinski (1859-1944) is part of Couchoud's *Christianisme* series.

26. *Jansenius*: Cornelius Jansen (1585-1638), Dutch theologian and bishop of Ypres, whose *Augustinus*, in which he sets forth his interpretation of St. Augustine's doctrines on grace, free will, and predestination, gave rise to Jansenism, of which Pascal was an adherent.

27. *"that they died as though they were overcome with sleep"*: Hesiod: *Works and Days*, tr. Hugh G. Evelyn-White (The Loeb Classical Library, 1929), p. 11, 116.

28. *Renan*: Unamuno supplies the following information in parentheses: *Feuilles détachées*, page 391. Actually, the quotation came directly from Houtin, 1924, footnote to p. 365. The primary source of the quotation is Renan's 1884 article on Amiel included in *Feuilles détachées*, and since Houtin does not provide the publisher and date of the book, neither does Unamuno.

Choses passées . . . Alfred Loisy: Loisy (1854-1940) was ordained in 1879, taught at the Institut Catholique and later at the Collège de France.

An outspoken Modernist, he gave up Christianity in 1908. *The New Catholic Encyclopedia* (Vol. 8, 1967, p. 973) says: "In his *Choses Passées* and *Mémoires pour servir à l'Histoire religieuse de notre Temps, 1860-1931* (3 v. 1930-31), there is a wealth of information about the history of Modernism and autobiographical details that show the tortured variations of his thought, his difficulties of conscience, and his relationship with scholars and ecclesiastics of his time."

29. *"La déesse France"*: From Maurras, op. cit., pp. 471-77.

Abbé de Saint-Cyran: Jean du Vergier de Hauranne (1581-1643), French theologian, born in Bayonne, friend of Jansenius, and a great influence at the convent of Port-Royal, seat of Jansenism.

30. *Bossuet*: Jacques Bénigne (1627-1704), French bishop and orator of great renown and influence; opponent of Fénelon.

Mazzini: Giuseppe (1805-72), outstanding Italian patriot. The quotation, from "Ai Giovani d'Italia" (*Scritti Scelti*, con note e cenni biografici di Jessie White V.ª Mario, Firenze, G. C. Sansoni editore, 1901, p. 265), to which Unamuno, great admirer of Mazzini, refers, ends thus: " . . . *noi non abbiamo che un solo padrone nel cielo, ch'è Dio, e un solo interprete della sua legge in terra, ch'è il Popolo*" (Mazzini's italics).

General Lizárraga: Unamuno's wife's name was Concepción Lizárraga, and therefore Unamuno's children's full family name is Unamuno y Lizárraga.

The Carlists are ultra-traditionalists. They have warred, mainly in the north of Spain, against the central power of Madrid. When Ferdinand VII died in 1833, leaving as his successor his small daughter

Isabel, later Isabel II, his brother Carlos, invoking the Salic Law, challenged the right of the young heiress to succeed her father, and claimed the throne for himself.

32. *her companion in sin*: David conceived Solomon adulterously with Bath-sheba. Cf. II Samuel 11.

35. *Lev Shestov*: see above, note to p. 16.

normal men: OC^1 and OC^2 and the Candamo edition have "anormales": "abnormal men." But the French of Cassou (and hence the English of the Pierre Loving translation), published before any Spanish edition, reads "ces pauvres hommes normaux" (*L'Agonie du christianisme* par Miguel de Unamuno, traduit du texte espagnol inédit par Jean Cassou, Paris, 1925, p. 54), translated, thus, by Pierre Loving "these poor normal men," which is to be expected in the context.

Phantasia, non homo: Satyricon, XXXVIII, 16, translated as "He was a fairy prince, not a mortal." (*Petronius*, tr. Michael Heseltine, revised E. H. Warmington, Loeb Classical Library, 1969, p. 71.)

Comte Joseph de Maistre: Cf. above, note to p. 4. De Maistre often writes of his contempt for human reason when left to its own powers, as for instance: "The more human reason trusts in itself and tries to rely on its own resources, the more absurd it is and the more it reveals its lack of power. That is why the world's greatest scourge has always been, in every age, what is called *philosophy*, for philosophy is nothing but the human reason acting alone, and the human reason reduced to its own resources is nothing but a brute whose power is restricted to destroying." (*Study on Sovereignty, The Works of Joseph de Maistre*, selected, translated and introduced by Jack Lively, New York, 1965, p. 105.)

Unamuno's library in Salamanca contains *Joseph de Maistre, Œuvres Choisies* (Paris, 1909), as well as Maistre's *Les Soirées de Saint-Pétersbourg*.

"*They have nothing but their reason*": There is a double meaning here, inasmuch as Spanish "tener razón," to possess reason, also means "to be right."

"*son poids*":

> Feeble souls enthusiasm fear
> afraid of its fervor and weight.

Alfred de Vigny: (1797-1863), French romantic poet and prose-writer, one of the few French writers Unamuno admired.

36. *St. Teresa of Jesus . . . love.*: *The Interior Castle* (*El castillo interior* or *Las moradas*, 1588), in *The Complete Works of Saint Teresa of Jesus*, translated and edited by E. Allison Peers from the critical edition of P. Silverio de Santa Teresa (London and New York, 1957), II, pp. 277-78.

And Goethe . . . builds: *Faust I*, ll. 338-43, 1336-37.

Nicolás Salmerón: (1838-1908), third president of the first Spanish Republic; an opponent of capital punishment, he resigned the presidency after only two months in office rather than sign death warrants handed down by the courts against separatist rebels who were fighting to overthrow him—a gesture unmatched in modern political history and inconceivable in the later totalitarian epoch. The complete idealist, he was editor of *La Justicia*, a utopian newspaper attracting all tendencies.

37. *Candace*: Acts 8:27 "queen of the Ethiopians." In Acts 8:26-40, the unnamed eunuch, "a man of Ethiopia, an eunuch of great authority under Can-

dace . . . who had the charge of all her treasure," was preached to and baptized by Philip.

39. *Gesù*: "The Church of Jesus, mother church of Jesuits in Rome, commenced in 1568 by Vignola as the first example of a style which was to find its full realisation in the Baroque." *New Illustrated Guide of Rome*, 1968, p. 127.

M. Accard . . . novels: Accard appears in Paul Bourget's *Physiologie de l'amour moderne* (1890) and is described as "un Bonaldiste Tainien," a manifest contradiction.

Paul Bourget (1852-1935), French novelist most celebrated for his *Le Disciple* (1889), a study of the deleterious effects of the teachings of Adrien Sixte, a determinist philosopher (presumably modeled after Taine) upon his disciple Robert Greslou.

Hippolyte Taine (1828-93), French philosopher and historian; strict determinist.

Bonald: Louis, vicomte de (1754-1840), French political writer, ardent defender of monarchy and Catholicism.

40. "La Crise de l'esprit": translated as "The Crisis of the Mind" in the volume *History and Politics*, translated by Denise Folliot and Jackson Mathews, New York & London, 1962; this edition points out that the essay was written at the request of John Middleton Murry for the *Athenaeum* (London), and published first in English, in two parts: I. "The Spiritual Crisis," II. "The Intellectual Crisis," in 1919; the translator's name is not given; it was later translated by Malcolm Cowley and published in the volume titled *Variety* (N.Y., 1927). The translation of the quotation here given is from p. 26 of the 1962 edition.

Auguste Comte: (1798-1857), French philosopher, father of Positivism. The quotation comes from
Maurras, op. cit., p. 481.

Louis Veuillot . . . God." Unamuno gives as his
source *Odeurs de Paris, livre II, La petite presse*,
IV. In Veuillot's *Œuvres Complètes* (Paris, 1926),
the quotation can be found in vol. XI, entitled *Les
Odeurs de Paris, Molière et Bourdaloue, Le fond de
Giboyers*, p. 56. Louis Veuillot (1813-83) was a
militant Catholic and journalist, director of *L'Univers*, in which he defended ultramontanism, and in
which he attacked Père Hyacinthe Loyson whom
Unamuno takes to be one of his "cardiac" writers and
about whom he read in the three volumes by Albert
Houtin (see especially chapter X of this volume).
Henri Rochefort was the Marquis de Rochefort-
Luçacy (1830-1913), journalist, politician, and
playwright; enemy of Napoleon III and of Léon Gam-
betta, supporter of General Boulanger; founded
L'Intransigeant in 1880 and was its editor from its
inception to 1907.

the self-same Veuillot: the quotations that follow
are from Veuillot's *Odeurs de Paris*, p. 32.

"*And why learn French?*": We follow the original of the first printed (French) edition of *Agony*;
the Spanish versions omit the question.

41. *justification*: The oblique reference is to *Die
christliche Lehre von der Rechtfertigung und Ver-
söhnung* (*The Christian Doctrine of Justification and
Reconciliation*) of the German theologian Albrecht
Benjamin Ritschl (1822-89), which Unamuno read
and several times mentions in *The Tragic Sense of
Life*. Essentially, Ritschl and his school of liberal
Protestant theologians (Wilhelm Herrmann, Julius
Kaftan, Adolf von Harnack, all of whom are alluded

to or discussed in *The Tragic Sense of Life*) thought of the religious life as a moral life. To such a limited view of religion Unamuno objected violently, for to him the only reason for religious belief was the possibility it offered of immortality.

Shestov: in his *La Nuit de Gethsémani*.

42. *Jenseits*: the entire title of Nietzsche's work is *Jenseits von Gut und Böse* (*Beyond Good and Evil*), 1886.

43. *Père Hyacinthe*: the Abbé Loyson (born Charles-Jean-Marie Loyson, 1827-1912) was first a Dominican priest and then became a Carmelite; he preached in Paris; in 1873 he left the Roman Church and joined the Old Catholic Church in Geneva; in 1879 he founded the Église Catholique Gallicane in Paris. Chapter 10 of the present book, "Père Hyacinthe," gives further biographical and bibliographical detail.

"good mother": from Houtin (1924), p. 250.

"this one": op. cit., p. 371.

44. *October 18, 1892*: op. cit., p. 374.

the will to believe: *The Will to Believe and Other Essays in Popular Philosophy*, 1897. William James was one of Unamuno's favorite philosophers and his library in Salamanca contains *The Will to Believe*, *The Varieties of Religious Experience*, and *Pragmatism*. Unamuno adapted James freely and often to his own needs: the first mention he makes of the American philosopher dates back to 1896 and the last is 1936.

45. *Schopenhauer . . . will*: In *The World as Will and Idea*, tr. R. B. Haldane and J. Kemp (London, 1957), I, pp. 425-26, Schopenhauer says: "The genital organs are, far more than any other external member of the body, subject merely to the will, and

not at all to knowledge. Indeed, the will shows itself here almost as independent of knowledge, as in those parts which, acting merely in consequence of stimuli, are subservient to vegetative life and reproduction, in which the will works blindly as in unconscious nature."

putabat se colleum Jovis tenere: In *Petronius*, with an English translation by Michael Heseltine, revised by E. H. Warmington (Loeb Classical Library, Cambridge and London, 1969), the pertinent line on p. 104 reads "Hoc facto putabat se solium tenere, . . ." which is translated "After doing this he thought he had himself seated on the throne of Jupiter. . . ." Page 105, note 2 says "But cod. *H* has *coleum*. So by a glorious piece of blasphemy 'thought he had Jupiter by the balls.' "

Gana!: a word of pure Spanish extraction and usage, even though its philological origins are "uncertain" (Corominas, *Diccionario etimológico de la lengua castellana*). The word suggests a strong but arbitrary desire; a whim, an appetite, a prurient itch. Cf. the *gana-Begriff*, the *gana* phenomena as described by Count Keyserling, in his *South American Meditations*, pp. 161 ff. Jung notes its usage more than once. *Gana* also exists, with the same meaning, in the Catalan language.

46. *Huysmans . . . faith*: Unamuno, who uses *en route* in the original, has in mind the novel *En Route* by Joris-Karl Huysmans (1848-1907). Published in 1895, it is the autobiographical account of a man's conversion to Catholicism.

organs of virility: The expression for which Unamuno gives the euphemism is "Eso no me sale de los cojones" which literally means: "It does not issue from my testicles," for the Spaniard invariably centers his virility in those latter organs rather than in the penis, and all measures and impulses are based on the scrotum, the cod. A massively comprehensive study of the Spanish usage in this area is contained in the *Diccionario secreto*, I (Madrid, 1968), by Camilo José Cela, which is devoted in its entirety (348 pp.) to the one Low Latin word *coleo, -onis,* Sp. *cojón, cojones,* testicles, and its "affinities" and to popular and historical usage in Spanish; the book (p. 115) gives the following for the expression here in question: ". . . que denotan deseos o gana o real gana de hacer . . . una cosa": "denoting desire or *gana* or *real gana* to do . . . something" with examples. Cela's definition could have been taken from this passage in Unamuno, so close is the linking of *gana* and *cojones.* And cf. note on *gana,* p. 258.

Journal Intime: Fragments d'un Journal Intime, précédés d'une étude par Edmond Scherer, dixième édition (Genève, 1908), 2 vols. In vol. II, p. 4 (letter of April 17, 1867) and p. 194 (letter of August 28, 1875) Amiel uses the Spanish word "nada." The above book is the one in the Unamuno library in Salamanca. Cf. below, note to p. 88.

47. *St. John of the Cross . . . Miguel de Molinos*: San Juan de la Cruz (born Juan de Yepes, 1542-91), one of Spain's greatest mystics and poet, a friend of St. Teresa.

Fénelon: François de Salignac de La Mothe-Fénelon (1651-1715), archbishop of Cambrai, author of *Télémaque* (1699); influenced by the quietism of Mme Guyon (1648-1717).

Miguel de Molinos: (1628-96), Spanish theologian whose quietism reached Fénelon through Mme Guyon; died in prison.

Ignacio Zuloaga: (1870-1945), Spanish painter.

The painting referred to here is the *Botero de Segovia*.

nothing about nothing: the colloquial Spanish sense of nihilism, of *nada*-ism, is well synthesized in the original textual phrase given by Unamuno, with its (permissible) double negative: "al no decir nada de nada."

free-thinker: The editor of the Spanish text here refers us to a related essay by Unamuno on this theme: "Filósofos del silencio," written in 1915, contained in *OC*, xi, 603-608.

sown its seed: post-coital *tristesse* is not from St. Paul here, though it may have come into Unamuno's mind in a Freudian age, where this kind of puritanism was propagated as a shibboleth by the Viennese doctor, who apparently was not aware that the non-Viennese world was widely free of this malady.

48. *comes caro*: from *On the Love of God* (*De diligendo Deo*), Ch. XI.

mens sana in corpore sano: Juvenal's *Satire on the Vanity of Human Wishes* (10).

"*to inform it*": Unamuno parenthetically adds: from *Llama* (the *Living Flame of Love*), commentary to the fourth verse of the third stanza. And cf. Jean Baruzi, *Saint Jean de la Croix et le problème de l'expérience mystique*. Paris, 1924, iv, Ch. IV: "The appetite for God is not therefore always appetite according to God."

49. *La Peau de chagrin*: Early in his exile Unamuno was reading this novel by Balzac, and it had a strong influence on his *Cómo se hace una novela* published in 1927 (to be included in vol. 6 of this series).

Mademoiselle Salomon of the *Curé de Tours*, mentioned farther on, is Mlle Salomon de Villenoix who took care of her mad fiancé for five years before he died and left her an old maid. As for Pope Hildebrand, at the end of *Curé de Tours* Balzac makes only a passing reference to him along with Alexander VI, to go on to say that "celibacy thus leads to that capital sin which, merging all a man's powers into a single passion, egotism, makes him either destructive or useless." (*Eugénie Grandet* and *The Curé of Tours*, tr. Merloyd Lawrence, Boston, 1964, p. 244).

51. *Peter*: called *Cephas* (stone) by Paul (I Cor. 15:5) as he was in John (1:42) by Jesus.

56. *But after the reign of Constantine, . . .:* The paragraph starting with these words reflects the influence of the eminent German Protestant theologian and historian Adolf von Harnack (1851-1930) whose *Dogmengeschichte* Unamuno read avidly in the last years of the nineteenth century. The edition of Harnack's work used by Unamuno is the *Lehrbuch der Dogmengeschichte* von Dr. Adolf Harnack, dritte verbesserte und vermehrte Auflage, Freiburg i. B. und Leipzig, Akademische Verlagsbuchhandlung von J.C.B. Mohr (Paul Siebeck). These books are among the most annotated in the Unamuno library at Salamanca, and their impact is patent throughout *The Tragic Sense of Life*.

Twelve Tables: the body of Roman law, framed by the Decemvirs between 451 and 449 B.C. They are a compilation of previously existing customary secular law, and religious considerations are secondary; they were inscribed on twelve bronze tables.

58. *the silence of the universe which so terrified*

Pascal: *Pensées*, 206: "Le silence éternel de ces espaces infinis m'effraie."

Lamennais: Félicité Robert de (1782-1854); first an apologist for ultramontanist Catholicism, he later broke with the Church and evolved a mystical humanitarianism. Very much read and quoted by Unamuno.

Renan: the quotation comes from the Journal of Père Hyacinthe, dated May 10, 1883, to be found in Houtin (1924), pp. 351-52. Since Père Hyacinthe simply gives a page reference (p. 195) out of Renan's *Souvenirs d'enfance et de jeunesse*, without specifying the edition, so does Unamuno.

59. *had children*: Père Hyacinthe had only one child, a son Paul, born October 19, 1873.

60. *In Jerusalem* . . . : The quotation that follows is from Houtin (1924), p. 89. The entry is actually dated May 12, Sunday, although Unamuno says May 13, and the explanation "wife of the Russian consul at Jerusalem" is a footnote on p. 89.

Balmes: Jaime Luciano (1810-48), a Neo-Scholastic; the book in question, *El protestantismo comparado con el catolicismo en sus relaciones con la civilización europea* (4 vols., 1842-44), is in large part a critique of Guizot's *History of Civilization in Europe*, and a polemic in favor of Catholicism as civilizing element of the West.

63. *Louis Veuillot writes*: The quotation that follows is from Albert Houtin, *Le Père Hyacinthe dans l'Église romaine, 1827-1869* (Paris, 1920), p. 306. Its original source is Veuillot's *L'Univers*, 26 juin 1869.

64. *Syllabus*: a digest of errors compiled by Pope Pius IX, and circulated in 1864: among the doctrines

condemned are Rationalism, Naturalism, Liberalism, Socialism, and Communism.

Sedan: Napoleon III was defeated by the Germans at the battle of Sedan, September 2, 1870, thus bringing the Franco-Prussian War to an end.

the agony of Christianity: the latter Spanish editions have "of a Christian"; but all the early editions, in Spanish and in the French (which Unamuno saw), have "Christianity."

Shestov: in *La nuit de Gethsémani*, Paris, 1923. Cf. note above, p. 257.

70. *"the race . . . Christianity . . ."*: Houtin (1922), p. 33. The entry is dated 15 juillet 1870.

"Europe is doomed . . . and true civilization.": Houtin (1920), p. 56.

Ultramontanism: from the point of view of non-Italian countries, that which lies across the Alps, in Italy: the Italianate faction of the Roman Catholic Church; and, finally, the name given by national church supporters to those who favored the pope as authority over all national churches; the Vatican Council of 1869-70 incorporated the principles of so-called Ultramontanism as dogmas, making the pope independent and superior to general councils and making him the source of all jurisdiction; the term is also used by certain revolutionaries (notably the followers of Daniel de Leon, 1852-1914) to label Roman Catholicism as a whole.

MENE, TEKEL, UPHARSIN: the Aramaic words written on the wall at Belshazzar's feast, interpreted by Daniel (5:25-27) to mean: numbered (and finished), weighed (and found wanting), divided (and given up to the Eastern invaders).

71. *Oswald Spengler*: (1880-1936), German phi-

losopher and historian. His *Untergang des Abend-landes* (1918-22) is in the Unamuno library.

Treitschke: Heinrich von (1834-96), German historian. Cf. the famous dictum of von Clausewitz (1780-1831) in *Vom Kriege*: "War is nothing more than the continuation of politics by other means."

72. *phalanstery*: etymologically, a phalanx/monastery; a community of families organized in accord with the socialist-monastic model of the French utopian Charles Fourier (1772-1837); "spontaneous," self-contained groups of 2,000 persons were the unit; all attempts, in France and the United States (Brook Farm, 1841-47) to form such communities, proved unavailing.

Ghibelline: both *Ghibellino* and *Guelfo* (the opposing party) are Italian words of German derivation, and the two parties (12th to 15th centuries) are definable by their attitude towards the German emperors: the Ghibellines for, the Guelphs against.

Celestine V: St. (1215-96); he was called out of his mountain retreat, where he was known among a few followers (later Celestines) for ascetic holiness, when the cardinals could not agree on a new pope; soon realizing he was a puppet to the King of Naples, he resigned.

che fece . . . il gran rifuto: *Inferno*, Canto III, 60.

non raggioniam . . . : *Inferno*, Canto III, 51. The English for both of Dante's lines is taken from the translation by Charles S. Singleton, *The Divine Comedy, Inferno* (Princeton, 1970), pp. 29 and 26, respectively.

73. *what I wrote*: in a special issue of the *Revue de Métaphysique et de Morale*, for April-May, 1923.

Pensée 64: Unamuno follows the numbering of the Brunschvicq edition of Pascal's *Pensées*.

St. Teresa: According to *OC*², Unamuno gives two citations, 499 and 868; the latter should be 867.

74. *Sabiude*: Raimundo Sabunde, or Raymunde de Sabunde, the Spaniard whom Pascal studied through Montaigne ("L'Apologie de Raymond de Sebonde"), was a fifteenth-century apologetic writer of great popularity (there were at least twelve editions of the original text of his *Natural Theology*, despite the suppression of the Prologue by the Council of Trent). The Spanish historiographer Marcelino Menéndez y Pelayo, in his classic work *Historia de los heterodoxos españoles* (Buenos Aires, 1951, Vol. III, pp. 251-54), discusses Sabunde as a "sectarian of Llull," and includes him in his survey of the great heterodox thinkers only because Sabunde found himself in the same situation as Llull, "of whose ideas and methods he is a faithful continuer"; his *Natural Theology* (*Theologia Naturalis Raymunde de Sabunde, Hispani, viri subtilisimi . . . Venetiis, apud Franciscum Tiletum*, 1581) is composed "as if all the dogma of the Christian religion were written in the great book of creatures," to again cite Menéndez Pelayo, who adds that Sabunde's attempts to demonstrate dogma by natural proof constitute a linking of Llull's sentiment with the burgeoning Renaissance. Our authority expends over two pages in proving that Sabunde was a native of Barcelona and that his language was Catalan, as observable in his erratic Latin.

Martini: a thirteenth-century Dominican from Catalonia. In H. F. Stewart's Introduction to his translation of Pascal's *Pensées* (N.Y., 1950, 1965, p. XIII), the author writes: "This *Dagger of the Faith*, slumbering in a MS. at Toulouse, was brought to light by François Bosquet, Bishop of Toulouse, and published in 1651, with 190 pages of learned observations by J. de Voisin of Bordeaux (Jurist and Cabbalist like his father), out of a total of 1,000. It is a treasury of Rabbinical lore which Pascal plundered with both hands. We need not assume that he personally possessed all these huge folios, which are not exactly bedside books." Menéndez Pelayo (op. cit., III, p. 227) writes: "Ramón Marti [*sic*] (1230-1286?), the great Hebraist . . . was author of an Arabic lexicon . . . and of a masterpiece of Rabbinical argument and erudition, an immortal monument to Spanish science, the *Pugio fidei*, much utilized by Pascal in his *Pensées*." And he adds that Spain owes a debt to Pascal for reviving the work. He cites the full title of the *Dagger of the Faith*, which begins *Pugio fidei, Raymundi Martini, ordinis Praedicatorum, adversus Mauros et Judaeos*.

Among the letters of Ignatius Loyola . . . : The English translation of the portions of the letter quoted by Unamuno, done by (selected and translated by) William J. Young, S.J., *Letters of St. Ignatius of Loyola* (Chicago, 1959), pages 289 and 290 respectively, runs as follows:

> I also desire that this be firmly fixed in your minds, that the first degree of obedience is very low, which consists in the execution of what is commanded, and that it does not deserve the name of obedience, since it does not attain to the worth of this virtue unless it rises to the second degree, which is to make the superior's will one's own in such a way that there is not merely the effectual execution of the command, but an interior conformity, whether to wish or not wish a thing done.
> But he who aims at making an entire and perfect

oblation of himself, in addition to his will, must offer
his understanding, which is a further and the highest degree of obedience. He must not only will, but
think the same as the superior, submitting his own
judgment to the superior, so far as a devout will
can bend the understanding. . . . Every truly obedient man should conform his thought to the thought
of his superior.

75. *scepsis*: Unamuno here furnishes a note: "The
meaning that I attribute to the word *scepsis*, σκέπσις,
differs considerably from what is commonly called
scepticism, at least in Spain. *Scepsis* signifies *research*, not *doubt*, unless by the latter be understood
methodical doubt in the manner of Descartes. In this
sense the sceptic is opposed to the dogmatist just as
the man in search is opposed to the man who asserts
prior to any research. The sceptic studies in order to
find a solution, and he may find none. The dogmatist
seeks nothing except proofs to sustain a dogma to
which he has given his allegiance prior to having
found any proofs. The first is fond of the hunt, the
second of the spoils. This is the sense in which the
word scepticism is to be taken when I use it in con-
nection with the Jesuits and with Pascal, and it is
with this same sense in mind that I call probabilism
a sceptical process."

probabilism: A Roman Catholic doctrine of moral choice. There are several forms of the doctrine,
but they all center on the choice of an action based
on probability sufficing (certainty being often impossible) for valid action. The probability is defined
differently by various schools of thought, and they
range from probability based on the opinion of a doctor of the Church, through the notion of a necessarily
equal probability between two choices to be made,
and the contrary view requiring that the absolutely

more probable (of two choices) be made, to the totally opposite belief that the morally safer choice be
made even if less probable.

76. *the eternal silence of infinite space terrified
him*: Pascal's *Pensée* 206.

thinking reed: *Pensée* 347.

"*shed those drops of blood*": *Le Mystère de Jésus*:
Pensée 553.

77. *can be rationally and scientifically proven*: The
Vatican Council text reads: "Naturali rationis huma-
nae lumine certi cognoscere posse," as Unamuno
footnotes.

78. *Pyrrhonists*: In his *History of Ancient Philosophy*, W. Windelband succinctly writes: "The first to
perfect the system and ethics of Skepticism was Pyrrho of Elis, whose working years were contempo-
raneous with the origin of the Stoic and Epicurean
schools. . . . As regards the relativity of all percep-
tions and opinions, Pyrrho asserted that if sense and
reason were deceptive singly, no truth could be expected from the two in combination. . . . Of contradictory propositions one is not more valid than the
other. We should on this account express nothing,
but should withhold our judgement. . . . The moral
worth of the abstinence of judgement consists in the
fact that it alone can produce equanimity (ἀταραξία)
which is likewise the moral idea of the Skeptics"
(translation by H. E. Cushman). The Pyrrhonists
of the seventeenth century followed the same mental
trajectory: an ethical quietism prevailed in both.

80. *La Nuit de Gethsémani*: published in Les
Cahiers Verts, publiés sous la direction de Daniel
Halévy (Paris, 1923). There is no copy in Unamuno's library at Salamanca. Most of the books read
at this time, during Unamuno's Paris exile, were left

behind there and never became part of the Salamanca library.

81. *Augustinian ethics*: Jansenism and Port-Royalism maintained that their doctrine was a restoration of the teachings of St. Augustine. A basic book for their teaching—and one condemned by the official Church—was Jansenius's book *Augustinus* (1642). In his Introduction to his translation of Pascal's *Pensées* (op. cit., p. XVI), H. F. Stewart notes: "The supporters of the book *Augustinus* and its teaching called themselves Augustinians, but the nickname Jansenist has stuck to them despite their protests." Even though Port-Royalism was initially more a state of mind, a spiritual temper, than a doctrine, it was their view of Augustinian ethics which led to their ultimate downfall within the Church.

82. *Juan Sala . . . flesh*: The poem referred to here is "La Fi d'En Serrallonga" by Joan Maragall (1860-1911), eminent Catalan poet and writer whom Unamuno admired greatly. It is to be found in the *Obres Completes de Joan Maragall* (Barcelona, 1929), I: *Poesies*, pp. 80-85; the passage in question occurs at the very end of the poem.

83. *Leo Taxil*: Gabriel Jogand (1854-1907), French anti-clerical pornographer; he "converted" to Catholicism and began a denunciation of the Freemasons basing himself on fraudulent documents. Taxil is mentioned in Houtin (1924), pp. 67-68.

84. *Father Astete*: Gaspar Astete, S.J. (1537-1601) whose catechism was widely used in Spain; according to Unamuno, who cites it very frequently throughout his work, it fostered passive acceptance of dogma and narrowness of thought.

Alain: Émile Auguste Chartier (1868-1951), French thinker and professor, most famous for his

Propos. The quotation is from *Propos sur le Chris-tianisme* (Paris, 1924), one of the *cahiers* on *Chris-tianisme*, published under the direction of P.-L. Couchoud, Ch. XLIV, "Pascal," p. 147: "Pascal fait opposition continuellement, essentiellement; hérétique orthodoxe."

85. *"faith of the charcoal burner"*: "la fe del carbo-nero," proverbial expression to denote unquestioning acceptance of religious dogma.

will dominate the bête . . . brute: Unamuno is referring here to Pascal's *Pensée* 358, "L'homme n'est ni ange ni bête, et le malheur veut que qui veut faire l'ange fait la bête." ("Man is neither angel nor brute, but as luck would have it he who would act the angel acts the brute.")

scientia media: The Spanish Jesuit Luis de Mo-lina (1536-1600) in his doctrine on grace, pre-destination, and free will developed the concept of *scientia media*, an antique notion previously elabo-rated upon by Pedro de Fonseca, which postulated a divine foreknowledge by God concerning free human acts, free within predetermined condition and circum-stance; man needs only divine cooperation, *concursus divinus*, and no positive divine predetermination, *praedeterminatio physica*.

86. *Suárez*: Francisco (1548-1617), Spanish Jesuit, influential scholastic philosopher who helped mold post-medieval legal doctrine. Julián Marías writes: "The most important Spanish theologian of the sixteenth century, and the only original thinker among them, he is the great figure of Spanish phi-losophy until the twentieth century. . . . In 1597 he published his *Disputationes metaphysicae*, first sys-tematic and independent interpretation of metaphys-ics since Aristotle." (*Diccionario de literatura espa-*

ñola, Madrid, 1964). Suárez also wrote several works of legal theory, which served in the evolution of political and international law. His extensive production is collected in 26 folio volumes in the Vives edition, Paris, 1856-66; a 23-volume eighteenth-century Venetian edition; and others. Whatever his importance, Unamuno could not abide his philosophy.

88. *Albert Houtin*: The three volumes by this author bear the following titles (given by Unamuno in the text, but without publication dates): *Le Père Hyacinthe dans l'Eglise romaine, 1827-1869* (Paris, 1920); *Le Père Hyacinthe, réformateur catholique, 1869-1893* (Paris, 1922); *Le Père Hyacinthe, prêtre solitaire, 1893-1912* (Paris, 1924). In the text Unamuno refers to these volumes as I, II, III, respectively.

Albert Houtin (1867-1926) was ordained priest in 1891 but several of his books, clearly Modernist, brought him into conflict with the Church, and he left the priesthood in 1912.

Amiel: Henri Frédéric (1821-81), Swiss writer, often alluded to by Unamuno. The edition which Unamuno had in his personal library, and which is still preserved in the Casa-Museo in Salamanca, is the one edited by the "Calvinist prude" referred to in the text: *Fragments d'un Journal Intime*, précédés d'une étude par Edmond Scherer, dixième édition (Genève: Georg et Cie., 1908), 2 vols. Since Unamuno brought back few or perhaps no books from his exile in France, we cannot specify which "new" edition of Amiel he was reading at the time he composed *The Agony of Christianity*.

90. *Mrs. Merriman*: Invited to preach in Rome in 1868, Père Hyacinthe there impressed a young American widow, née Emily Jane Butterfield, born

in Oswego, N.Y., on June 2, 1833, and widowed on October 18, 1867. She had one son by her first marriage, Ralph Merriman. Emily Merriman became Père Hyacinthe's "pénitente" and was received into the Catholic Church on July 14, 1868, in Paris, with the priest as her *parrain*. She married him in London on September 3, 1872, and died on December 3, 1909.

Of her, Houtin (II, 19) writes: ". . . tantôt séduisante, tantôt mystérieuse et solennelle, elle lui apparut comme une 'femme providentielle,' une 'prophétesse,' une 'prêtresse,' chargée de faire de lui un apôtre des temps modernes, l'annonciateur du 'Millenium,' 'un prophète.' "

93. *the Psalmist*: Père Hyacinthe's quotation, which he attributes to Psalm 21, and in his own italics, runs as follows: "Je m'acquitterai de mes vœux, en présence de ceux qui craignent le Seigneur: mon âme vivra pour lui, et *ma race le servira!*" In *La Sainte Bible* (nouvelle édition publiée sous la direction de S. Ém. le Cardinal Liénart par *La Bible pour tous*, Paris, 1955), Psalm 22:26 reads "Aussi devant la foule assemblée tu seras l'objet de ma louange,—j'accomplirai mes vœux en présence de ceux qui te craignent"; and 22:30 reads "Et mon âme vivra pour lui—et ma postérité le servira."

to that son whom he saw die: Unamuno is quite mistaken here, and below, since Paul Loyson (1873-1921) survived his father (1827-1912).

the latter . . . even a poet: Unamuno is again confused here. The poet was Charles Loyson, Père Hyacinthe's paternal uncle who died seven years before the priest's birth. Père Hyacinthe's father, Louis-Julien (1792-1852) was a teacher at the lycée Louis-le-Grand in Paris, inspector at Orléans, and "recteur d'Académie" at Metz and Pau. His mother was first Charles's fiancée and, at his death, accepted the hand of his brother, Louis-Julien.

94. *Msgr. Darboy*: Georges Darboy (1813-71); Archbishop of Paris; an opponent of the doctrine of papal infallibility at the Vatican Council of 1870, he submitted to the dogma once it was proclaimed; he was among sixty-three hostages shot by the Communards in the Paris Commune of 1871.

Darboy favored Père Hyacinthe and invited him to preach at Notre Dame early in the priest's career.

95. *a widower bereft of a son*: Unamuno, of course, is wrong; see previous note.

96. *ex opere operato*: "by virtue of the thing done," irrespective of the merit of the person doing it. In theology, used primarily of the sacraments, which are not invalidated by the defects of the minister.

ex opere operantis: in terms of the above definition, "by virtue of the person carrying out the work."

fiction of a Mass: This is exactly what Unamuno's fictional Don Manuel Bueno was to do in the novelette *San Manuel Bueno, mártir* (1933).

97. *Deduc me . . .* : "Lead me, Lord, along thy way and I shall enter into thy truth!"

98. *"I cannot recreate the world . . ."*: Actually Père Hyacinthe's words are: "Voici l'une de mes plus cruelles angoisses: je sens en moi la puissance créatrice, et les obstacles du dehors m'empêchent de l'exercer. Le monde qui est dans ma pensée, je ne puis le créer, ou, si je le crée, c'est dans les paroles qui passent, non dans les faits qui demeurent!"

Calderón: The poet does not say "sin" but "crime": "Pues el delito mayor/del hombre es haber nacido," *La vida es sueño*, I.

99. *Ollivier*: Olivier Émile Ollivier (1825-1913), French liberal imperialist; premier of liberal cabinet in final year of Napoleon III in 1870; led France into Franco-Prussian War; issued eighteen-volume *L'Empire libéral* (1895-1918) as apologia for his contradictory role; married to a daughter of Liszt.

Seillière: Baron Ernest (1866-1955), French anti-Romantic critic (*Le Mal romantique*, 1908); author of nearly 100 volumes.

René: Romantic hero of the novelette of the same name (1802) by François René, vicomte de Chateaubriand (1768-1848), whose works had a profound influence upon the adolescent Unamuno.

100. *Sheol*: Hebrew Hades, the grave; the underworld; the abode of the dead. As, in the Revised Version, Psalm 16:10, "For thou wilt not leave my soul to *Sheol*." Not used in King James English.

101. *Obermann*: Romantic hero of the novel of the same name (1804) by Étienne Pivert de Sénancour (1770-1846). This novel was one of Unamuno's favorite books throughout his life.

104. *Never was . . . Acropolis!*: the reference is to Renan's "Prière que je fis sur l'Acropole quand je fus arrivé à en comprendre la parfaite beauté," in Chapter II of *Souvenirs d'Enfance et de Jeunesse*, *Œuvres Complètes de Ernest Renan*, ed. Henriette Psichari, Paris, n.d., Vol. II, pp. 755-59. The emotions behind the "Prière . . ." are explained by the following words of Renan (op. cit., p. 753): "Quand je vis l'Acropole, j'eus la révélation du divin, comme je l'avais eue la première fois que je sentis vivre l'Évangile. . . ."

Unamuno, all his life a professor of Greek, had, by his own confession, little sympathy for the "Hellenic" spirit and never evinced any enthusiasm for the splendors of ancient art.

106. *Hesiod*: the quotation is of verses 232-35. And for discussion on the question of "legitimate" and "well-formed," cf. Hésiode, *Les travaux et les jours*, edition nouvelle, par Paul Mazon, Paris, 1914, note du vers 235, p. 81.

108. *"Christianity is like a cholera . . ."*: Houtin (1924), pp. 258-59; dated 1888, not 1880 as the Spanish text says. On p. 252, Houtin identifies Augustin Gazier as "professeur honoraire à la Sorbonne," author of the *Histoire Générale du mouvement jan-séniste depuis ses origines jusqu'à nos jours* of which he quotes from Tome II, published in 1922.

113. NICODEMUS THE PHARISEE: "Nicodemo el fariseo" (in *OC*, III, 121-53) is the only extant essay of a series of *Meditaciones evangélicas* (*Meditations on the Gospel*) which Unamuno had planned, as he informed his friend Pedro Jiménez Ilundain in a letter dated January 3, 1898 (in Hernán Benítez, *El drama religioso de Unamuno*, Buenos Aires, 1949, pp. 258-60). In a letter to Federico Urales (probably of 1901, and included in Urales's *La evolución de la Filosofía en España*, Barcelona, 1934, II, pp. 203-13), Unamuno avows: "About four years ago, I passed through a deep personal crisis which it would take too long to describe in detail. It was a period of terrible anguish which is reflected in my 'Nicodemus' (an essay which reveals, not my current state of mind, but what I felt then)."

This spiritual crisis of 1897 is best studied in Unamuno's Journal or *Diario íntimo* which, after many years, is now available in Vol. VIII of the Escelicer edition of the *Obras Completas*, and in the Libro de Bolsillo of Alianza Editorial (Madrid, 1970). A good deal of what Unamuno says in *Nicodemus* is adumbrated in the diary.

Nicodemus was read at the Madrid Athenaeum on November 13, 1899, and then, with some additions at the beginning and end, was published in the *Revista Nueva* on November 25, 1899.

124. *Richard of St. Victor*: theologian, born in Scotland, date unknown, died in Paris, 1173. Became prior of the Abbey of Saint-Victor in 1162. The process of the elevation of the soul to the vision of God is described in his *Benjamin minor* and *Benjamin maior*, while his *De Trinitate* influenced St. Bonaventure and the Franciscans.

148. FAITH: The essay "La fe" (in *OC* xvi, 99-113) was the third and last of three essays published in 1900 as *Tres ensayos*: the other two are "¡Adentro!" and "La ideocracia" to be found in *OC* iii, pp. 418-27 and 428-40 respectively. Unamuno had read and been deeply affected by the *Dogmengeschichte*, (3 vols., 1886-89) of the church historian and theologian Adolf von Harnack (1851-1930), and was beginning his reading of Kierkegaard; both influences pervade his later *The Tragic Sense of Life* and other key works.

In his letter to the eminent Uruguayan essayist José Enrique Rodó, Unamuno affirmed: "The concept of faith in the third of my *Three Essays* [*Tres ensayos*] is, at bottom, genuinely Lutheran. With the reading of the *Dogmengeschichte*, vast horizons have opened up to me." Indeed, the portion of "Faith" which emphasizes the evolution of earliest Christian faith into structure, curialism, and dogma, reflects the enormous impact of Harnack's work.

Brand: Ibsen's *Brand* was, one might say, Unamuno's favorite play by his favorite dramatist. In a letter to the Spanish critic and novelist "Clarín" (Leopoldo Alas, 1852-1901), dated April 3, 1900,

Unamuno says: "Now that I can already translate Dano-Norwegian or Norso-Danish I am going to immerse myself in the theologian and thinker Kierkegaard, principal source of Ibsen, who as a young man said that he aspired to be Kierkegaard's poet, as I have read in Brandes's book on Ibsen which is where I began to study Danish (a very easy task since I know German and English). Many of my meditations in this area are condensed in the third of my *Three Essays*, entitled 'Faith.' "

believe . . . beget: in the original Spanish the play of words is between "creer" (believe) and "crear" (create, beget); our English is merely an approximation.

vortex: *OC²* has "tormento," torment; but the first edition of the essay reads "torbellino," whirlwind or vortex.

151. *It was the time . . .* : Unamuno adumbrated some of the ideas in this essay—especially the evolution of *pistis* to *gnosis*—in his earlier essay "¡Pistis y no gnosis!" dated January, 1897, to be found in *OC²*, IV, pp. 1019-25, where the paragraphs reproduced in the later "Faith" are indicated by asterisks.

155. *credo quia absurdum*: "I believe because it is absurd," a phrase from Tertullian, very frequently quoted by Unamuno.

"faith of the charcoal-maker": "la fe del carbonero," proverbial expression to denote unblinking acceptance of religious dogma.

156. *ita ius esto*: This will be the law.

the Stagirite: Aristotle, who was born in Stagira, Macedonia.

157. *Krausist*: one connected with or influenced by Krausism, introduced into Spain by Julián Sanz del Río (1814-69) after a sojourn in Belgium and

Germany. Krausism, based on Sanz del Río's interpretation of the ideas of an obscure German philosopher Karl Christian Friedrich Krause (1782-1832),
became the basis of the spectacular development of
free secular higher education among other progressivist phenomena, and was the target for the ire of
many conservatives, above all the great scholar Marcelino Menéndez y Pelayo (1856-1912).

159. *Hello*: Ernest Hello (1828-85), French
Catholic satirist, author, and mystic. He was one of
the earliest adherents of Lamennais and de Maistre,
and wrote biographical studies of Renan and Lacor-
daire.

Qui ex Patre Filioque procedit: ". . . who proceeds from the Father and the Son." The phrase
is from the Nicene Creed as recited and sung in the
Roman Catholic Church. In its original formulation
by the Council of Nicaea (A.D. 325), the Nicene
Creed did not include this refinement of the dogma
of the Holy Spirit and His relationship with the other
two Persons of the Trinity. Gradually, however, between the sixth and ninth centuries, the phrase here
cited by Unamuno crept into use in the Church in the
West and was one of the principal contributing factors (in the popular mind perhaps the chief of them)
to the schism between the Churches of the East and
of the West.

Unamuno's point here is, of course, that to the
ordinary Christian, whether the Holy Spirit "proceeds" (in the language of the theologians) from the
Father and the Son, or from the Father only, is a matter of small daily importance.

161. *in my native Basque country*: Unamuno was
writing from Hendaye, in the French Basque coun-

try. A Basque born in Bilbao, he is here appropriat-
ing the entire Basque country, French and Spanish,
to himself.

165. WHAT IS TRUTH?: The essay "¿Qué es ver-
dad?" (in *OC²*, III, 992-1009) was published in *La
España Moderna*, Madrid, March 1, 1906.

stopping for answer: cf. "What is truth? said
jesting Pilate; and would not stay for an answer."
Francis Bacon, *Essays*, "Of Truth."

Zeferino González: (1831-94), theologian, cardinal and primate of Spain. Both volumes of the
Filosofía elemental, written when the author was
Bishop of Córdoba and dated Madrid, 1876, are in
the Unamuno library in Salamanca.

167. *say they mean*: ". . . no quieren decir más de
lo que dicen": a play on words; *querer decir* = to
mean, but Unamuno repeats the *decir* (in *dicen*)
which literally = to say ("they say").

172. *This very day*: December 16, 1905, as the
text makes clear: "16 de diciembre."

177. *the right of the creed*: Without taking certain
liberties, Unamuno's wordplay can not be transmitted
into English ("Hay gentes que dicen pelear no por el
hecho, sino por el derecho; no por el huevo, sino por
el fuero. Si quedara el huevo del hecho escueto y claro,
no haría falta el fuero del derecho"; literally: "There
are people who say they fight not for the deed but for
the principle, not for the egg but for the law. But if
the egg of the deed were plain and clear, there would
be no need for the law of principle"). Its assonant
rhymes and perfect rhymes, its suggestion of outer
and inner, and its hint of popular refrain can not
be exactly conveyed. A literal translation does not
give the spirit, and our equivalent sound translation

omits a certain amount of overtone, though it conveys the essence of the metaphoric equation.

178. *St. Aloysius Gonzaga*: Luigi Gonzaga, 1568-91, Italian Jesuit, member of the family which ruled Mantua from the fourteenth to the eighteenth centuries, eldest son of the Marquis of Castiglione, who intended him for a military career; died while caring for victims of the plague in Rome.

Cf. Unamuno's autobiographical *Recuerdos de niñez y de mocedad* (*Memories of Childhood and Adolescence*) in *OC²*, i, pp. 314 ff.

179. *The Varieties of Religious Experience*: London & Glasgow, 1963, p. 345. James (p. 342) calls the saint by his French designation, as he found it in his chief source, "Meschler's *Life of Saint Louis of Gonzaga*, French translation by Lebréquier, 1891, p. 40."

185. THE SECRET OF LIFE: The essay "El secreto de la vida" (in *OC²*, iii, 1027-1042) was published in *La España Moderna*, Madrid, July, 1906.

What needs air and light . . . : Manuel García Blanco, the editor of the *OC*, appends this note: "This same theme was treated by the author in the poem 'No busques luz, mi corazón, sino agua' ["Seek not Light, Oh my Soul, but Water"], included in his book *Poesías*, 1907."

197. *acedia*: "*Acedia, the malady of Monks*," Baudelaire, in *The Intimate Journals*, XIV, tr. Christopher Isherwood (London, 1930). Cf. "On the Forms of Spanish Sorrow: Acedia," in vol. 3 of this series, pp. 405-11.

202. THE PORTICO OF THE TEMPLE: The essay "El pórtico del templo" (in *OC²*, iv, 503-508) is date-lined "Salamanca, July 1906."

204. *Fray Alonso de Cabrera*: (1549?-98), Dominican, preacher to King Philip II of Spain, delivered the latter's funeral oration. The quotation comes from *Sermones del P. Fr. Alonso de Cabrera* (Madrid, 1906), pp. 5 ff.

206. *"He who can, does. He who cannot, teaches.":* From "Maxims for Revolutionists" (appended to *The Revolutionist's Handbook*, ascribed to John Tanner) in *Man and Superman* (London, 1947), p. 213, first published in 1903.

Krausists: those inspired by the liberal philosophy evolved by Julián Sanz del Río (1814-69) from the ideas of an obscure German philosopher Christian Friedrich Krause (1781-1832). Some of the most "progressivist" intellectuals of Spain were Krausists, among them Joaquín Costa (1844-1911), and Francisco Giner de los Ríos (1839-1915), who founded the famous Institución Libre de Enseñanza (1876), an institution free of state and church and a revolutionary step in Spanish education.

209. MY RELIGION: The essay "Mi religión" (in *OC²*, XVI, 115-24) is datelined "Salamanca, 6 November 1907," and was published in *La Nación*, Buenos Aires, December 9, 1907.

211. *Inconceivable . . . we-shall-not-know*: Unamuno, who in his early days was a great admirer of Herbert Spencer and indeed translated many of his works into Spanish, is here (and elsewhere) vehemently rejecting the agnosticism of Spencer and his school.

212. *In this matter I am with Kant*: In Chapter I of his *Tragic Sense of Life* (1913), Unamuno says that Kant made the "jump" from his *Critique of Pure Reason* in which he "pulverized" the traditional proofs

of the existence of God, to his *Critique of Practical Reason* where he reconstructs "the God of conscience, the Author of the moral order. . . ."

214. *Life of Don Quixote and Sancho*: 1905. Vol. 3 of this series.

215. *modernist nonsense*: Unamuno looked with great scorn upon the aestheticism of the Modernist school of poetry and prose whose outstanding exponent was the Nicaraguan-born poet Rubén Darío (1867-1916).

217. *My good friend . . . at all.*: In *OC*² the editor Manuel García Blanco supplies the following note: "He refers to the reviews which he wrote for *La Lectura* of two books of the Chilean writer B. Vicuña Subercaseaux, included now in Volume VIII of the *Obras completas*." These two reviews are "Un libro chileno sobre Chile: *Un país nuevo*, por B. Vicuña Subercaseaux" (June, 1904), pp. 267-83, and "Un escritor chileno afrancesado: *La ciudad de las ciudades*, por B. Vicuña Subercaseaux" (February, 1906), pp. 317-37.

218. THE VERTICAL OF LE DANTEC: The essay "La Vertical de La Dantec" (in *OC*², IV, 828-37) was published in *La Nación*, Buenos Aires, May 29, 1911.

Félix Le Dantec: (1869-1917), a French biologist, disciple of Pasteur, taught at various universities including the Sorbonne. He gave up scientific research for philosophical speculation, was a determinist and a defender of Lamarckian theories. His book *L'Athéisme* was published in Paris, 1906.

225. *he tells us a little later*: op. cit., p. 59.

226. *Our popular libraries*: "nuestras bibliotecas económicas y de avulgaramiento," literally "our cheap and popularizing libraries." Unamuno is speaking of

the "progressivist" libraries which were set up to foment workers' education and secular knowledge in his day. They were by nature anti-religious.

Señor Morote: Luis Morote y Greus (1862-1914), Spanish journalist and writer; was published in many journals, especially in *El Mercantil Valenciano*, for which Unamuno also wrote. There are two books by Morote in Unamuno's library: one is *La moral de la derrota* (Madrid, 1900), and the other, done in collaboration with Adolfo Buylla and Adolfo Posada, is *El Instituto de trabajo, datos para la historia de la reforma social en España* (Madrid, 1902).

"Time and Space died yesterday": from the "Initial Manifesto of Futurism" signed "F. T. Marinetti, Editor of *Poesia*" (first published on the front page of *Le Figaro*, Paris, February 20, 1909) quoted here in the translation published in the catalogue of the Sackville Gallery, London, in March, 1912. The context of the sentence cited by Unamuno reads: "We stand upon the extreme promontory of the centuries! . . . Why should we look behind us, when we have to break in the mysterious portals of the Impossible? Time and Space died yesterday. Already we live in the absolute, since we have already created speed, eternal and ever-present. We wish to glorify War— the only health giver of the world—militarism, patriotism, the destructive arm of the Anarchist, the beautiful Ideas that kill, the contempt for woman." Cf. *Futurism*, by J. C. Taylor, New York, 1961, p. 124. The term "Futurism" itself was "coined in the autumn of 1908 by the bilingual Italian poet, editor, and promoter of art, Filippo Tommaso Marinetti": op. cit., p. 9.

227. *Haeckel*: Ernst (1834-1919), German biologist—"ontogeny recapitulates phylogeny." His pop-

ular *The Riddle of the Universe* (German, 1899; English tr., 1901) helped to spread the ideas of Darwinism.

Claude Bernard: (1831-78), French physiologist whose *Introduction à l'étude de la médecine expérimentale* (1865) set down the fundamental principles of scientific research and exercised a crucial influence upon Zola and many naturalists.

230. REBEKAH: The essay "Rebeca" (in *OC²*, IX, 59-63) was published in *Los Lunes de "El Imparcial,"* Madrid, March 2, 1914.

231. *Ernest Renan*: "In the apologist who turns apostate . . ." comes from Renan's article "M. de Lamennais," which appeared as "M. de Lamennais et ses Œuvres posthumes," in *Revue des Deux Mondes*, August 15, 1857, and is now in *Essais de Morale et de Critique* (1859), *Œuvres Complètes de Ernest Renan*, ed. Henriette Psichari, Paris, n.d., II, pp. 109-10. Renan (1823-92), was born in Tréguier, Brittany, and attended three seminaries (among them Saint-Sulpice) in Paris, but decided against the priesthood and devoted himself for the rest of his life to research and writing. He is very frequently quoted by Unamuno.

Lamennais: Félicité Robert de (1782-1854), priest and writer, broke with the Church about 1832. His *Essai sur l'indifférence en matière de religion* (1817-23) and *Paroles d'un croyant* (1834), which along with other works are in Unamuno's library, were carefully read, pondered, and quoted.

Tertullian: (c. 160 - c. 230), one of the Fathers of the Latin Church; he modified the school of Montanus (Montanism), a second-century Phrygian who claimed that the Paraclete, the Holy Spirit, dwelt in him; Unamuno made much of Tertullian's famous

paradox: "Certum est quia impossibile est": "It is
certain because it is impossible." *De Carne Christi*,
V. The saying is usually modified to read: *Credo
quia impossibile*: I believe because it is impossible.

233. *Manzoni . . . Fifth of May*: Alessandro Manzoni (1785-1873), poet and novelist, best known for
his *I Promessi Sposi*. The poem referred to in the text
is "Il Cinque Maggio" and was written upon receipt
of the news of Napoleon's death on May 5, 1821,
on the island of St. Helena.

the Unique Napoleon: Unamuno says "Napoleón
el Unico" which suggests not only that he was
"unique" but "the only one," thus barring any con-
fusion with Napoleon III.

"Due secoli":

> Two centuries
> one against the other pitted
> willingly submissive to him
> waited on him for their fate.
> He commanded silence
> and as judge and arbiter
> took his place among them.

wearing an air of defeat: Tertullian's sense of
"defeat" is perhaps summed up in the martyr's creed
enunciated in his sentence: "Semen martyrum est
sanguis Christianorum": "The blood of martyrs is
the seed [of the Church]."

234. *And Rebekah . . . whom Jacob might espouse*: Gen. 27:46. Unamuno says Esau instead of
Jacob.

Words of a Believer: *Paroles d'un croyant* of
Lamennais.

235. SPIN FROM YOUR ENTRAILS!: The essay
"¡Hila tus entrañas!" (in *OC*², IX, 86-89) was published in *Nuevo Mundo*, Madrid, April 11, 1919.

Diapsalmata: the opening section of *Either/Or*; the English given here is from the translation from the Danish by D. F. and L. M. Swenson, Princeton, 1944; it opens the ante-penultimate paragraph of *Diapsalmata*.

On the enormous influence of Kierkegaard on Unamuno, see above, p. 276.

1843: The original title page of *Either/Or*, Part I, is dated "Copenhagen, 1843." The citation which follows constitutes the beginning of the first paragraph on p. 24, of the Swenson translation.

In 1870 Walt Whitman was saying: The poem is entitled "A Noiseless Patient Spider" and according to Emory Holloway, editor of *Walt Whitman, Complete Poetry and Selected Prose and Letters* (London, 1967), p. 406, the date of composition of the poem is 1862-63, while the date of its final revision and inclusion in *Leaves of Grass* is 1881.

The edition of *Leaves of Grass* which Unamuno owned and which is now in the Unamuno library was a gift from Professor Everett Ward Olmstead of Cornell University in 1906. For a complete discussion of Unamuno and Walt Whitman, see Manuel García Blanco: *América y Unamuno* (Madrid, 1964), pp. 368-405.

236. *fearful cavern*: the action takes place in Part II, Ch. XXII, of *Don Quixote*. We use the English of Charles Jarvis, in his second volume, London, 1742, p. 116.

Index

A page number followed by *n* refers to the notes at the end of the text. If the item which is indexed appears only in a note, the page number is given as, for example, 23*n*. If the item appears in the text and in a note, the form is 23 & *n*.

Index

Cassius, 107

Cassou, Jean, 14*n*, 35*n*

Castilian-Catholic Basque, ix

Castilla (La Nueva and La Vieja), 157

catechism, 11, 83, 84*n*

Catholic: Celt, ix; Rousseau, 99; sadness, 43

Cave: of the Darksome Future, 237; of the Future, 237; of Montesinos, 236

cavern, fearful, 236 & *n*

Cedron, 141

Cela, Camilo José: *Diccionario secreto*, 46*n*

Celestine V (Pietro del Murrone), 72 & *n*

Cervantes Saavedra, Miguel de: *Don Quixote*, 23

charcoal burner, faith of, 85 & *n*, 155 & *n*

Chateaubriand, François René, vicomte de, 70, 89, 99 & *n*, 101

Chile, 209, 217 & *n*

Chosen People, 21

Christ, 10*n*, 53, 57, 60, 71, 75*f*, 83, 86, 95, 98, 104, 107, 151, 154*f*, 165, 169*f*, 185, 208, 211*f*; and agony, 9*ff*, 41, 92, 102, 143; as born of woman, 51; brandishing, 48; and casting of first stone, 139; and celibacy, 67; as Child Jesus, 11, 68, 162; on Cross, 65, 81, 109; David as pre-figuration of, 34, 37; and Eucharist, 18, 92; in God, 35; historical, 22*f*, 51; Kingdom of, 18, 20, 55*f*, 64, 81, 123, 126, 168; and Mary Magdalen, 25, 51*f*, 126, 139, 145*f*; and miracles, 58, 109, 130, 140, 171; and mob,

141*ff*; on Mount of Olives, 61, 109; "My God, my God, why hast thou forsaken me?" 10; and Nicodemus, 123-46; as non-patriot, 56, 58*f*; as non-political, 58; and Pilate, 142, 163, 165; and resurrection, 17*ff*, 52, 81*f*, 92, 103; and Second Coming, 18, 151, 153; and socio-economic matters, 56, 58*f*; Spanish, 10, 102; struggle against Ultramontane Pharisees and rationalist Sadducees, 97; from Tangiers, ix; tempted by Pharisees, 19; as Word, Logos, 51*f*

Christian Democracy, ix, 55, 57

Christian Fathers, 103

Christianisme, 4, 14*n*

Christianity: agony of, 4*ff*, 19*f*, 28*f*, 59, 64, 79, 81*ff*, 87*f*, 96*f*, 101, 104; in agony as in Christ, 10; and agony of Spain, 102, 108; and anti-Christianity, 15; apolitical, 61; as beehive, 68; become Catholic and Roman, 61; Chateaubriand as falsifier of, 89; civilization and culture of, 60; *corrida* of, vii; crusade as agonic act of, 88; like disease, 108 & *n*; as doctrine, 14; essence of, 18*f*; Europe equivalent to, 70; differentiated from Evangelism; 18; fatherhood and agony of, 88; in France, 104; geniuses of, 137; Gentile, 97; and "glad tidings," 17; as grace and sacrifice, x, 57; and Jesuit-

Index

Index